Crossing the Highland Line

Cross-Currents in Eighteenth-Century Scottish Writing
Selected Papers from the 2005 ASLS Annual Conference

Edited by
Christopher MacLachlan

Association for Scottish Literary Studies
Occasional Papers: Number 14

ASSOCIATION FOR SCOTTISH LITERARY STUDIES

First published in Great Britain, 2009
By the Association for Scottish Literary Studies
Department of Scottish Literature
7 University Gardens
University of Glasgow
Glasgow G12 8QH, UK

ASLS is a registered charity no. SC006535

British Library Cataloguing in Publication Data
A CIP record for this book is available
from the British Library

ISBN 978 0 948877 88 9

The Association for Scottish Literary Studies acknowledges
the support of the Scottish Arts Council towards the
publication of this book.

Typeset by Ellipsis Books Limited, Glasgow, UK

Contents

Introduction

The essays presented here have their origins in papers given at a conference entitled 'Crossing the Highland Line' organised by the Association for Scottish Literary Studies and held at Sabhal Mòr Ostaig on the Isle of Skye, 20–22 May 2005. Those who attended the conference will have very happy memories of a most successful gathering, not least because of the wonderful weather. Few of us will forget the excellent conference dinner in the splendid dining hall of the college, with its vast picture windows looking out over the Sound of Sleat towards the hills of Knoydart. As we ate and talked and listened to traditional Gaelic singing, we watched the reflection of the hills in the glassy sea fade in the evening sun from glowing gold to purple shadow.

The title of the conference proved very well chosen for it became clearer and clearer as the conference went on that Scottish writing in the eighteenth century could no longer be thought of as divided by any sort of line, cultural or geographical, between Highlands and Lowlands. Time and again the papers, and the discussion of them, revealed connections and influences between those who wrote in Scots and English and those who wrote in Gaelic. This was not just a matter of borrowings and translations but also of the way writers in all traditions faced and dealt with the problems and challenges and the changing political and social culture of the period.

Of course the Gaelic writers seem to have been the more bilingual, and so more able to import into their works direct allusions to those of Lowland writers. The Lowlanders, ignorant of the Gaelic language, were far less responsive to the new, or indeed the old, writing of the Highlands and paid a price for their ignorance in their reliance on Macpherson's so-called translations of Ossianic verse. Yet, if we look beyond Ossian and the travesty of the Highlands it made so dominant in the minds of the rest of Britain and Europe, and consider instead the state of Scottish poetry in the eighteenth century, the parallels between the Scots' relationship with English poetry and that between the Gaelic poets and *their* southern neighbours are striking. Just as the Scots had to assert voices for themselves yet could not help borrowing the accents of the dominating English, so the Gaels also had to try to build on their own traditions while responding to developments in taste and technique elsewhere.

In the end, however, this is not a simple matter of one group's relations with another but more a sign that all of them, Scots, Gaelic and English, participated in the processes of eighteenth-century literary history, and notably its transformation of neoclassicism into romanticism and its development from a literature of aristocratic patronage to one based on markets and public reputation. The careers of individuals, whether Highland or Lowland, show similar tensions and difficulties. The treatment of their poetry, and the purposes to which it is put in the period, also show strong similarities. This is a time of satire and political commentary but also of the celebration of nature and community, and of the individual and his or her sensibility and feelings. Old forms are put to new uses and the poetry of the folk, especially song, becomes a powerful inspiration in the literature of the period.

The conference began, as this book does, with Edward Cowan's trenchant, wide-ranging survey of the Highlands in modern Scottish history, and historiography. The political background to relations between Highlands and Lowlands is sketched with a sharp eye on the attitudes of historians and other outsiders to the Highlands and with anticipatory flourishes towards the literary debates that will come later in the collection. Gerard Carruthers begins these in the second essay, an eloquent plea on behalf of James Thomson, too easily dismissed as an Anglo-Scot, but here presented as both a major writer and a major Scottish writer, an essential part of the development of Scottish, and British, writing in the eighteenth century.

Ronald Black, in an article given here in both Gaelic and English, then makes the case for seeing the career of one of the greatest Gaelic poets of the eighteenth century, Alastair Mac Mhaistir Alastair, or Alexander MacDonald, as dedicated to making Gaelic culture a living part of Scottish culture as a whole. Connections between his poetry and British and European literature are fully displayed. Christopher MacLachlan tries to add to this by examining the literary activity in Edinburgh during the time in which MacDonald is known to have been in the capital. The Jacobite theme present in this poet's work is evident again in that of the subject of the fifth essay, John Roy Stuart. Neil Macgregor's essay, in effect a literary biography of the soldier and poet, is generous in its use of quotation to give an immediate impression of his character and art. As if to close a group of essays in which Jacobitism is prominent, we then have Murray Pittock's 'Jacobite song: was there a Scottish *aisling*?', exploring a possible connection or parallel between Scottish and Irish Jacobite culture, with all the political implications that might lie behind such a link.

Donald Meek's discussion of Dugald Buchanan is evidently based on his work on the texts of the poems. In attempting to remove the masks which have obscured 'the real Dugald Buchanan' Professor Meek brings to the fore his debts to English-language poets and makes Buchanan a prime example of a poet who crosses the Highland line. The most notorious example is, however, the subject of Kenneth Simpson's essay on Ossian, but there is no apology here for taking James Macpherson's creation seriously as a part of Scottish literature and showing the Ossianic in relation to Scottish and

English writers of the eighteenth century, and beyond. The modernity of Gaelic culture is a theme of Meg Bateman's essay on Duncan Ban MacIntyre. In exploring the poet's attitude to nature in an essay whose form is based on that of pibroch, the very shape reinforces the point that the continuities of Gaelic culture add weight to what seems the contemporary relevance of its environmentalism.

Margery Palmer McCulloch's essay on women poets and songwriters in the Lowlands makes the case for Janet Little, Isabel Pagan and Lady Nairne. Unfortunately for the reader, the musical examples, so finely performed by the speaker at the conference, to the delight of those present, can only be set out here in notation form. In the next essay Mairi MacArthur surveys eighteenth-century travel in the Highlands, listing the major visitors who have left some record of their journeys and briefly describing the conditions of travel and the attitudes brought to, and from, the Highlands.

The Gaelic oral tradition is the topic of Domhnall Uilleam Stiùbhart's essay, a subject which, as he says, crosses many boundaries. The essay reaches back into the sixteenth century before moving energetically forward to 1800, showing themes and ideas in Gaelic song and how they mingled with those of Scots and English ballads. Lastly, in another essay that owes much to the writer's renewed attention to the texts of his poet, William Gillies, by means of a close study of three poems, flags up the bicultural issues and aspects of the work of William Ross, bringing the collection to a fitting close in an assessment of the cross-currents in the work of this eighteenth-century writer.

The Association for Scottish Literary Studies, which is supported by the Scottish Arts Council, is grateful to the Catherine McCaig's Trust for financial assistance with the publication of this book. Thanks are due to the following for their co-operation in the planning of the conference from which the book derives: Dr Michel Byrne, Duncan Jones, James Alison and Alan MacGillivray. Thanks also to Mark Wringe for his help in planning the conference and in making all the arrangements at Sabhal Mòr Ostaig. The editor would also like to record his thanks to Ian MacDonald for his help, especially with the contributions in Gaelic.

Neither the book nor the conference from which it grew would have existed without the enthusiasm and energy of a tireless worker for Scottish literature, Ronald Renton. It is entirely fitting therefore that this book is respectfully dedicated to him, with much gratitude and admiration for all his work on behalf of the ASLS and Scottish literary studies.

EDWARD J. COWAN

Contacts and tensions in Highland and Lowland culture

In 1896 the formidable ministerial team of A. and A. Macdonald published the massive history of their clan. In volume one they traced the history of the Lordship of the Isles from Somerled, founder of Clan Donald, to John last Lord of the Isles who was forfeited in the 1490s and who died in Dundee in 1503 to be buried in Paisley Abbey. Since Somerled himself had been killed at nearby Renfrew in 1164 this was dramatically satisfying but the coincidence reinforces the point that from the time of the early *Scoti* to that of Para Handy the Clyde represented a crucially important political and cultural frontier between Gael and Lowlander and one furthermore that was often crossed in both directions. In the opinion of the Macdonalds, Somerled was 'the instrument by which the position, the power, the language of the Gael were saved from being overwhelmed by Teutonic influence, and Celtic culture and tradition received a new lease of life'. To his successors, the Lords of the Isles, he bequeathed a supremely important legacy: 'It was theirs to be the leading spirits in resistance of the Gaelic race, language, and social life to the new and advancing order which was already moulding into an organic unity the various nationalities of Scotland – the ever increasing, ever extending power of feudal institutions'.[1]

The Macdonalds had another beef constantly reiterated throughout their *History* in that they attached very little value to the opinions of Scottish historians regarding the history of the Highlands. 'Ignorance of the language, customs and traditions of the people has so tainted their utterances; racial hatred has likewise blinded them to facts, that their deliverances on the difficult problems of Highland History are in the main quite unreliable.'[2] The learned authors rather ruined their own case, however, by quoting, among other suspect Sassenach authorities, Sir Walter Scott's dismal effusion *The Lord of the Isles*. The poem, originally to be entitled *The Nameless Glen*, a concept as oxymoronic as Wordsworth's 'untrodden ways', is a disappointing affair with a limp plot, dreary characterization and predictable, tiresome descriptive passages, demonstrating above all that the genre was well and truly played out. Scott more or less admitted as much when he confessed that he completed it 'unwilling and in haste, under the painful feeling of one who has a task which must be finished, rather than with the ardour of one who endeavours to perform the task well'.[3] Historical it emphatically was not. But in the opinion of the Macdonalds the fall of the lordship marked the end of an

1

era, and the collapse of the dynasty 'which for hundreds of years had continued to represent, in a position of virtual independence, the ancient Celtic system of Scotland'. The consequence was to be 'prolonged outbursts of anarchy and disorder'.[4] Almost every writer who mentions the end of the lordship, and emotionally Scott was certainly of their number, has felt compelled to compose some sort of plaintive epitaph for a way of life that was no more. Whether viewed from 1815 or 1896 however, the metaphor was somewhat weakened by overuse. As we all know, 'It is no joy without Clan Donald', but despite successive obituaries they were an unconscionable time a-dying, and of course they never did, as neither arguably did the culture with which they had supposedly been entrusted. An epitaph resurrected and reapplied from generation to generation rapidly loses its effectiveness yet it is trotted out again and again with reference to the last Macdonalds of Islay,[5] to the departure of Alasdair mac Colla following the Montrose campaigns in 1644–5,[6] to Glencoe,[7] Culloden[8] and the Clearances[9] and it is a theme of numerous Gaelic poems some of which are discussed elsewhere in this volume.

While there were undoubtedly tensions between Highland and Lowland Scotland, as between both and their southern neighbour, we should not approach the eighteenth century with the expectation that those who lived in that era actually believed, or were even aware, that they might be the last of their kind. Some of the events of the century, especially the Jacobite risings,[10] were anachronisms that should never have happened and which artificially prolonged a view of the Gaels and their way of life which historians of the sixteenth century believed to be redundant two hundred years before Culloden.[11] The eighteenth century could not represent the end of all things because many of these things had already ended.

The eighteenth century in Scotland remains somewhat under-investigated in comparison with others.[12] This holds true whether it is the 'short' eighteenth century – 'Between the Unions 1707–1801' – or the 'long' which is under review. The latter has been deemed to coincide with the period 1688–1832, between a revolution that was far from 'glorious', which resulted in James VII fleeing the throne to establish the Jacobite court in exile, and the death of Sir Walter Scott. This was the century of political union, of Jacobite rebellion, of Enlightenment and the supposed retreat from superstition, of agricultural improvement and the first real stirrings of industrialization. It was a period when the Scottish Kirk became polarized between Moderates and Evangelicals in an unholy dialectic about the role of the church in modern society which would culminate in the posturing of Disruption in 1843, proving once again how the love of Christ could so easily metamorphose into contempt for one's neighbours. Those of residual covenanting sentiment squared off against the forces of scepticism and atheism. Robert Wodrow published his momentous *History of the Sufferings of the Church of Scotland* in 1722, inspiring much venom and many derivatives such as John Howie's *The Scots Worthies* of 1775 which would remain a best-seller for a century or more, blasting many an Enlightenment tract off the bookstalls. For light relief as well as spiritual edification folk purchased chapbooks, the first cheap literature. The chapman Dougal Graham is regarded in some quarters as the greatest practitioner of prose in the Scots language.[13] The intense flash of genius that was Robert Fergusson burned out in an insane asylum in 1774 after a mere twenty-four years. In his poems he satirized Enlightenment ideas, fearing that they were not necessarily in Scotland's best interests. Like Allan Ramsay, Fergusson was to have a profound effect upon Robert Burns whose more pessimistic poetry provides ample testimony that the ideals of the *philosophes* concerning progress and the perfectibility of humankind were manifestly falling far short. Travel-writers stalked the country in unprecedented numbers, scouring its burghs, castles and glens for curiosities, exotica, evidence of the supernatural, and increasingly for scenery. James Boswell and Samuel Johnson produced two of the greatest pieces of travel literature about one journey to the Hebrides, inspiring legions of disciples to write far too many pages on the basis of far too little knowledge. The terrible twosome were moved to mount their expedition through reading Martin Martin's *A Description of the Western Islands of Scotland*, 1695 and 1716, which remained for long one of the very few explorations of the Gàidhealtachd and its culture by a Gaelic-speaker. By century's end, in the aftermath of Culloden and the Ossianic phenomenon, writers were penning obituaries for a way of life that appeared to be on the verge of extinction. Boswell and Johnson were not alone in detecting a rage for emigration, from the Highlands, but just as significantly, from Lowland Scotland also.

Frank McLynn has highlighted the vitality of the mid-eighteenth century in its wider context by scrutinizing the year of Burns' birth, 1759, as the date to which we can trace the beginnings of the British Empire, when Britain, for good or ill, became the Master of the World as the French were defeated in India, North America, Latin America and the Caribbean, and British ideas of 'Freedom and Civilisation' allegedly triumphed over French 'Despotism and Barbarism'. Seapower ensured that seven million Brits defeated twenty-five million French to establish English as the language of world domination. Wolfe, the veteran of Culloden, triumphed on the Heights of Abraham utilizing Highland soldiers that he famously considered 'hardy, intrepid . . . and no great mischief if they fall. How can you better employ a secret enemy than by making his end conducive to the common good?'[14] James Cook, whose father came from the Scottish Borders, was honing skills which would render him the greatest navigator and explorer in world history. The Carron Ironworks was set up at Falkirk and Benjamin Franklin received an honorary degree from St Andrews. Nature conspired in the portentous as earthquakes hit Scandinavia, Tripoli, and the eastern Mediterranean where one caused a tsunami. Vesuvius erupted and Halley's Comet reappeared.[15]

'This is the historical age', David Hume famously wrote at the height of the Scottish Enlightenment, 'and we are the historical people'. Historians are interested in why

3

things happened but in the comparatively large and growing historiography of the Enlightenment there is still some disagreement on how to account for the remarkable outpouring of philosophy, history, science, sociology, economics, speculative works and publications on general improvement in Scotland between about 1730 and 1790. The Scottish historian perusing studies of the Scottish Enlightenment has the uneasy feeling that he is contemplating an unfamiliar landscape, that he does not recognize the Scotland under discussion.[16] Many scholars writing on the eighteenth century seem to know very little about earlier Scottish history. There is something sinister about the word 'enlightenment' itself, the label 'Scottish Enlightenment' having first been applied as recently as 1900.[17] Present light implies past darkness as Corinthians makes explicit, rendered in the Lorimer translation, God 'lat licht shine oot o the mirk'. Enlightenment writers would themselves popularize this view of a Scotland somehow benighted during the first 1700 years of her existence, frozen in darkness until the Union of the Crowns in 1603 when the first rays of a new dawn tentatively caressed her blighted landscape, gradually bathing her in dazzling light following the 1707 Union of Parliaments. The single most popular explanation for Enlightenment is that it is a consequence of union with England, supposedly a vastly superior and culturally more advanced country than her bleak neighbour to the north. The argument suggests that it is only after the Scots purge their systems of religious controversy, notably of the theologically hair-splitting Calvinistic variety, that they can turn their minds to greater things. Whether the enema was administered at the Glorious Revolution in 1688 or at the Union of 1707 is still a matter of debate. Thereafter it was to be the Moderate party in the Kirk which would prove itself the powerhouse of Enlightenment.

There is much perception in the late David Daiches' thesis on the paradox of eighteenth-century Scottish culture, that the Scots were on the one hand a proud patriotic people securely rooted in their past, but who, on the other, aspired to be Britons who could take advantage of the new commercial opportunities afforded by the Union of 1707.[18] Furthermore the Scots, or more correctly, perhaps, their writers, had long been accustomed to questioning the nature of their culture and society in comparison with their English neighbours to the south, and just as importantly, their Gaelic-speaking countrymen and women, to the north and west. Questions about identity and human nature led naturally to the investigation of climate and environment, to the forces of production, to science and geology, and the relationship between all of the foregoing.

Scotland was a small country in which all or most of the thinkers knew one another personally through either the speculative clubs or the universities. The latter around 1730 moved from the regenting system to specialized professors. The so-called 'enlightened' all believed in progress and the perfectibility of Humankind but, however problematic they found the contemplation of the British present, they also retained a strong sense of the Scottish past. David Hume's world was not all that far removed from that of Duns Scotus, with whom he was, in a sense, engaged in dialogue, as he was with all of his philosophical predecessors.

Indeed the Enlightenment period exhibited something of a vogue for the past. One of the most significant literary productions of the eighteenth century was, without doubt, James Macpherson's *Fragments of Ancient Poetry* in 1760,[19] allegedly translated from the Gaelic compositions of the bard Ossian. The issues concerning authenticity or forgery have been often rehearsed. Macpherson's achievement was not only a significant contribution to the development of the Romantic Movement but also the initiation of a widespread craze far beyond the bounds of Scotland for the recovery of folk literature and oral tradition. But Macpherson made an equally important contribution in giving people a glimpse of a world that was believed to antedate those of Greece and Rome. In a word he extended time, significantly adding to the Scottish and the world timeline. He was the British Homer, a title which underlined the absence of any English competitors who could match his achievement.

A similar contribution was to be made by the geologist James Hutton, who did not publish his results until 1785 although in the tight wee world of Scottish intellectuals his theories had become quite well known considerably earlier. In his *Theory of the Earth* Hutton investigated erosion and stratification. He argued that the Earth is formed out of the detritus of a former world and that one day the debris of this world will build another in the future. He thus discovered and communicated the idea that geological time is virtually infinite and, since one lifetime is irrelevant in the context of the succession of worlds, it is unknowable. To quote his famous dictum in his investigation of the theory of the Earth he found 'no vestige of a beginning – no prospect of an end'.[20] It is tempting to suggest that between them James Macpherson and James Hutton conspired in the destruction of time, and thus, potentially, of history itself, as they were then understood. It might have been expected that historians would have changed their ideas in order to grapple with this astonishing and profound revelation, but such was far from being the case.

Scotland's two greatest historians of the age, though there were several others, were William Robertson and David Hume. Robertson wrote *A History of Scotland* (1759) followed by histories of the reign of Emperor Charles V, of America and of India. Hume in 1763 produced *A History of England to the Revolution of 1688*, the last part of which, on the sixteenth and seventeenth centuries, was published first so that he worked backwards, so to speak, to complete his *History* from the time of Julius Caesar. Despite the title the study did contain material on Scotland. Like Hutton, Hume was aware that because of the shortness of human life no individual could ever grasp the experience of all previous ages without the assistance of history. 'A man acquainted with history may, in some respect, be said to have lived from the beginning of the world, and to have been making continual additions to his stock of knowledge in every century.'[21] Both Robertson and Hume were firmly rooted in their own present. Both regarded early history as being akin to childhood, medieval and early modern times to adolescence, and their own era to full adult maturity. They thus subscribed to a theory of progress though both were spared the realization that progress is in certain respects, not least with respect to ethics and morality, an illusion. Robertson observed that 'no period in the history of one's own country can be considered as altogether uninteresting. Such transactions as tend to illustrate the progress of its constitution, laws or manners, merit utmost attention.'[22] Upon publication, his *History of Scotland* was given a rapturous reception, praised for its judiciousness, balanced moderate tone, and for its clarity of style. It treats of Scottish history from 1542 to 1603 with a preface on the medieval period, incorporating an undue proportion of material on the life of Mary, Queen of Scots though the exposition is scrupulously fair and even-handed.

Robertson opined that existing histories were marred by polemic and bias. There is some truth in his claim since Scottish historians tended to behave like advocates. They entered the courtroom with a distinct point of view, ready to demolish the opposition, and they supported their arguments with proofs, often full transcripts of documents inserted into their texts. They have been unfairly dismissed as antiquarians but they were nothing of the kind. Robertson and Hume often wrote with a certain aloofness which gives the impression that they were not really engaged with their subject. The former transcribed his documents in an appendix. It was said of Hume that he never dirtied his hands in an archive.

Robertson dismisses the first 900 years of Scottish history as 'pure fable and conjecture and ought to be totally neglected or abandoned to the industry and credulity of antiquaries'.[23] However, the picture gradually becomes clearer as it emerges that Scotland's problem was the overwhelming power and ambition of the nobility. He repeatedly tells his readers that 'under the aristocratical form of government established among the Scots, the power of the sovereign was extremely limited'.[24] The Reformation simply increased aristocratic authority. Even under James VI 'all the defects in the feudal aristocracy were now felt more sensibly, perhaps, than at any other period in the history of Scotland and universal licence and anarchy prevailed to a degree scarce consistent with the preservation of society'.[25] In the conclusion to the entire work it is revealed that the process of taming the magnates began in 1603 once James gained access to English resources. As elsewhere in Europe the feudal aristocracy was 'undermined by the progress of commerce'. Stuart absolutism did the rest. Seventeenth-century Scotland was a miserable place – 'its kings were despotic; its nobles were slaves and tyrants; and the people groaned under the rigorous dominations of both'. The nobility fought back at the Crown during the Covenanting Revolution but were financially bankrupt by 1660. Their power was finally broken by the Union of 1707. 'As commerce advanced in its progress, and government attained nearer to perfection [feudal privileges] were insensibly circumscribed and at last, by laws no less salutary to the public than fatal to the nobles, they have been almost totally abolished. As the nobles were deprived of power, the people acquired liberty.'[26]

Robertson's rather astonishing condemnation of the aristocracy has not, perhaps, received the attention it deserves. We might wonder how his views were received by his noble contemporaries, since the Moderate party in the Kirk, of which he was the leader, tended to gravitate towards aristocratic circles. There may of course have been an element of flattery in all of this in that, in Robertson's version of Scottish history, the nobility had enjoyed an heroic, if anarchic past, in which they could possibly take a perverse pride while rejoicing that they were now members of polite society.

There was, however, an ambivalence about the historian's attitude to his nation's past. He observes that, despite the chaos, Scottish geography, 'mountains and fens and rivers, set bounds to despotic power and amidst these is the natural seat of freedom and independence'. According to him the nobility 'owed their personal independence to those very mountains and marshes which saved their country from being conquered'.[27] He admits to the realization that the nobility, for all their faults, checked the excesses of the monarch and preserved the constitution and liberties of Scotland.[28] There is a refreshing and touching honesty in Robertson's declared self-doubts as a historian. He may even be questioning his own commitment to progress when he reflects that 'the vices of another age astonish and shock us; the vices of our own become familiar and excite little horror'.[29] He was potentially in something of a bind in admitting that the barbarous past had provided the cradle of freedom and independence while progress implied submission to authority. Indeed his views were arguably not all that far removed from those of his precursory historians two hundred years earlier.

There are other parallels for Robertson was also a practitioner of conjectural history, that is, a historiography which speculated on the origins of society and government using a comparative anthropology which might draw upon evidence derived from the classical models of Greece and Rome, or borrow from information derived from the New World, in the form of encounters with, or descriptions of, the practices and 'manners' (an Enlightenment obsession) of native Americans.[30] American 'Indians' were often cited by writers of the Scottish Enlightenment, particularly those in pursuit of 'conjectural history'. The latter, in a word, involved the substitution of anthropological material when discussing historical periods for which there was little or no evidence. Thus it was conjectured that the stage of advancement reached by certain sections of the native population of the Americas might approximate to that of Scotland at otherwise unrecorded phases of her past – and one not that distant when surveying the history of the Gaels. Scottish emigrants who described their experiences of the First Nations of Canada in the eighteenth and nineteenth centuries may actually have believed that they were somehow perceiving an earlier stage of their own history. The scientific interest was present as early as the 1620s when William Alexander and Robert Gordon,[31] in their respective tracts, pointed to the nobility of the native peoples, their potential value as allies, and the desirability of learning something of their language. It is striking in subsequent literature that Scots wrote most approvingly of native culture and customs suggesting a certain empathy, extending to linguistics, ethnography and anthropology, all of which were reinforced by Enlightenment writers. The identification of Gael and Amerindian received a huge if undeserved boost in the work of David Malcolme, minister of Duddingston, Edinburgh, who in the early eighteenth century interviewed the veterans of the Darien expeditions (1698–1700) on the matter of language. He subsequently convinced a committee of the Church of Scotland that the natives of Darien did indeed speak Gaelic, as did, by extension he reasoned, the inhabitants of the entire American continent.[32] This extraordinary and utterly deluded notion was to long enjoy considerable currency and is not yet completely discredited in certain quarters.

It is often assumed that Lowlanders regarded Gaels with universal contempt as barbarous, illiterate, idle vagabonds, energized only by war or the prospect of cattle raids. However, in the sixteenth century a clutch of brilliant Scots Latinists, all of whom spent a good deal of their time furth of Scotland, studying in France and Spain, detected admirable values and qualities in the Gaels or, as they called them, the 'Auld Scots', thus anticipating, in some respects, the approach of enlightened conjecturalists.

Their attitudes are best summed up in the writings of two of their number, Hector Boece, Principal of Aberdeen University, and George Buchanan, the brilliant humanist and tutor of James VI.[33] Boece was convinced that the Gaels preserved values which his contemporary Lowland countrymen had lost. The Scots in the past, through ingenuity, wisdom and their capacity for warfare, had resisted the incursions of the English, with strength, vigour and 'sovereign virtue', qualities which were no more; they were now drowned in all manner of avarice and lust. Their heroic ancestors had practised temperance, the fountain of all virtue; moderation governed their most mundane activities such as sleep, eating and drinking. Plain bread made from native cereals sustained them. Hunting for meat made them strong as did their habit of consuming it half raw. They had only two meals a day, breakfast and supper, 'throw quhilk thair stomok wes nevir surfetly chargit'. When celebrations were called for they consumed whisky, not made of costly spices but of such natural products as grew in their own backyards. Otherwise they drank ale but were often content with water. Each warrior brought his own oatmeal on campaigns.

In peace-time they strenuously exercised. Since they were hatless, baldness was unknown and feet, likewise, were bare except in the coldest weather. Clothes were made from home-grown products. Children were trained from their earliest years to sleep on the ground or on bunches of straw without any covering. Each mother breast-fed her own child, wet-nurses being unknown. Injury to one was deemed to affect all, compensation being sought in blood. All were prepared to die for their chiefs. Women fought alongside the men unless they were pregnant. All fought without deceit or treachery.

It was indicative of the antiquity of his ancestors that they used the rites and manners of the Egyptians whose hieroglyphs, Boece believed, had been transferred to Pictish stones, but unfortunately that crafty manner of writing had now been lost, along with their ancient language when Lowlanders acquired the Saxon tongue. About the time of Malcolm Canmore (1058–93), due to increased interaction with the English, the old ways became contaminated, so generating Scotland's present predicament; 'where our ancestors had sobriety, we have insobriety and drunkenness, where they had plenty with sufficiency, we consume immoderate courses with superfluity, as if he who is most noble and honest can devour and swallow most and seeks out so many luxurious dishes as to make the stomach receive more than it can sufficiently digest'. Folk now tuck away double dinners and suppers so that fish, fowl and animals are endangered due to their voracious consumption. The current craze for foreign foods and wines, drugs and medicines has a debilitating impact upon health and well-being, the material displacing the spiritual.

George Buchanan was actually a Gaelic speaker from the southern end of Loch Lomond. In various tracts and a *History of Scotland* (1582) he argued that ideas about the ancient Scottish constitution were preserved within the clan system in which unsatisfactory chiefs could be deposed by their own followers, thus providing justification for the removal of Mary, Queen of Scots by her subjects in 1567. He derived much of his information from Boece but he was particularly fascinated by the fact that the Gaels had preserved their language, manner of living, and even their costume, uncorrupted for a period of over two thousand years.

Indeed, as I have suggested elsewhere,[34] in the works of these historians – and others could be cited – there seems to be a process underway which involves the sentimentalization of the Gael, almost in anticipation of the romanticization of the inhabitants of the Highlands which took place following the defeat of the last Jacobite rebellion in 1745–6. For the earlier period the iconic event corresponding to the battle of Culloden was the collapse of the Lordship of the Isles at the end of the fifteenth century when it appeared that the assimilation of the Gàidhealtachd was only a matter of time. Indeed, at the Union of the Crowns in 1603, the great feudal lawyer Sir Thomas Craig could confidently anticipate a time in the not-too-distant future when Gaelic would have fallen into desuetude: 'There is not a single chieftain in the Highlands and Islands who does not speak, or at least understand, English . . . I have not the slightest doubt that before the century is over Gaelic will no longer be spoken on the mainland and islands of Scotland'.[35]

Craig was to be proved wrong but contemporaneously James VI was striving to

9

ensure that Gaelic's days truly were numbered as he mounted a remarkable and deplorable attack upon Scottish traditional society, not only in the Gàidhealtachd but in the Borders and the Northern Isles as well. Rhetoric matched action as the agents of Scottish government referred to the 'clans' of the Borders, 'companies of wicked men coupled in fellowship by occasion of their surnames or near dwellings together, or through keeping society in theft'. Clans were not perceived at this point as exclusively Gaelic, though those of the north and west were memorably demonized as 'infamous bykes of lawless limmers', wasp-nests of lawless rogues. The bandits of the ancient southern frontier were dismissed as 'gangs', the first usage of the modern term.

James was initially asked by Elizabeth to curb those clans who were supplying gallowglasses, Hebridean mercenaries, in support of Irish resistance to English rule. One such was that of MacDonald of Islay and Kintyre, also known as the MacDonalds of Dunyveg and the Glens (i.e. Dunyveg in Islay, Scotland, and the Glens of Antrim in Northern Ireland). Clan MacGregor was another that James had in his sights. He granted commissions to the Campbells to hunt down members of both clans. Savage campaigns of state-inspired terror ensued. As I have previously argued James VI, at the beginning of the seventeenth century, evolved a threefold policy towards Gaelic Scotland which can be summed up as – plantation, deculturalization, and extirpation.[36] Plantation, akin to similar schemes going on at exactly the same time in Ireland and the American colonies, involved the establishment of Lowland burghs in the Highlands and Islands, for example Campbeltown in Kintyre and Stornoway on the Island of Lewis, though other places were also mooted. The idea was that protestant colonists, mainly from Ayrshire and Fife, would be 'planted' in order to transform the existing population. Thus commerce and the Scots language would drive out barbarism exactly as had been envisaged with the establishment of bastide towns by the English in Wales and Ireland during the Middle Ages.

Deculturalization aimed at the destruction of Gaelic culture as signalled in the controversial measures laid out in the 'Statutes of Iona' in 1609. James was convinced that one way to accomplish the disempowerment of the chiefs, once and for all, was to abolish the heritable jurisdictions, which gave them the power of life and death over their clans-folk. The 'Statutes' envisaged the more systematic dismantling of much that the Gaels held dear including the sending of children to be educated in the Lowlands, the prohibition of firearms, the maintenance of the Church (anathema to those chiefs who were Catholic), the establishment of inns (to facilitate travel in the Highlands), curbing the number of a chief's retainers, the discouragement of bards who were thought to cause trouble and violent eruptions through their scurrilous poetic compositions, and the consumption of 'strong wynis and acquavitae'. These conditions were further reinforced seven years later when the chiefs were required to appear before the Privy Council in Edinburgh when ordered to do so, to reduce the size of their households, and to purge their territories of beggars and idlers. They were forbidden to bear weapons except in the king's service while their clansmen were effectively disarmed. Each chief was compelled to specify his main residence and to repair his dwelling house, and each was permitted the use of one galley. Chiefs were allocated a drink ration; their clansmen were to abstain.

That all of this was deliberate and no accident is suggested by a document entitled 'instructions concerning the isles', either written by James himself, or more likely with his cognizance, in February of 1609. In this document he introduced the third plank of his policy, namely extirpation. Referring to the rude, barbarous and uncivil people, 'wild savages voyde of Godis feare and oure obedience', he thinly hinted that pacification of the western Gàidhealtachd might be carried out on the model of the Ulster plantation and he did not rule out a 'final solution'. 'We wilbe spairing to dispose upon ony pairt of these Yllis, and unwilling to extermine, yea skairse to transplant the inhabitants of the same, *bot upon a just caus*' (my italics). He then provided a brief analysis of Hebridean society, which he divided into chiefs, tacksmen (though he did not use the term) and labourers. The last would be permitted to remain. Those in the intermediate group who, from the eighteenth century, aware that their role was redundant, would often lead group migrations across the Atlantic, were to find respectable work, otherwise they would be transported or banished. Chiefs must submit to having their holdings reduced, a form of dispossession, and if they resisted they were also to be exiled.

King James can be seen as the architect of governmental policy toward the Gàidhealtachd which would be implemented by successive generations. The plantation of burghs and towns went on apace. Deculturalization, the suppression of the language and customs of the Gaels, has persisted into very recent times. Extirpation meant 'rooting out' or, in the final resort, destruction. James himself stated that he would be unwilling to exterminate recalcitrant Gaels except with 'just cause', an idea which so often depends upon the beholder. Such cause was easily distinguished with reference to clans such as the MacGregors and the MacDonalds of Islay, both of which were brutally persecuted by the Campbells with the cooperation, and sometimes the coercion, of the Crown. While far from successful in the short term James' policies were echoed in the motivation behind such events as the Massacre of Glencoe (1692), the aftermath of the Jacobite Risings and the Highland Clearances.

It seems fairly obvious that the clan system might well have atrophied had not the Stuarts required military manpower during the British civil wars of the mid-seventeenth century. James Graham, Marquis of Montrose, rallied the loyal clans – in several cases the same as those who would declare for Charles Edward Stuart in 1745. Some of these same loyal clans came to the fore in 1689 in support of James VII and II who, in England, was deemed to have abdicated, but in Scotland had forfeited his right to the kingship, a martyr to Catholicism and his own capriciousness. Following

11

the defeat of John Graham, Bonnie Dundee, at the battle of Killiecrankie in 1689 and the subsequent suppression of the first Jacobite Rising, William of Orange's government took steps to punish the participants. The authorities' first instinct was to go after all the clans that had supported the exiled James Stuart. There was then a half-hearted attempt to buy them off. In the view of the secretary of state, Sir John Dalrymple, the Master of Stair, the money would have been as well spent in ravaging the Highlands as in trying to pacify them. He contemplated the complete extirpation of the Jacobite clans of the Great Glen,[37] utilizing troops based at Inverness and Inverlochy.

In the event an example was to be made only of the MacDonalds of Glencoe whose chief had been late in tendering his oath of allegiance to the new regime, news which gladdened Stair's black heart: 'It is a great work of charity to be exact in rooting out that damnable sect, the worst of the Highlands.' The same emotive terminology was reflected in the official instructions issued by the king noting that it would be 'proper vindication of the public justice to extirpate that set of thieves'. The orders to the troops on the ground who would actually carry out the heinous deed were equally explicit. 'The orders are that none be spared of the sword, nor the government troubled with prisoners'; it was for the good and safety of the country 'that those miscreants be cut off root and branch'.[38] The massacre was disgraceful, but this was by no means the last occasion on which this particular weapon would be used in the history of British imperialism, a blunt instrument devised by James VI and now used to bludgeon the loyal followers of his grandson, James VII.

Equally unsubtle were the missionary endeavours promoted by the Kirk from 1709 when the Society for the Propagation of Christian Knowledge in Scotland launched its activities in the north. Education was its major remit though, unfortunately, through the medium of English rather than Gaelic. Thus began the assault on language that would survive within living memory.

It was to be expected that those who supported the Jacobite Rising of 1715, and the minor postscript which came to grief in Kintail in 1719, would pay the price for their failure. Although there were a number of executions almost all commentators are agreed that the government's response was on the whole merciful. The Disarming Act of 1716 may be thought to have enforced the intent of the Statutes of Iona with considerable rigour but, although compensation was paid for weapons surrendered, it was somewhat ineffective. Notoriously the clans handed in broken or damaged items and hid the more effective specimens in the thatch of their houses for a future occasion. Simon, Lord Lovat, proposed raising Independent Companies from among the Highlanders to act as a type of militia. This had been tried in William's reign but they quickly deteriorated into gangs of blackmailers and extortionists. Both initiatives were to be managed much more effectively from 1724 by General Wade who is much better known for having designed and constructed the first decent system of communications throughout the Highlands. His scheme involved the building of roads and bridges but also inns, as James VI had envisaged. All of these developments were later to be given highly effective novelistic treatment in Neil Munro's *The New Road.*

The government-perpetrated atrocities which took place on the field of the battle of Culloden (1746), as well as the vicious policies that were pursued thereafter, have often been rehearsed. Alan Macinnes has stated that 'the immediate aftermath of the 'Forty-Five was marked by systematic state terrorism, characterized by a genocidal intent that verged on ethnic cleansing'.[39] Personally I am not entirely convinced by his argument, nor do I commend the practice of transferring newspaper headlines to history texts, but we are probably all guilty of the practice and he has a point of view, perhaps better represented by his admission that 'this genocidal campaign was more noted for intent than achievement',[40] a statement that might also be usefully applied to the outcome of James VI's ambitious project. Certain it is that the victorious Duke of Cumberland actually contemplated the transportation of all the Jacobite clans in Lochaber; he did not share his royal ancestor's stated, though doubtful, unwillingness 'to extermine, yea skairse to transplant the inhabitants'. What is not in doubt is that the punitive legislation after the rebellion sounded the final death knell of the Old Highlands, even though many had detected its echo long before. The Disarming Acts, the abolition of heritable jurisdictions, first mooted by James VI in 1598, and again in 1609, the suppression of military tenures and the outlawing of tartan, all represented legislation which was intent upon the suppression of culture as much as on the prevention of future rebellion.

Meanwhile plantation went on apace. To be sure the government gave up on the idea of colonization on the Campbeltown model but the process can be detected particularly in those towns which housed forts and thus garrisons, such as those of Cromwell at Fort William and Inverness, which, however short-lived, doubtless had some impact as the military always does. Daniel Defoe noted that the people of Inverness 'speak as good English as at London, and with an English accent; ever since Oliver Cromwell they are in their manners and dress entirely English'.[41] Defoe probably exaggerated since presumably his own linguistic skills did not permit him to communicate with anyone in Gaelic. Most remarkable of all is the massive structure of Fort George, east of Inverness, which commenced building in 1748. Nothing offers greater testimony to the paranoia of the British authorities concerning another uprising in the Gàidhealtachd. Equally astonishing is the fact that garrisons were still maintained at the castles of Braemar and Corgarff late in the reign of Victoria to guard against the native population. The amount of money expended on the so-called defence of the Highlands – defended, be it noted, against *the enemy within* – must represent one of the greatest single outlays by imperial Britain, taking into account the miles of road, the amount of engineering and quarrying, the number of bridges erected and drains installed, as well as the building or rebuilding of forts, not to mention the maintenance of troops and the gangs of labourers required for the various projects. The construction of Fort George alone, some twenty years in the making, cost over £200,000, more than £1 billion at present day prices.[42]

Captain Edmund Burt, who worked on the communications system, was the author of the much quoted *Letters from the North of Scotland* published in 1754,[43] almost twenty or thirty years after the original letters were written, mostly in the 1720s, the last in 1737. He reported that the Gaels adapted well as wage earners and eagerly grasped the opportunities afforded by commerce, since roads built for the movement of troops would also serve for the conveyance of trade goods and people. Although it seems that almost nothing is known about the writer his missives reveal many of the tensions between Highland and Lowland, and between Scotland and England. There is a thin narrative thread running through the sequence as Burt moves from initial suspicion and fear of the inhabitants and their environment which evolve into sympathy with the human plight and a culminating awareness of the awesome beauty of the scenery.

He considered that a Highland chief did not think 'the present abject disposition of his clan towards him to be sufficient', but believed that poverty would intensify their obedience and 'accordingly makes use of all oppressive means to that end' (p. 27). He thought the Gaels had a good conceit of themselves with pretensions to gentle blood even when employed in menial occupations (p. 40). He reported four or five fairs per year in Inverness when the Highlanders brought their commodities to market, 'but good God! You could not conceive there was such misery in this island' (p. 45); the poorest and scantiest of goods were offered for sale. Burt was not unsympathetic to the Gaels but he depicts them as enduring conditions of abject misery, ill-clad, malodorous, barefoot, ill-fed, living in filthy hovels, with most people suffering from the itch. He described how the turf roofs of houses harboured insects and how worms dropped from the divots in dry weather, though the latter was in short supply for he mentions how the populace 'enjoyed nine months of winter and three months of bad weather', while a shower might last nine or ten weeks (p. 303). The locals liked to perform tasks to the sound of the pipes (p. 213) and he included a famous passage on the indecent brevity of the kilt (p. 232). He noted belief in witchcraft, fairies, second sight, prophecy and goblins among the 'poor superstitious people who do not even have the good sense to grow potatoes'. Burt teased his correspondent by recalling how once their ideal 'poetical mountain' had been Richmond Hill (p. 158). The reality of the Caledonian landscape was altogether more savage, frightening and repulsive: 'as I believe I am the first who ever attempted a minute description of any such mountains I cannot but greatly doubt of my success herein' (p. 155); '. . . of all views, I think the most horrid is, to look at the hills from east to west, or vice versa, for then the eye penetrates far among them, and sees more particularly their stupendous bulk, frightful irregularity, and horrid gloom, made yet more sombrous by the shades and faint reflections they communicate one to another' (p. 157).

The locals referred to the soldiers as 'poke puddings' because they ate so much (p. 64). When one Scot told Burt that he wanted his job he cheerfully replied that he would gladly surrender it and resign, as would all his fellow countrymen, provided that in return no Scot had any government employment south of the Tweed. Should this happen there would be plenty of room for all the English soldiers back home. As it was the Highlanders seemed to believe that 'every gain they make of the English is an acquisition to their country' (pp. 55–6). These anecdotes neatly introduce the topic of the Highland economy, on which Burt is exceptionally interesting. It was later to become a cliché that all Gaels (males at least) were indolent, alien to capitalism and did not understand the work ethic, claims still occasionally made in some of the literature by people who should know better. Early in his correspondence he relates that the chiefs forbid their clansmen to become involved in trade or trades since to do so would loosen the feudal bonds (p. 27). Such chiefs considered any kind of trade demeaning (p. 40). On the other hand he did distinguish young men who were good tradesmen, though the best of them usually emigrated (p. 60). Later he noted that the economy was improving because of the presence of the soldiers who teach the locals new trades and handicrafts (p. 132). Also wages were rising. Writing in the 1720s Burt explicitly denied that the Gaels were work-shy:

It is a received notion (but nothing can be more unjust) that the ordinary Highlanders are an indolent, lazy people: I know the contrary by troublesome experience – I say troublesome, because in a certain affair wherein I had occasion to employ great numbers of them, and gave them good wages, the solicitations of others for employment were very earnest, and would hardly admit of a denial: they are as willing as other people to mend their way of living; and, when they have gained strength from substantial food, they work as well as others; but why should a people be branded with the name of idlers, in a country where there is generally no profitable business for them to do?

Hence I have concluded, that if any expedient could be found for their employment, to their reasonable advantage, there would be little else wanting to reform the minds of the most savage amongst them. For my own part, I do assure you, that I never had the least reason to complain of the behaviour towards me of any of the ordinary Highlanders, or the Irish; but it wants a great deal that I could truly say as much of the Englishmen and Lowland Scots that were employed in the same business. (pp. 199–200)

On one occasion Burt had a native guide who had lost his house and his living as a result of the '15 Rising even though he had not been involved in the 'scrape' as it was called; hence he had become a mountain guide. He was convinced that there would not be another war, by which he meant another Jacobite Rising. When asked to expand on this view he replied that 'he believed the English did not expect one, because they were fooling away their money, in removing great stones and blowing up of rocks'. Burt reflected that once the roads were completed such guides would become redundant (p. 110). Burt's occupation as a roadmaker does not intrude until the final letter of the series. He related, as does Wade's memorial at Aberfeldy, that since 1726 some 250 miles of road had been constructed (p. 279), and in some memorable passages described in colourful detail a selection of the engineering problems encountered. He depicted with some precision the road over the Corrieyairack Pass from Dalwhinnie to Fort Augustus which required the construction of seventeen traverses (p. 288). Although Burt was understandably proud of such achievements, Thomas Telford, the Scottish Borderer who would be responsible for the next phase of Highland road building as well as for the construction of the Caledonian Canal, would later condemn Wade's roads for their inconvenient steepness.[44] Burt reveals that already in his day there had been discussions about cutting a navigable waterway through the Great Glen but he thought the mountains would act as a wind funnel which would thus endanger shipping (p. 293).

That Burt had travelled some way since he first arrived in the Highlands to build his roads is indicated by one passage in which he confessed defeat in trying to convey the magnificence of the Great Glen:

This opening would be a surprising prospect to such as never have seen a high country, being a mixture of mountains, waters, heath, rocks, precipices, and scattered trees; and that for so long an extent, in which the eye is confined within the space, and, therefore, if I should pretend to give you a full idea of it, I should put myself in the place of one that has had a strange preposterous dream, and, because it has made a strong impression on him, he fondly thinks he can convey it to others in the same likeness as it remains painted on his memory; and, in the end, wonders at the coldness with which it was received. (p. 290)

In this passage, we may think, Burt attained some sort of Caledonian epiphany; the nightmare had become the dream.

The Gaels have all too often been portrayed as the victims of history but it could be argued that they colluded in the romanticization of themselves in the inventive verse translations of James Macpherson or in the celebration of a world that had gone in the works of Walter Scott. So too, however, did the whole of Scotland. In the face of military conflict and the threat to the British state it is all too easy to stress the very real tensions between Highlands and Lowlands in the eighteenth century but both parts of the nation were subjected to similar forces and influences. The inhabitants of both regions knew that the world was changing – economically, socially, materially, culturally and intellectually. By century's end, although travellers continued to stream into Scotland and the Highlands in particular in search of scenery and superstition, it was no longer legitimate to view the Gaels as remote dwellers of distant

16

glens untouched by the outside world. Their men had fought for the British army on several continents; many folk had emigrated to parts of the world that once barely registered with them. The Gael had shown that he could be commercialized as easily as any other Scot. Arguably the Highland evictions yet to come could be seen as a more intensive version of the 'Lowland Clearances'[45] experienced elsewhere in Scotland. Those enlightened individuals whom Johnston and Boswell met on their travels attended the same schools and universities as their Lowland counterparts. And all were aware, as Thomas Carlyle dutifully noted of his father in *Reminiscences*, the world could not and would not last as it was, and that mighty changes, of which none saw the end, were on the way.

Notes

[1] A. & A. Macdonald, *The Clan Donald*, 3 vols., Inverness, 1896–1904, vol. 1, 55.

[2] Macdonald, *Clan Donald*, vol. 1, 50.

[3] Walter Scott, *The Poetical Works of Sir Walter Scott with the author's introduction and notes*, ed. J. Logie Robertson, London, 1913, 474.

[4] Macdonald, *Clan Donald*, vol. 1, 280.

[5] Charles Fraser-Mackintosh, *The Last MacDonalds of Isla*, Glasgow, 1895.

[6] Edward J. Cowan, *Montrose: For Covenant and King*, London, 1977: Edinburgh, 1995.

[7] Paul Hopkins, *Glencoe and the End of the Highland War*, Edinburgh, 1986.

[8] John Prebble, *Culloden*, London, 1961.

[9] Eric Richards, *The Highland Clearances, People, Landlords and Rural Turmoil*, Edinburgh, 2000.

[10] Bruce Lenman, *The Jacobite Risings in Britain, 1689–1746*, London, 1980.

[11] Edward J. Cowan, 'The Discovery of the Gàidhealtachd in Sixteenth Century Scotland', *Transactions of the Gaelic Society of Inverness*, lx (2000), 259–84.

[12] For a recent survey which contains an excellent bibliography see David Allan, *Scotland in the Eighteenth Century: Union and Enlightenment*, Harlow, 2002.

[13] Edward J. Cowan and Mike Paterson, *Folk in Print: Scotland's Chapbook Heritage*, Edinburgh, 2007.

[14] John Prebble, *Mutiny: Highland Regiments in Revolt 1743–1804*, London, 1975, 94.

[15] Frank McLynn, *1759: The Year Britain Became Master of the World*, London, 2004, 1–5, 20–21.

[16] Edward J. Cowan, 'Burns and Superstition' in *Love & Liberty: Robert Burns: A Bicentenary Celebration*, ed. Kenneth Simpson, East Linton, 1997, 231.

[17] R. B. Sher, *Church and University in the Scottish Enlightenment*, Edinburgh, 1985, 4.

[18] David Daiches, *The Paradox of Scottish Culture: The Eighteenth Century Experience*, Oxford, 1964.

[19] James Macpherson, *The Poems of Ossian and related works*, ed. Howard Gaskill, with an introduction by Fiona Stafford, Edinburgh, 1996, 1–31.

[20] Stephen Baxter, *Revolutions in the Earth: James Hutton and the True Age of the World*, London, 2003, 142.

[21] Alexander Broadie, *The Scottish Enlightenment, The Historical Age of the Historical Nation*, Edinburgh, 2001, 47.

[22] William Robertson, *The History of Scotland*, 3 vols., London, 1759, vol. 3, 186.

[23] Robertson, *History*, 1, 203.

[24] Robertson, *History*, 1, 405–6.

[25] Robertson, *History*, 3, 93–4.

[26] Robertson, *History*, 3, 181–6.

[27] Robertson, *History*, 1, 222–3.

[28] Robertson, *History*, 1, 405.

[29] Robertson, *History*, 2, 156.

[30] See H. M. Hopfl, 'From Savage to Scotsman: Conjectural History in the Scottish Enlightenment', *Journal of British Studies*, 17 (1978), 19–40.

[31] Sir William Alexander, *An Encouragement to Colonies*, London, 1624; Robert Gordon of Lochinvar, *Encouragements For such as shall have intention to bee undertakers in the new plantation of Cape Briton, now New Galloway in America By Mee Lochinvar*, Edinburgh, 1625.

[32] David Malcolme, *An essay on the antiquities of Great Britain and Ireland: wherein they are placed in a clearer light than hitherto. Designed as an introduction to a larger work, especially an attempt to shew an affinity betwixt the languages, &c of the ancient Britains, and the Americans of the Isthmus of Darien. In answer to an objection against revealed religion* . . . , Edinburgh, 1738.

[33] For full references to what follows see Cowan, 'Discovery of the Gàidhealtachd', 260–78.

[34] Cowan, 'Discovery of the Gàidhealtachd', 278–9.

[35] Sir Thomas Craig, *De Unione Regnorum Britanniae Tractatus*, (ed.) C. Sanford Terry, *Scottish History Society*, Edinburgh, 1909, 289.

[36] Edward J. Cowan, 'Clanship, kinship and the Campbell acquisition of Islay', *Scottish Historical Review*, lviii (1979), 132–57.

[37] This point is admittedly contentious though I am not convinced by the argument advanced by Hopkins, *Glencoe*, 310–11 and note 12.

[38] The extreme violent language used by Stair and others is adequately documented by Hopkins, *Glencoe*, 308–50. See also D. J. Macdonald, *Slaughter Under Trust*, London, 1965, and John Prebble, *Glencoe, the Story of the Massacre*, London, 1966.

[39] Allan I. Macinnes, *Clanship, Commerce and the House of Stuart, 1603–1788*, East Linton, 1996, 211.

[40] Macinnes, *Clanship*, 212.

[41] Quoted F. H. Groome, *Ordnance Gazetteer of Scotland: A Survey of Scottish Topography, Statistical, Biographical, and Historical*, 3 vols., Edinburgh, 1886, vol. 2, 305.

[42] Chris Tabraham and Doreen Grove, *Fortress Scotland and the Jacobites*, London, 1995, 98.

[43] Edmund Burt, Burt's *Letters from the North of Scotland*, London, 1854: rep. Edinburgh, 1998, referenced in text.

[44] Anthony Burton, *Thomas Telford*, London, 1999, 106–7.

[45] Edward J. Cowan, 'Agricultural Improvement and the Foundation of Early Agricultural Societies in Dumfries and Galloway', *Transactions of the Dumfriesshire and Galloway Natural History and Antiquarian Society*, 3rd Series, vol. liii (1977–8), 166.

GERARD CARRUTHERS

'Poured out extensive, and of watery wealth': Scotland in Thomson's *The Seasons*

It is somewhat ironic that James Thomson, a poet of empirical landscape observation, paying close attention not only to the natural environment but also to the human
geography of Great Britain, should be a writer nowadays of rather uncertain territory. Among the number of great writers produced by Scotland in the eighteenth
century, Thomson is not today much loved either by critics or among the large popular
audience for eighteenth-century poetry in his cradle-country. In Scotland there is no
clamour for editions or statues of Thomson the way there is for the commemoration
of Allan Ramsay, Robert Fergusson, Robert Burns or Duncan Ban Macintyre. Even
James Macpherson is better served than Thomson in the attention paid by Scottish-
published editions, critical books and journal articles. Scotland has become adept at
writing out its most successful international writers and, in extent second only to
Walter Scott, the influence of James Thomson is *the* major 'Scottish' one standing at
the centre of western literary history. I have written elsewhere about the problematic
reception of James Thomson in the country of his birth, and how this has much to
do with the cultural nationalism of the Scottish criticism of the twentieth century.[1]
In such criticism, Thomson is not seen as authentically Scottish enough in his émigré,
'non-vernacular', British nationalist status. However, the canonicity of Thomson in
his Scottish and British contexts is worth revisiting because it is much less simple than
the still prevalent, old-fashioned discussions of bifurcated eighteenth-century Scottish
literary identity would have us believe.

Scottish commentary of the last one hundred years sees Allan Ramsay and James
Thomson representing the polar extremes of early eighteenth-century cultural attitude
in Scottish poetry: the 'vernacular' versus the 'non-vernacular'. However, we should
be aware of similarity between the two in that Thomson, like Ramsay, was a path-
breaking poetic revivalist. Where Ramsay re-mints the 'Christ's Kirk' and 'Habbie
Simson' stanzas for Robert Fergusson, Robert Burns and many others, Thomson,
more than anyone else, through the influence of 'The Castle of Indolence' (1748),
repopularises the Spenserian stanza so that Fergusson in 'The Farmer's Ingle' and
Burns in 'The Cotter's Saturday Night' come to employ this vehicle. Certainly, the stanza
choices of Ramsay and Thomson represent different ideological badges, the identities of Tory, Stuart-loyalism and Whig dissenting Protestantism, respectively, but the

project of revival in Scotland works across ideological lines and flows sometimes into a common reservoir, as we see clearly in the case of Fergusson, the inheritor of both Ramsay and Thomson (indeed, Fergusson's natural scene-painting owes much more to the sensuous detail observation of Thomson than Ramsay's more generalised pastoral writing). The revival of 'Habbie Simson' and 'Christ's Kirk' stanzas is also part of the same broad cultural movement with the revival of the Spenserian stanza. All three reutilisations can be read against the desire, widely abroad in eighteenth-century Britain, to return to a kind of cultural purity or refreshed primitivism after the inextricably confused cultural utterances (usually involving the vexed and bloody interpretation of sacred scripture) during the internecine turbulence of the seventeenth century. In the 'Spring' (1728) part of *The Seasons* Thomson may be explicitly referring to the Iron Age:

> Of iron war, in ancient barbarous times,
> When disunited Britain ever bled,
> Lost in eternal broil, ere yet she grew
> To this deep-laid indissoluble state
> Where wealth and commerce lift the golden head,
> And o'er our labours liberty and law
> Impartial watch, the wonder of a world! (ll. 842–8)[2]

We must, however, read these lines mindful of the recent and prolonged British civil wars of the century before. The impetus behind the Augustan age sought to put the horror of the previous century with its seemingly ever-fragmenting sects and ideologies behind it. A more settled, certain world was desired and this helps account for the newly heightened pastoral sensibility, both in the 'Scottish' stanzas of 'Christ's Kirk' and 'Habbie Simson' resurrected by Ramsay, associated, to a large extent, with robust peasant good living, and in Thomson's passion for the man he held to be the greatest pastoral writer of the British Isles, Edmund Spenser. More widely, of course, we have also in the early eighteenth century the fervent return to Virgil, including the observation of agricultural process, which we might read broadly as representing the British desire for a more settled landscape and a new empiricism centred on the rational observation of nature as opposed to the opaque urgings of the word which had prevailed during so much of the previous century.

Thomson's poetry in *The Seasons* owes much to the likes of Newtonian-influenced books such as William Derham's *Physico-Theology* (1713) and this title succinctly relays the shift towards a more rational form of religion and physically contiguous (rather than spiritually inspired) intercourse with the world in the period of early Enlightenment.[3] *The Seasons* is something of an 'artless' production, as it objectively surveys the British landscape and civic scene within the cycle of the year. In so far as imaginative

22

'art' is involved in Thomson's text, subjective personification of the elements is usually rather 'standard' and immediately accessible. Virgilian method – the observation of agricultural process and the deriving of moral import from this – represents again a highly received, rather obvious didactic mechanism.

It is possible to suggest more particularly, however, that we might see Thomson's moderate Presbyterian devotional eye (an aspect of Scottish literary identity to which modern Scottish criticism has been blind). For instance, we might turn to 'A Hymn to the Seasons', which concludes Thomson's greatest work:

> Mysterious round! what skill, what force divine,
> Deep-felt in these appear! a simple train,
> Yet so delightful mixed, with such kind art,
> Such beauty and beneficence combined,
> Shade unperceived so softening into shade,
> And all so forming an harmonious whole
> That, as they still succeed, they ravish still.
> But, wandering oft with brute unconscious gaze,
> Man marks not thee, marks not the mighty hand
> That, ever busy, wheels the silent spheres,
> Works in the secret deep, shoots steaming thence
> The fair profusion that o'erspreads the Spring,
> Flings from the sun direct the flaming day,
> Feeds every creature, hurls the tempest forth,
> And, as on earth this grateful change revolves,
> With transport touches all the springs of life. (ll. 21–36)

God is found in nature skilfully, deeply, harmoniously at work creating beauty and bounty with 'kind art'. Man with his 'brute unconscious gaze' in the face of such benevolence, however, is a rather sinister presence and this conjunction hallmarks Thomson's Christian vision in *The Seasons*. For thinkers like Thomson the world, or reality, was a text inadequately regarded by humanity most especially in the ideology- and sectarian-bound generations that had preceded his in Britain.

Thomson's response to recent British history informed by his moderate Presby- terianism, where divine providence and purpose are to be read in the world, is the context in which his attention to nature is crucial. There has sometimes been a distracting tendency in Thomsonian criticism to read his impetus in *The Seasons* as part of a Scottish tradition going back to medieval writers like Gavin Douglas and Robert Henryson.[4] Such single-track nationalising, however, is the kind of thing that has often closed down sensitivity in Scottish criticism to the profound differences through the generations in Scottish literature, and to the fact that the best writing responds to its contemporary situation (much more than 'tradition') and, at the same time, often has to 'remake' its links in its own country. Let us observe two aspects of Thomson remaking literary space for himself in the Scottish context. The first of these is, in a sense, fairly 'minor' but regards a volume that deserves to be paid more attention. This is the *Edinburgh Miscellany* (1720) to which Thomson and several friends including fellow divinity student Patrick Murdoch contributed. Also present were Robert Blair (later Church of Scotland clergyman and the author of the didactic, meditative poem 'The Grave' (1743), which was to be so memorably illustrated by William Blake), David Malloch (later Mallet), who later collaborated with Thomson on the play *Alfred, A Masque* (1740), which included the notorious 'Rule Britannia', and James Arbuckle, an Ulster poet at the University of Glasgow. The circumstances surrounding the production of the *Edinburgh Miscellany* are hazy, including the precise editorship, if any. Add to the volume's throwaway title, a preface that is slightly comic in its vagueness about who has written the materials within and we can perhaps see some deliberate impression-making going on.[5] None of the contents are hugely interesting, comprising imitation Horatian odes and very standard pastoralising, but the volume overall can be read as an attempt to kickstart the Augustan vision in early eighteenth-century Scotland. The studied effect of the volume, cumulatively, is that of not trying too hard, of letting the audience assume that such poetry production is simply 'natural' to Scotland. There is probably a bit more co-ordination going on, however, found in the bringing together of Edinburgh college student Thomson and Glasgow University student Arbuckle, a man likewise of liberal Presbyterianism. For both Arbuckle and Thomson notions of 'liberty', of stoical self-restraint and of the good of the commonwealth come to be writ large in their writings. What we glimpse, arguably, in the *Edinburgh Miscellany* is a platform for a nascent progressive Whig mentality abroad in Scotland, embracing poetry in a way that the older, more Calvinist Presbyterian mentality of Scotland would not (at this time and for several decades to come this harsher religious mindset remained prominent among the city-fathers of Edinburgh).

If the linkage of Thomson with Scotland's medieval past has been urged unconvincingly by some commentators, there is nonetheless an explicit point of contact that again, even more clearly, shows Thomson helping redraw Scottish cultural heritage in the early eighteenth century. This happens in the context of Thomson's most extensive treatment of Scotland in the 'Autumn' (1730) section of *The Seasons*. He describes Scotland:

> Her airy mountains from the waving main
> Invested with a keen diffusive sky,
> Breathing the soul acute; her forests huge,
> Incult, robust, and tall, by Nature's hand
> Planted of old: her azure lakes between,

Poured out extensive, and of watery wealth
Full; winding deep and green, her fertile vales,
With many a cool translucent brimming flood
Washed lovely, from the Tweed (pure parent-stream,
Whose pastoral banks first heard my Doric reed,
With, sylvan Jed, thy tributary brook)
To where the north-inflated tempest foams
O'er Orcas or Betubium's highest peak –
Nurse of a people, in misfortune's school
Trained up to hardy deeds, soon visited
By Learning, when before the Gothic rage
She took her western flight; a manly race
Of unsubmitting spirit, wise, and brave,
Who still through bleeding ages struggled hard
(As well unhappy Wallace can attest,
Great patriot-hero! ill requited chief!)
To hold a generous undiminished state,
Too much in vain! Hence, of unequal bounds
Impatient, and by tempting glory borne
O'er every land, for every land their life
Has flowed profuse, their piercing genius planned,
And swelled the pomp of peace their faithful toil:
As from their own clear north in radiant streams
Bright over Europe bursts the boreal morn. (ll. 881–909)

Remarkable here is the appearance of William Wallace, which follows on from two important earlier Scottish literary appearances: Allan Ramsay's 'The Vision' (1715) recalled the example of Wallace as it lamented the Anglo-Scottish parliamentary union of 1707 and William Hamilton of Gilbertfield published his edition, 'translated' into English, of Blind Hary's 'Wallace' in 1722. Ramsay resurrects the great Scottish hero to serve anti-unionist purposes and soon Ramsay's friend Hamilton 'modernises' or Presbyterianises Wallace to appeal to a mainstream eighteenth-century Scottish audience in an edition that becomes hugely popular over the next half century or so.[6] Generally, Thomson is allowed access to Wallace by this manoeuvre of Hamilton's, which Thomson expands in the overall context of *The Seasons* so that Wallace is inserted into a canon of 'patriots' resisting forces of tyranny larger than themselves. These include Francis Drake, John Hampden, the pivotal parliamentary hero of the civil war, and Algernon Sidney, one of the most conscientious judges at the trial of Charles I. Cleverly, in a similarly catholic manoeuvre, Thomson also includes in this pantheon Thomas More: 'Who with a generous though mistaken zeal,/Withstood a brutal tyrant's useful rage' ('Summer' (1727), ll. 1489–90), so that with some important qualification even More the canonised Roman saint can be used as a hero against unreasonable and unlimited authority. If More can be brought in from the cold, then so too can another 'rebel' against the English king: Wallace. What we find here, in fact, is the start of a Wallace venerated by Scottish Whigs (such as Robert Burns) and even by English Whigs who by the 1790s are able to cite the great Scottish guerrilla leader as among those fighting in the long and arduous line that opposes unconstitutional autocracy.

In the passage I have just cited writ large also is what I would call 'water pastoralism'. England might be a 'green and pleasant land' agriculturally superior (Scotland is uncultivated or 'incult'), but the northern nation has resources in its water, in the creatures which throng its sea, rivers and lochs. If only Britain would wake up to this; instead, however, the nation is 'Shamefully passive, while Batavian fleets/Defraud us of the glittering finny swarms/That heave our friths and crowd upon our shore' (ll. 921–3). Thomson here can be linked to Allan Ramsay in 'The Prospect of Plenty' and Robert Fergusson in 'The Rivers of Scotland' (both poems, among the best in their respective author's oeuvres, though shamefully overlooked by standarising critics and anthologisers who can't see past the notion of eighteenth-century vernacular Scots poetry in its non-pastoral, supposedly urban centre of gravity). Scotland, according to Thomson, is still waiting to catch up with the rest of Europe, still waiting to enjoy a 'boreal', or fully post-glacial state, where industry and agricultural improvement might be introduced. A hardy, often learned people are just waiting to be led in the right direction. For this leadership, Thomson turns to the Duke of Argyll, a commander at the Battle of Malplaquet in Flanders in 1709 when the British defeated the French. Argyll comes from the same hardy stock as Wallace, according to Thomson, and what is interesting here is that Thomson is not the first to yoke the pair together. Allan Ramsay makes the same explicit connection in his Horatian ode, 'To John, the second Duke of Argyll', published in 1720, and so we have a second piece of evidence that Thomson had been reading his Ramsay. (The first bit of evidence is Thomson's early piece – written in 1719 – 'Elegy on James Therburn in Chatto' – a fragment in the 'Habbie Simson' stanza). It is interesting too that, as with Allan Ramsay yet again (Ramsay both corresponded with and celebrated in his poetry this individual), another Scottish leader of progress is cited in Ducan Forbes of Culloden, improver both of agricultural and legal theory (see 'Autumn', ll. 945–9). Twentieth-century Scottish criticism often painted a kind of Scottish nationalist, proto-demotic literary impetus (Ramsay *et al.*) versus Anglified, proto-capitalist Scottish literature: Thomson. In fact, both Ramsay and Thomson seek to draw continuity between the ancient Scottish patriotic past and what they took to be the best of progressive Hanoverian Britain. This commonality of effort proves, I think, the overwhelming desire for unity between past and present and, again, in the face of seventeenth-century British history the desire for a cultural wholeness that transcends merely the Scottish situation (even the part-time Jacobite, and part-time anti-Unionist, Allan Ramsay ultimately has a bigger agenda in wishing an end to British faction and throwing in his lot with an ideal *Pax Hanoveriana*).

The language of being a 'Briton', however, so fashionable in the eighteenth century has become retrospectively debased in the light of the nineteenth-century imperial enterprise. For Thomson and others of the Real Whig or Commonwealth political persuasion, however, the badge of 'Briton' was meant to represent the aspiration of industrious, non-luxurious living founded on reasonable thinking and conscientious political involvement – these attributes being recommended to all classes of British society. *The Seasons* has a strong surrounding context to it, very well elucidated by Glynis Ridley, of critiquing unchecked mercantile and capitalistic venture (including slavery) that Thomson associated with the ministry of Sir Robert Walpole who enjoyed a huge personal ascendancy because of a bored, non-English speaking George I, and then afterwards because of George II, who also frequently absented himself from the political process.[7] *The Seasons* is not, as some critics like to imply, the production of a Scotsman on the make in London, but is a poem of opposition, and was understood as such in the eighteenth century. We need to regain a sense of Thomson's reception in the eighteenth century. I've mentioned already his part in the coinage of William Wallace as part of the pantheon of heroes for those in the 1790s opposing the corrupt British political system of patronage and rotten boroughs; Thomson plays a part also in popularising King Alfred as an icon for the reform movement. Alfred, unlike George I or II, so far as Thomson was concerned, was a hands-on king, of strong military bent, and also fostered learning including the promotion of a vernacular literary language – Anglo-Saxon. It is precisely because of Thomson's championing of King Alfred that Robert Burns is enabled to do likewise in his 'Ode [For General Washington's Birthday]'.

Thomson himself, indeed, becomes something of an icon for liberty in the 1790s. For instance, I have recently come across a very interesting document in Glasgow University Library among a series of pamphlets gifted to the University by David Steuart Erskine, the Earl of Buchan. In 1780 the Society of Constitutional Information published a speech by the Reverend George Walker in Mansfield, Nottinghamshire, which demands the extension of the franchise and complains that political debate is being stifled. Published along with this speech is James Thomson's preface to John Milton's *Areopagitica*, which Thomson had published in 1738 at a time when it was feared that widespread censorship was about to be enacted by the Walpole administration in the face of criticism of his foreign policy. Thomson in his preface talks of 'the human rights' that are involved in the freedom of the press. 'Take away the Liberty of the Press', he says, 'and we are all at once stript of the Use of our noblest Faculties: our Souls themselves are imprisoned in a dark Dungeon: we may breathe, but we cannot be said to live.' In 1780, the Society of Constitutional Information found abiding relevance in Thomson; in 1791 the reformist Earl of Buchan, who had been involved in the SCI, sought to inaugurate an annual commemoration of Thomson for which Robert Burns wrote a poem. In 1793–4 one of the most outspoken writers urging extension of the franchise was a man named James Thomson Callender. Callender was the friend of the reformist lawyer Thomas Muir, and like Muir suffered exile after being charged with sedition. Callender might actually have been the nephew of James Thomson, author of *The Seasons*; whether or not he was, he enjoyed being thought of in this light, and so we see the striking purchase of James Thomson as a spokesman and icon of political progress.[8]

Thomson's status is somewhat neutralised, however, in the course of the nineteenth century. 'Rule Britannia' is read in the light of empire (when in fact it is about an often beset nation ruling the waves in self-defence, rather than ruling anyone else's land). Matthew Arnold's invention of 'Celtic Literature' with its special ability in portraying nature has several critics see Thomson in the light of this 'Celtic' made manifest, obviously enough, in the natural description of *The Seasons*. There is a big irony, however, in that, as Derick Thomson and others have shown, Duncan Ban McIntyre, Alexander MacDonald and Dugald Buchanan (in common with just about every other important poet in the British Isles in the eighteenth century) owe a debt to Thomson's method of didactic interaction with the natural environment.[9] So far as much twentieth-century Scottish criticism is concerned, however, Thomson takes the 'natural' Celtic heritage (in his genes as it were) and presses it into British service. He is read, then, as a part of the story of the Highlandisation of Scottish and, indeed, of British culture (helping invent a romantic landscape in which what is masked is the true nature of the Scoto-British commercial and imperial enterprise).[10] There was, however, a synthetic construction of the 'Celtic' with regard to Thomson, and we see this clearly in response to Thomson's death in August 1748, when William Collins wrote a rather fine elegy which begins 'In yonder grave a Druid lies'. Again, this speaks of the allegiance of the two men – Thomson and Collins – to the 'Patriot' or Real Whig party, where, as a result of early eighteenth-century antiquarianism, the Druids were read as tenacious opponents of a corrupt Roman empire (associated in the minds of the Real Whigs with the Walpole ministry). The extrapolation of Thomson's cultural identity as a Presbyterian Real Whig, taking cognisance of cross-border political and literary canons to which he wished to express allegiance, the attempt by him and others to carve out a sense of pure or 'druidic' Britishness, which is to say politically liberal and generous Britishness in the face of the feud and faction of the seventeenth century, remains inadequately appreciated. Unfortunately these co-ordinates have been lost amidst the narrow national terms of reference involved in the predominant narratives of much modern Scottish criticism:

'Scotland' – good; 'Britain' – bad.
'Vernacular' – good; 'Augustan' – bad.
'urban focus' – true; 'pastoral focus' – false.
'Genuine' 'Celtic' – good; 'Celtic mythicisation' – bad.

In an age perhaps where we are beginning to understand identity in more complex fashion, as the eighteenth century itself did; in an age where there is a new emphasis on 'four nations' history and culture that no longer accedes either to the notion of an all-conquering English-centred Britishness, nor to the absolute cultural separateness of England, Ireland, Scotland or Wales we ought to be able to reread James Thomson as, yes, a complex Scottish writer, but not as someone to be effectively excluded from discussions of Scottish literature for being not Scottish enough or for being too British.

Notes

1   Gerard Carruthers, 'James Thomson and Eighteenth-Century Scottish Literary Identity' in Richard Terry (ed.), *James Thomson: Essays for the Tercentenary* (Liverpool University Press: Liverpool, 2000), pp.165–190.

2   James Thomson, *The Seasons and The Castle of Indolence*, edited by James Sambrook (Oxford University Press: Oxford, 1987); all subsequent references to this edition.

3   Alan Dugald McKillop, *The Background of Thomson's Seasons* (Archon Books: Hamden, Connecticut, 1961), see especially p.7 & pp.81–2.

4   See, for example, R.R. Agrawal, *Tradition and Experiment in the Poetry of James Thomson (1700–1748)* (Institut für Anglistik und Amerikanistik: Salzburg, 1981), pp.11–12.

5   See James Sambrook, *James Thomson 1700–1748: A Life* (Clarendon Press: Oxford, 1991), pp.17–19.

6   For a very useful account see Elspeth King's introduction to *Blind Harry's Wallace* by William Hamilton of Gilberfield (Luath Press: Edinburgh, 1998), pp.xi–xxix.

7   Glynis Ridley, '*The Seasons* and the Politics of Opposition' in R. Terry (ed.), *James Thomson: Essays for the Tercentenary*, pp.93–116.

8   See the modern biography of Callender Thomson by Michael Durey, '*With the Hammer of Truth': James Thomson Callender and America's Early National Heroes* (University Press of Virginia: Charlottesville & London, 1990).

9   See Derick S. Thomson (ed.), *Gaelic Poetry in the Eighteenth Century* (Association for Scottish Literary Studies: Aberdeen, 1993).

10   See, for instance, the comments of Andrew Noble on Thomson in his 'Urbane Silence: Scottish Writing and the Nineteenth-Century City' in George Gordon (ed.), *Perspectives of the Scottish City* (Aberdeen University Press: Aberdeen, 1985), p.66.

RAGHNALL MACILLEDHUIBH

Compàirteachadh an urraim:
Mac Mhgr Alastair 's a' Ghalldachd

Tha mi toirt an tiotail agam, 'Compàirteachadh an Urraim', bhon roi-ràdh a sgrìobh
Alastair ris an leabhar as ainmeil aige, *Aiseirigh na Seann Chànain Albannaich*, a thàinig
a-mach ann an 1751 's a tha 'na chomharradh-tìre ann an litreachas na Gàidhlig. 'S e
sgrìobhadh ann am Beurla, ged a tha a' bhàrdachd air fad san leabhar ann an Gàidhlig
a-mhàin, tha e 'g ràdh an toiseach gu bheil e 'n dòchas gun toir na dàin dibhearsain
do na thuigeas iad, agus miann do chàch a' chànan ionnsachadh, ma bheirear a chreid-
sinn orra sin gun d'fhiach a leithid de bhàrdachd an spàirn. Tha e an uair sin a'
bruidhinn air an nòisean a bh' aige duanaire eachdraidheil de bhàrdachd Ghàidhlig
fhoillseachadh anns am bi beachdan léirsinneach agus eadar-theangaichean Beurla. Tha
e 'g ràdh: 'If such a series can be made out, besides the general agreeableness of the
thing itself, nothing perhaps will better contribute to discover the progress of genius,
through all its different degrees of improvement, from extreme simplicity, to whatever height we shall happen upon examination to find it, amongst this people . . . An
agreeable inquiry, surely! and one would think not displeasing, even to the inhabitants
of the lowlands of Scotland, who have always shared with them the honour of every
gallant action, and are now first invited to a participation of their reputation for arts.'
   Thoir an aire nach e tiotal an leabhair *Aiseirigh na Seann Chànain Ghaidhealaich* ach
Aiseirigh na Seann Chànain Albannaich. Se th' ann an 'aiseirigh' ach 'éirigh a-rithist' no
'dàrna éirigh'. Tha tarraing sa bhàrdachd dhaibhsan a tha a' creidsinn ann an Seumasachd
agus ann an saorsa na toile. Bha Gaidhil agus Gaill an cogadh còmhla, tha Alastair ag
ràdh, chan ann a-mhàin air Sliabh a' Chlamhain, aig an Eaglais Bhric 's ann an Cùil
Lodair, ach ann an 'every gallant action' – 's e ciallachadh gun teagamh Sliabh an t-
Siorraim, Worcester, Inbhir Chéitinn, Flodden, Allt a' Bhonnaich, Drochaid Shruighlea
agus iomadh blàr eile eatarra sin.
   Se an *Aiseirigh* a' chiad chruinneachadh de bhàrdachd no rosg saoghalta Gàidhlig
a chaidh fhoillseachadh riamh, agus tha na Gaill air am fiathachadh gu pàirt a ghabhail anns a' cho-ghàirdeachas. Tha an t-ùghdar an dòchas gum bi miann a' Ghaill gu
Gàidhlig ionnsachadh air àrdachadh le cruinnichean den t-seòrsa seo cho math ri gaol
bràthaireil na seirbheis airm 's nan amasan compàirtichte poileataigeach. B'iad tri prìomh
amasan nan Seumasach Albannach cur ás do dh'Achd an Aonaidh, tilleadh nan
rìghrean Stiùbhartach, agus saorsa creidimh. Bha Alastair an-seo a' cur amas cultarach

31

riutha sin: gur e nàisean aonaichte dà-chànanach no trì-chànanach a bhiodh anns an Alba ùir neo-eisimeilich a thigeadh ás a-seo, le co-ionannachd don Ghàidhlig 's don Bheurla, neo gu dearbh don Ghàidhlig, don Bheurla 's don Albais. Tha seo 'na mhiann brìoghmhor cultarach gus an latha an-diugh, mar a tha am Bile Gàidhlig a tha dol 'na lagh an ath mhìos a' leigeil fhaicinn, ged a dh'fheumas mi ràdh gu bheil mi air mo chur gu eudòchas leis na chuir eachdraidh chultarach na h-Alba de charan mìchiatach bho chaill am pàrtaidh aig Alastair blàr Chùil Lodair.

Ach an nì a tha mi ag iarraidh a dhèanamh sa phàipear seo, se feuchainn ris na ceuman a lorg tron deach am miann cultarach seo a ruigheachd ann an inntinn Alastair.

Rugadh Alastair 'na mhac ministeir mu 1698 agus dh'fhàs e suas ann am mansa Dhail Eilghe ri taobh Loch Seile ann am Mùideart. Bidh e air foghlam trì-chananach fhaighinn, ann an Gàidhlig, Beurla agus Laideann, anns an stuidear aig athair, cho math ri foghlam susbainteach tro mheadhan na Gàidhlig, mar a chanamaid ris an-diugh, ann an taighean-céilidh na dùthcha. An uair sin chaidh a chur air falbh gu Oilthigh Ghlaschu. Chan eil lorg sam bith gun do chlàraich no gun do cheumnaich e; an aon rud a tha fios againn se gun do fhritheil e clasaichean, ach chan eil dad ás an rathad mu dheidhinn sin. Chuir an t-Urr. Tómas MacCalmain nach maireann air shùilean dhuinn gun do rinn Alastair a dhà dhe na h-òrain aige, 'Òran a' Gheamhraidh' agus 'Allt an t-Siùcair', air na fuinn 'Tweedside' agus 'The Lass o' Patie's Mill', a bha ann an 1822 agus fada roimhe air an cluich leis na cluig, a' chiad fhear Di-Ciadaoin 's an dàrna fear Diar-Daoin, ann an Stìopall na Toll-Bhùtha aig Crois Ghlaschu, beagan cheudan slat bhon t-Seann Cholaist air an Àrd Shràid. 'May we not think of him,' bheachdaich MacCalmain, 'sitting uncomfortably on a hard bench in a dull classroom, while the professor drearily discoursed in Latin about Aristotle and the rest, letting his mind wander to his beloved Highlands and Allt an t-Siùcair, as the chimes of 'The Lass o' Patie's Mill' tinkled faintly through the window?'

Dé bhiodh e air a leughadh sna bliadhnachan sin timcheall air 1712? Leigeadh Màrtainn Màrtainn, *A Description of the Western Islands of Scotland*, 1703, fhaicinn dha gun robh feòrachas mór am measg eòlaichean na Rìoghachd ùir Aonaichte gu tuil-leadh fios a bhith aca mu na h-eileanan, gu sònraichte a thaobh cho fada 's gun robh iuchair na slàinte aig na Gaidhil. Leigeadh James Watson, *A Choice Collection of Comic and Serious Scots Poems*, 1706, fhaicinn dha gun robh bàrdachd an t-sluaigh chumanta ga meas airidh air gléidheadh le bhith ga cruinneachadh 's ga clò-bhualadh. Leigeadh Edward Lhuyd, *Archaeologia Britannica*, 1707, fhaicinn dha gu saidheansach gun robh teaghlach air leth ann de chànanan Ceilteach, ás an robh Gàidhlig na h-Alba, Gaeilge, Gàidhlig Mhanainn, Cuimris, Còrnais agus cainnt na Breatainne Bige uile a' soirbheachadh. Leigeadh Alexander Pope, *The Rape of the Lock*, 1712, fhaicinn dha gum faodadh aoir bhàrdail a bhith éibhinn, eirmseach, eireachdail agus ann an clò, uil' aig an aon àm.

Thathar a' cumail a-mach gun deach na bliadhnachan oilthigh aig Alastair a thoirt gu crìch le pòsadh tràth, ach an aon phòsadh aig Alastair mu bheil fianais shoilleir againn, ri Sìne Dhòmhnallach a mhuinntir Ghlinn Éite, tha e coltach gun robh e ann an 1727 no timcheall air. Is math dh'fhaodte gun robh e ann an trioblaid air sgàth ho-ro-gheallaidh air choreigin còmhla ri caileig, ach tha e nas coltaiche leamsa gur e chuir crìoch air a chùrsaichean foghlaim ach an tachartas deagh-aithnichte sin air 6 Sultain 1715, togail bratach Rìgh Sheumais air Bràighe Mhàirr, a' stiùireadh gu blàr Shliabh an t-Siorraim air 13 Samhain. Ma tha mi ceart ann a bhith cur breith Alastair ann an 1698, bhiodh e seachd bliadhn' deug a dh'aois, sean gu leòr air son claidheamh a chur uime 's a dhol far an robh athair 's a bhràthair as sine, Aonghas Beag, ann an réisimeid Mhic 'ic Ailein. Ann an dà dhàn thràth, 'Dìomoladh Chabair Féidh' agus 'Moladh an Leoghainn', tha trì reifreansan gu math mionaideach ri latha Shliabh an t-Siorraim, 's a thuilleadh air a-sin, anns na cuimhneachain a sgrìobh Alastair mu Bhliadhna Theàrlaich tha dà reifreans eile ris a' bhlàr anns a' chiad phearsa iolra. 'As we enter'd this pavilion we were most chearfully welcom'd by the Duke of Athole to whom some of us had been known in the year 1715.' Agus a-rithist, 's e bruidhinn air Dùn Bhlàthain: 'It was in this neighbourhood that many of our fathers and severalls of us now with the Prince fought for the same cause just thirty years ago at the battle of Sheriffmuir.'

Bha Sliabh an t-Siorraim 'na latha sgriosail do Chlann Raghnaill, 's bha a bhuil aige air a' chòrr de bheatha Alastair. Chaidh an ceann-feadhna, Ailein, a mharbhadh 's an oighreachd arfuntachadh. Thathar a' creidsinn gun robh Ailein ag iarraidh air Alastair a dhol 'na phreantas aig Fearchar MacCulaich, an nòtair ris an robh gnothaichean lagha na h-oighreachd an urra. Bha feum eadhan na bu mhotha aig Raghnall Mac 'ic Ailein, a lean Ailein mar cheann-feadhna, air luchd-lagha, oir bha esan air fògradh. Dh'eug e aig St Germains ann an 1725, agus chaidh a leantainn le cho-ogha, Dòmhnall Bheinne Bhadhla, a bha cuideachd anns na h-oghaichean do Mhgr Alastair. Tha e soilleir gun d'fhuair Alastair trèanadh air choreigin san lagh, oir sgrìobh e co-dhiù aon phàipear laghail a bhuineas ri cùisean Chlann Raghnaill 's a tha air mhaireann an-diugh. Math dh'fhaodte gun tug e greis ag ionnsachadh a chiùird anns an t-seòmar sgrìobhaidh aig fear-lagha air choreigin ann an Dùn Éideann anns na bliadhnachan a lean aramach '15. Tha litrichean ann a tha a' leigeil fhaicinn gun robh Alastair ag obair ás leth Penelope, bantrach Ailein, a' déiligeadh ris an riaghaltas, a' feuchainn ri snaoim na cùis amallaich seo fhuasgladh agus oighreachd arfuntaichte Chlann Raghnaill fhaighinn air ais. Bhiodh an t-uabhas siubhail an lùib seo eadar Beinne Bhadhla, Uibhist a-Deas, Mùideart, Inbhir Nis, Dùn Éideann agus dh'fhaodte cuideachd Lunnainn. A réir aon tobair fhiosrachaidh ás an naoidheamh linn deug, John Reid, bha Alastair 'na mhaor fearainn ann an Canaigh ann an 1725 no roimhe, 's ma tha sin fìor, bha an dreuchd aige fo Chomiseanairean nan Oighreachd Arfuntaichte.

Leis na thug seo dha de dh'eòlas an t-saoghail, bha Alastair an teis-meadhoin an

33

atharrachaidh chultaraich. Fhritheil e oilthigh Gallda san deichead a lean an t-Aonadh, nuair a bha Gaill a' tòiseachadh a' deilbh ìomhaigh ùr phoileataigeach agus chultarach dhaib' fhéin. Agus chì sinn le sùil air ais gur e blàr mór Shliabh an t-Siorraim, seach blàr beag Chùil Lodair an ceann deich air fhichead bliadhna eile, a dh'fhàg gach nì bha cinnteach ann an saoghal nan Gaidheal air talamh bog na mì-chinnt. Tha e soilleir nach fhaca Alastair e fhéin riamh 'na bhàrd tradiseanta aig nach robh mar dhreuchd ach moladh nam fear ainmeil agus cuimhneachadh dhaibh na bha dùil aig an t-sluagh bhuapa. Sann anns na 40an a-mhàin, nuair a chaidh e 'na fhear-propaganda mór Seumasach, a mhol e daoine idir, mar bu thrice am Prionnsa Teàrlach. B' fheàrr leis cha mhór dad sam bith ach fir ainmeil a mholadh – boireannaich, pìob Mhic Cruimein, peata calamain. Ann an 'Guidhe no Ùrnaigh an Ùghdair don Cheòlraidh' tha e toirt rann do gach té dhe na naoi 'miùsas' – 'naoinear inghean Iupiter àird / 'S Mnemosyne caoimh' – le rannan do dh'Apollo 's do Minerva cuideachd. Diathan na Gréige 's na Ròimhe – bha seo ùr ann an Gàidhlig. 'S tha am marbhrann a rinn e dhan chalaman 'na dhìteadh air dualchas na bàrdachd mholaidh, aig an robh mar phrìomh amas a bhith a' cur foirmlean deas-ghnàthail an gnìomh.

> Chan e gun chiste no anart bhith còmhdach do chré
> Fo lic anns an ùir
> Tha mise, ge cruaidh e, an-diugh 'g acain gu léir –
> Ach do thuiteam le cù.

Ann am facail eile se 'm bàs fhéin a tha cunntadh 's chan e mion-chleachdaidhean an tòrraidh. Mar sin tha Alastair a' dlùthadh ri seòrs' ùr de bhàrdachd Ghàidhlig a bh' air a ghluasad le smuaintean pearsanta agus faireachdainn a' chridhe seach amasan fuara agus adhbharan sòisealta. Tha innteachaileachd a' dol air adhart an-seo cuideachd, oir tha fios gur e bàrdachd dhìomhair an duine fa leth tha seo seach teachdaireachd phoblach a tha ri sgaoileadh chun an t-sluaigh tro mheadhoin a' chiùil. Tha e 'g ràdh:

> Na tugaibh dhomh saothair nì glagan sa chluais
> 'S de thuigse bhios fàs.

Ach anns a' cheann thall se rathad mòintich tha seo seach rathad mór an rìgh. Tha an nì nach *eil* Alastair ag iarraidh a dhèanamh nas soilleire an-dràsta na na *tha* e ag iarraidh a dhèanamh. Mar sin tha e frionasach.

> Cainnt shnasta da m' dhìth, ge stràcte mo thoil –
> Tha mi falamh de sgil:
> Is nì gun susbaint ealdhain gun sgoil
> Air suibsec mar mhil.

34

COMPÀIRTEACHADH AN URRAIM: MAC MHGR ALASTAIR 'S A' GHALLDACHD

Am measg an fhéin-sgrùdaidh seo air fad, tha Alastair a' coimhead na tha bàird Ghallda a' dèanamh, agus anns a' chiad rann de 'Mhìomholadh Móraig' tha e ag ainmeachadh fear dhiubh. Ach mus gabh mi an rann, feumaidh mi innse dhuibh dé thachair. Bha Alastair air òran mór molaidh a dhèanamh do bhoireannach, Mórag, a mhol e bho bonn gu bàrr. Thuirt e aig an deireadh gur ann air Mórag a bhiodh e smaointinn nuair a bha e fhéin agus Sìne a' dèanamh gaoil. Ghabh Sìne gu dona ri seo, mar a shaoileadh sibh, agus aig toiseach 'Mìomholadh Móraig' se guth Sìne a chluinneas sinn.

> A Mhùideartaich dhuibh dhàna
>   Nan geurfhacal,
> Sguir de d' bhùrt 's de d' thàlmhagadh
>   Pléideasach.
> Tàmh de d' sgeig dhiom tràth
> Neo ruigeam Ailean Bàrd
> 'S gach filidh ga bheil càs
>   An Dùn Éideann dhiom:
> Bheir iad ort gun sgàin
> 'S gum fail thu uil' o d' chnàibh
> 'Nad mhaol-lòbhran grànda
>   Maol déistinneach.
> Sin an duais atà
> Agadsa 'nad ghràdh
> 'S 'nad mholadh magail bàth,
>   A bhalaich bheul-fharsaing.

Chan eil teagamh sam bith nach e Ailean Ramsay a th' ann an 'Ailean Bàrd'. Uair eile chì sinn Alastair a' gabhail nòisean do dh'òran gaoil fon tiotal 'SONG. Tune – Throw the Wood Laddie' anns a' chiad leabhar den *Tea-Table Miscellany* aig Ramsay, a thàinig a-mach ann an 1724 's a reic 'na mhìltean. Tha Ramsay a' tòiseachadh:

> As early I walk'd,
>   on the first of sweet May,
> Beneath a steep mountain,
> Beneath a clear fountain,
> I heard a grave lute
>   soft melody play,
>   Whilst the Echo resounded
> the dolorous lay.

Tha Alastair a' cur 'Òran an t-Samhraidh' air fonn 'Through the Wood, Laddie', agus mar sin tha e san aon mheadarrachd. Tha e tòiseachadh:

> An déis dhomh dùsgadh sa mhadainn
> 'S an dealt air a' choill,
> Ann am madainn ro shoilleir,
> Ann an lagan beag doilleir,
> Gun cualas am feadan
> Gu leadarra seinn,
> 'S mac-talla nan creagan
> Da fhreagradh 'Bròn Binn'.

Tha seo faisg air a bhith 'na eadar-theangachadh de Ramsay – tha 'n *lute* a' dol 'na feadan, ach tha 'n *Echo* 's an *dolorous lay* ann. Se 'Am Bròn Binn' an t-ainm aig laoidh Gàidhlig mu Rìgh Artair. Mar sin, tha Alastair a' ruamhar 'na dhualchas gu eadar-theangachadh a lorg air Ramsay. Tha seo gu leòr air son a chur a' dol: chan eil an còrr den òran an eisimeil Ramsay idir. Mar sin faodaidh sinn a ràdh gun deach 'Òran an t-Samhraidh' a dhèanamh ann an 1724 no as a dhéidh, agus tha fios againn gun deach 'Òran a' Gheamhraidh' a dhèanamh ann an 1743. Cha do rinn duine òrain dhan t-samhradh no dhan gheamhradh ann an Gàidhlig roimhe – mar a chì sinn a-rithist, tha e soilleir gur ann bhon obair aig James Thomson, a dh'fhoillsich 'Winter' ann an 1726 agus 'Summer' ann an 1727, a bha am brosnachadh a' tighinn.

Mar a chunnaic sinn, sann mu 1727 a phòs Alastair Sìne. Rugadh am mac, Raghnall Dubh, ann an 1728, agus bho 1729 a-mach bha Alastair ag obair an diofar àiteachan ann am Mùideart agus Àird nam Murchan 'na mhaighstir-sgoile 's 'na cheistear don Chomann an Albainn gu Craobh-Sgaoileadh an Eòlais Chrìostaidh, an SSPCK. Dh'fheumadh e bith-bheò chunbhalach, agus an toiseach, taing dhan Royal Bounty aig Rìgh Seòras, bha an t-airgead math: £16 sa bhliadhna, a' dol suas gu £18 ann an 1732 mus deach e sìos a-rithist.

Tha seo a' ciallachadh ann am briathrachas an latha an-diugh gun deach Alastair 'na thidsear Beurla. Aig an àm a chaidh a stéidheachadh ann an 1709 b'e amas a' Chomainn a' Ghàidhlig a thoirt ás a freumh, agus air son siud a thoirt gu buil dh'òrdaich e gur ann tron Bheurla bhiodh an teagasg air fad 'na chuid sgoiltean. Bha e follaiseach ann an ùine ghoirid ge-tà gur e buil a' phoileasaidh seo gun robh sgoilearan ag ionnsachadh earrannan móra dhe na sgriobtairean Beurla gun an sgot as lugha aca dé bha iad a' ciallachadh. Gu nàdarra, bha móran mhaighstirean-sgoile a' bruidhinn Gàidhlig nuair a bha iad a' teagasg, agus thug an fheadhainn bu dhìlse 's bu chiallaiche dhiubh a-staigh leughadh a' Bhìobaill, nan salm 's an leabhair-cheist Ghàidhlig mar ìre letheach-shlighe gu Beurla ionnsachadh. Thòisich an suidheachadh seo a bhith air a riaghailteachadh ann an 1723 nuair a chaidh a mholadh gum bu chòir iarraidh air sgoilearan dearbhadh cho math 's a bha iad a' tuigsinn nan teacsaichean Beurla le bhith cur Gàidhlig orra. Dà bhliadhna as a dhéidh sin, ann an 1725, thòisicheadh a' tuigsinn cho riatanach 's a bha leabhar-briathrachais Gàidhlig gu Beurla, agus chaidh a cho-dhùnadh gum bu chòir a dhèanamh le facail Ghàidhlig a chur an àite na Laidinn anns an *New Vocabularie for the Use of Schools* aig Seumas MacEoghain, 's gum bu chòir iarraidh air Cléir Latharna faighinn air fear de na buill acasan an obair a ghabhail os làimh.

Tha e follaiseach nach robh Alastair ag eas-aontachadh ris na dòighean ciallach seo a bhathar a' cur an gnìomh a-nis air son poileasaidh a' Chomainn a thoirt gu buil, oir se esan a nochd anns a' cheann thall mar ùghdar an leabhair-bhriathrachais aca, *Leabhar a Theagasc Ainminnin*, a thàinig a-mach mu dheireadh ann an 1741. Bhiodh na buannachdan economach a thigeadh an lùib eòlais air Beurla follaiseach gu leòr. Bha a h-uile sgoil anns an do theagaisg Alastair riamh am broinn fichead mìle bho Shròn an t-Sìthein, far an robh an York Building Company a' mèinneadh air son luaidh bho chaidh am fearann a cheannach le Sir Alastair Moireach á Stanhope ann an 1724. Mun tàinig 1733 bha na mèinnean gan ruith leis an sgrìobhaiche-litrichean ainmeil Shasannach Caiptean Burt, a bha fad iomadh bliadhna an sàs ann an iomairt mhór eile an latha ud air Ghaidhealtachd, togail rathaidean. An dearbhadh as fheàrr a th' againn gun robh beachd tur fàbharach aig Alastair air leasachadh economach agus teagasg na Beurla se an dàn Beurla a leanas, a chaidh fhoillseachadh timcheall air 1751 bho phàipearan Alastair Mhic Dhonnchaidh nach maireann, Tighearna an t-Sruthain.

MacDonald the Bard's Salutation to General Wade.

HAIL! Fav'rite of GREAT-BRITAIN's Throne,
    Prime Executor of her Law!
Whose Skill and foreward Zeal alone
    Could Fierceness to Submission draw.

Thro' rugged Rocks you forc'd a Way,
    Where Trade and Commerce now are found,
The Indigent look brisk and gay,
    Since Plenty does thro' you abound.

The steepest Mountain opes her Womb,
    To let her Sons and Hero meet;
Who could have dream'd it was her Doom,
    E'er to have vy'd with LONDON Street.

Mar a chuir Dòmhnall Uilleam Stiùbhart air shùilean dhuinn, is fheudar gur e am Bàrd

37

Dòmhnallach seo Mac Mhgr Alastair fhéin. Ma théid argamaid gur e bàrdachd Chuigseach tha seo, gabhaidh a chur an aghaidh sin nach robh Seumasach na bu mhotha ri linn na Tighearna an t-Sruthain fhéin. Ann am meadhoin agus air taobh siar na Gaid-healtachd bho 1735 gu 1745 bha daoine a' gabhail gu toilichte ri leasachadh econa-mach, a' gabhail air an taobh muigh ris na cumhachdan a bh' ann, agus a' strì fo rùm gus an rud ris an canar an-diugh 'régime change' a thoirt gu buil. Mar sin, mar a chuir mi 'n céill ann am pàipear a dh'fhoillsich mi mu Mhac Mhgr Alastair ann an Raineach, air a rathad dhachaigh bho na coinneamhan ann an Dùn Éideann air 16 agus 20 Samhain 1738 far an tug e seachad a làmh-sgrìobhainn den *Leabhar a Theagasc Ainminnin* don Chomann 's an d'fhuair e duais £10 air son a thrioblaid, tha e glé choltach gun tug e greis ann an cuideachd Thighearna an t-Sruthain fhéin. Chuir mi air tuairmse cuideachd gun robh Alastair 'na làn bheachd nuair chaidh e Dhùn Éideann gun robh an *Leabhar a Theagasc Ainminnin* a' riochdachadh mùthadh air poileasaidh a' Chomainn, 's gun deònaicheadh iad a-nis teacsaichean Gàidhlig mar 'Na Seachd Maighstirean Glice' fhoillseachadh mar eisimpleirean de stoidhle mhath Ghàidhlig air son a' chànan a theagasg ceart 'na chuid sgoiltean, oir thug e leis làmh-sgrìobhainn dheth sin cuideachd. Tha e follaiseach dhuinn an-diugh gur e amas a' Chomainn ann a bhith comiseanadh 's a' foillseachadh an *Leabhar a Theagasc Ainminnin* ach rathad na cloinne gu Beurla a dhèanamh réidh, ach chitheadh Alastair e 'na cheum air adhart dhan Ghàidhlig cuideachd, agus mar a chuir mi an céill sa phàipear sin, chan eil e ann an nàdar an neach-iomairt Ghàidhlig a bhith riaraichte le aon ghéilleadh. Cho-dhùin mi: 'It would have been made very clear to him by the Society that the change of policy had nothing to do with teaching the graces of the Gaelic language. In disgust, perhaps, he would have found other uses for the manuscript. Exactly six-and-a-half years later he rose in armed rebellion against everything that the SSPCK stood for.'

Air an aon chuairt gu Dùn Éideann tha mi cinnteach gun robh Alastair air lethbhreac a cheannach, neo fhaotainn mar ghibht bhon ùghdar, den *Essay on the Antiquities of Great Britain and Ireland*, a bh' air ùr fhoillseachadh aig an Urr.Dàibhidh MacCaluim neo Mac Comb, ministear Duddingston. Bha ùidh mhór aig MacCaluim ann an Gàidhlig; dh'fheuch e 'na leabhar ri leigeil fhaicinn cho aosta 's a bha na cànanan Ceilteach, agus ri sgeul sgriobtaireil a' chruthachaidh a dhearbhadh le bhith nochdadh gun robh ceangal eadar iad sin agus cànan Darien. Leis cho dlùth 's a thàinig seo air shàiltean an *Leabhar a Theagasc Ainminnin*, chaidh Alastair a bhrosnachadh gu 'Moladh an Ùghdair don t-Seann Chànain Ghàidhlig' a dhèanamh, anns a bheil e ag ràdh, am measg eile,

> Mhair i fòs
> 'S cha téid a glòr air chall
> A dh'ainneoin gò
> Is mì-rùin mhòir nan Gall.

Si labhair Alba,
   'S Galla-bhodaich fhéin,
Ar flaith, ar prionnsa
   'S ar diùcanna gun éis.

An taigh comhairl' an Rìgh
   Nuair shuidheadh air binn a chùirt,
Si Ghàidhlig lìobhtha
   Dh'fhuasgladh snaoim gach cùis.

Si labhair Calum
   Allail a' Chinn Mhóir,
Gach mith is maith
   Bha 'n Alba, beag is mór.

Si labhair Gaill is Gaidhil,
   Neo-chléirich agus cléir,
Gach fear agus bean
   A ghluaiseadh teang' am beul . . .

Si labhair Àdhamh
   Ann am Pàrras fhéin,
'S bu shiùbhlach Gàidhlig
   O bheul àlainn Eubh'.

Och tha bhuil ann:
   Is uireasbhach, gann, fo dhìth
Glòr gach teanga
   A labhras cainnt ach ì . . .

Chan fheum i iasad
   'S cha mhó dh'iarras uath' –
O, 'n t-seanamhair chiatach,
   Làn de chiadaibh buaidh!

Tha i fhéin daonnan
   Saidhbhir, maoineach, slàn,
A taighean taisge
   Dh'fhoclaibh gasta làn . . .

A' chànain cheòlmhor
Shòghmhor 's glòrmhor blas
A labhair móirshliochd
Scóta 's Ghaidhil Ghlais.

'S a réir Mhic Comb,
An t-ùghdar mór ri luaidh,
Si as freumhach òir
'S ciad ghràmair glòir gach sluaigh.

Tha an dàn seo 'na bhun fheallsanachd do dh'Alastair. Tha e ga chur aig toiseach na
h-*Aiseirigh*, 's tha e buileach ann an gleus ris na smuaintean 'na roi-ràdh mun Ghàidhlig
mar dhìleab chumanta na Galldachd 's na Gaidhealtachd, mar ulaidh nàiseanta a chaidh
a ghléidheadh leis na Gaidhil 's a bha a-nist deiseil air son a toirt air ais don nàisean
gu léir. Leamsa tha ìomhaigh na 'seanamhar chiataich' air leth drùidhteach. Tha fios
ge-tà gum faodadh Alastair a bhith neo-shupailte uaireannan. An-seo, air son a' chiad
uair, tha e a' fiathachadh a' Ghaill gu compàirteachadh ann am mìorbhailean na Gàidhlig,
ach aig an aon àm chan urra dha e fhéin a chumail bho bhith cleachdadh nam faclan
a chaidh bhon uair sin cho ainmeil, 'mì-rùn mór nan Gall'. Seo an seòrsa neo-chunbha-
lachd a tha 'na phàirt de phearsantachd an duine, ach feumar a ràdh cuideachd gu
bheil e nochdadh duilgheadas a tha còmhla ruinn fhathast an-diugh, faireachdainnean
làidir a' falbh dà dhiofar rathad aig an aon àm. Se an 'Caledonian antisyzygy' a bh'
aig Gregory Smith air. Eisimpleir eile dheth se mar a tha Alastair a' cumail a-mach
mun Ghàidhlig 'nach fheum i iasad', oir a-nuas gu 1747 bha e dèanamh òrain a bha
làn de dh'iasadan Beurla. Car son a tha e dèanamh seo? Uill, tha 'Òran a' Gheamhraidh'
air a bhreacadh le faclan Beurla leithid *planet, globe, sign, tropic* agus *hymns*, agus mar a
chuir Jack MacQueen an céill, seo faclan a bhiodh James Thomson a' cleachdadh tric
anns na *Seasons*. Urram do MhacThómais? Ach ann an 'Òran Bachail' tha Alastair ag
ràdh:

Is tu chuireadh an *curaids* san t-sluagh
'N àm cogadh ri aodann nan ruag.

'S tha eisimpleirean air leth iongantach 'na 'Òran do Raghnall Òg Mac Mhic Ailein',
a bha 'na thagradh do Raghnall Òg a bh' air fògradh san Fhraing – seadh, thachair e
rithist – sreingean a tharraing agus obair a lorg dha as déidh achd a' mhathanais anns
an Ògmhios 1747. Tha e 'g ràdh am measg eile:

Leoghann guineach calma luaineach
Tuilbheum sgrios-mharbhach san ruaig thu,

Beithir bheumannach 'n àm fuathais
Phas a *chùrs'* an *colaist* cruadail.

As déidh dha Raghnall a mholadh, tha Alastair a' dòrtadh a-mach na dìblidheachd phearsanta aige.

'S ged a tha mi ann am' dhùthaich
Is beag an-seo their *how do you do* rium;
Is buileach a chaill mi mo chùrsa,
Mi gun *phump* gun chairt gun stiùir orm.

Chan fhaic mise gu bheil adhbhar sam bith aige uiread Beurla ùisneachadh. Gus am bi làn sgrùdadh air a thoirt air a' phuing cha chan mise ach seo: shaoil Alastair gur e rud math a bh' ann tòrr Beurla ùisneachadh, ach shaoileadh feadhainn eile gur e droch rud a bh' ann, agus chan eil aon fhacal Beurla ann am 'Birlinn Chlann Raghnaill', an dàn as motha 's as cudromaiche aige, a chaidh a dhèanamh sna 50an.

Chan eil sin ri ràdh nach eil buaidh na Beurla ri fhaicinn sa 'Bhirlinn', ach se buaidh a th' ann a bhuineas do dh'fheallsanachd litreachais. Anns an leabhar bhuadhach aig Tòmas Blackwell, *An Enquiry into the Life and Writings of Homer*, 1736, mhìnich an t-ùghdar na bu chiall don tèarm 'epic'. Feumaidh i cogaidhean móra, tha e 'g ràdh, nithean tha iongantach agus mìorbhaileach, ach chan e idir fealla-dhà no cainnt lìomhta. 'A Poet describes nothing so happily, as what he has seen; nor talks masterly, but in his native Language, and proper Idiom; nor mimicks truly other Manners, than those whose Originals he has practised and known . . . Is what we call *Heroism* indeed any thing else, than *A disinterested Love* of Mankind and our Country, unawed by *Dangers*, and unwearied by *Toils*? If it is not, the social Passions, and noblest affections must prevail in an *Epic-Poem*.'

Tha a' 'Bhirlinn', a thòisich Alastair a réir choltais ann an Canaigh nuair fhuair e obair ann 'na bhàillidh mu 1750, 'na leithid a bhàrdachd. Ann am beagan agus 600 sreath tha e 'g innse mar tha a' bhirlinn air a beannachadh 's air a h-iomradh gu àite seòlaidh, mar a tha an sgioba air an cur air leth, mar a tha iad a' seòladh bho Uibhist a-Deas air Latha Fhéill Brìghde, agus mar a tha iad a' tighinn tro stoirm mhór gu caladh sàbhailte ann an Carraig Fhearghais an Éirinn. Bha a' mhórchuid dhen dàn air a gabhail seach air a seinn, 's tha a' mheadarrachd ag atharrachadh bho earrainn gu earrainn. Tha e 'g obair air ìre samhla cho math ri ìre tuairisgeul, 's tha e cliùiteach air son na tha e tarraing bho thobraichean litreachas nan Gaidheal. Mar as motha dheth seo a thig gu solas an latha, sann as fheàrr a chì sinn mar a chruthaich Alastair léirsinn ùr iomlan á bloighean aosta. Sann mar seo a chuir e argamaid an céill air son aonachd nan Gaidheal agus uachdaranachd nan daoine thar an ceannardan. Tha e toirt fios gu leòr dhuinn gu leigeil fhaicinn gu bheil a' bhirlinn 'na samhla do long-stàite Chlann Raghnaill, 's mar sin 'na samhla do na Gaidhil 's do dh'Alba cuideachd, 's i ga stiùireadh le sgioba ghaisgeil tro uisgeachan cunnartach Bliadhna Theàrlaich. Mar a tha an stoirm ag èirigh gu h-àirde tha gach creutair mara as grainnde ag èirigh gu uachdar a' chuain 's a' cuartachadh na luinge. Tha cunntas ga thoirt orra ann an còig rannan, a' tòiseachadh:

> An fhairge uile 's i 'na brochan
> Strioplach ruaimleach,
> Le fuil 's le gaorr nam biast lorcach
> Droch dhath ruadh oirr'.

An sealladh a tha romhainn an-seo se an casgradh a thugadh air arm Iain Chope air Sliabh a' Chlamhain. Ach tha na béistean mun luing a' dol nas lìonmhoire, nas mìchneasta, nas fuaimniche, nas eagallaiche. Seo Cùil Lodair, le beagan cuideachaidh, saoilidh mi, bho phìos beag clasaigeach de sgrìobhadh Seumasach ann an am Beurla, *Alexis*, a chaidh a sgrìobhadh ann an 1746 leis an Urr. Raibeart Foirbeis bho stuthan a fhuair e bho Alastair Dòmhnallach, fear Chinnsebuirg. Se 'Alexis' am Prionnsa Teàrlach, agus tha na 'Sea-Monsters' air am mìneachadh mar 'Ships of War'. Tha Fionnghal a' Phrionnsa ag ràdh: *'Providence*, I hope, will carry *Us* safely, and preserve *Us* from the *Sea-Monsters* which swim round this Island, and would be greedy of such a Prey as the great *Alexis.*' Agus tha an t-ùghdar ag ràdh: 'Upon their setting out a thick *Mist* descends, by which Means they get safely through the *Sea-Monsters*, who would have been ready to devour them.'

Rann no dhà nas anmoiche sa 'Bhirlinn' 's tha Mac Mhgr Alastair a' tòiseachadh a' bruidhinn air 'Sinn dallte le cathadh fairge', 'Peileirean beithrich', 'Fàileadh is deathach na riofa / Gar glan thachdadh', 'cogadh', 'Talamh, teine, uisge 's sian-ghaoth / Ruinn air togail', 's mu dheireadh, 'sìth'. Chan e long tha seo idir: cha bhi riofa siùil a' dol 'na theine. Se Cùil Lodair a th' ann. Agus seo na tha dèanamh *epic* dhen 'Bhirlinn'. Tha e mu dheidhinn gaisgich a tha tighinn ás le'm beatha 's a' dèanamh eachdraidh nuair tha gach nì 'nan aghaidh, 's tha e air a chur ri chéile bho eileamaidean beul-aithriseach a tha gan toirt beò le mac-meanmna làidir aon duine 's leis an eòlas phearsanta aige air cogadh. Chuir Iain Dòmhnallach, fear Àird na Bìthe ann an Gleanna Garadh, a chorrag air a' phrìomh thobar brosnachaidh aig Alastair nuair thuirt e ris:

> Gun tug thu bàrr air Hòmar
> Ge b'e ceòl-fhear mòr sa Ghréigis e.

Faodar a' 'Bhirlinn' fhaicinn ma-tà mar thinne san t-slabhraidh a tha ceangal Hòmar, Blackwell, Seumas Mac a' Phearsain agus Elias Lönnrot. Is cinnteach gun cuala Mac a' Phearsain e ann an taighean-céilidh Bhàideanaich 'na òige; chan eil e coltach gum

42

fac' e ann an sgrìobhadh e mun deach fhoillseachadh le Raghnall Dubh ann an 1776, anns an duanaire a gheall athair. Cha deachaidh dad cho adhartach fheuchainn a-rithist ann am bàrdachd Ghàidhlig gus an d'rinn Somhairle MacGill-Eain colmadh eadar briathrachas diadhaireachd nan Saor-Chléireach, John Donne 's nan òran tradiseanta Gàidhlig gu àmhghar pearsanta a chur an céill ann an 'Dàin do Eimhir' agus fearg phoileataigeach a chur an céill anns a' 'Chuiltheann'.

Dh'atharraich Alastair Mac Mhgr Alastair bàrdachd Ghàidhlig gu bràth. Ann an iomadh seòrsa dòigh nach do dh'ainmich mi an-seo, nochd e na h-àbhaistean, na stoidhleachan 's na h-amasan a bha gu bhith aig bàird Ghàidhlig fad dà cheud bliadhna eile. Rinn e seo le bhith a' gabhail ri buaidhean bhon chòrr de dh'Albainn 's bho thall thairis. Thug iad seo slat-thomhais dha air gach nì a b' fheàrr 's a bu mhiosa 'na dhualchas fhéin. Na nithean a b' fheàrr, dh'ùisnich e gu'n cùl iad. Ach tha mi dol a chrìochnachadh leis an smuain seo. Nuair a bha e siubhal còmhla ri bantrach Mhic 'ic Ailein tràth 'na bheatha gu bailtean mar Dhùn Éideann 's Lunnainn, nuair a bha e an sàs 'na dhuin' òg pòst' ann an teagasg, agus anns na naoi mìosan iongantach ud nuair a mheàrrs e gu Derby ann an arm a' Phrionnsa 's a ghabh e pàirt 'na othaich-ear anns na trì blàir mu dheireadh a chuireadh riamh am Breatainn, bha e beò air an stairsnich eadar saoghal na Gàidhlig agus saoghal na Beurla. Is fheudar gun robh sgot air choreigin aige co ris a bha Alba dol a bhith coltach anns na bliadhnachan ri teachd. Chuala mi bho chionn ghoirid ga ràdh gun tug Alba ìomhaigheachd chultarach na Gàidhlig oirre fhéin as déidh Chùil Lodair. An nì a thachair ann an da-rìribh se gun do rinn Alba taghadh-shiristean air cuid de dh'earrannan de dh'ìomhaigheachd chultarach na Gàidhlig – a' phìob mhór, an tartan, an t-éideadh Gaidhealach, an t-saighdearachd, an t-uisge-beatha, dìlseachd do chinnidhean, fraoch mar shamhla nàiseanta. Nuair a sgrìobh e mu 'chompàirteachadh an urraim', tha e soilleir gun robh Alastair a' roi-fhaicinn rudeigin mar seo a' tachairt ('s tha mi creidsinn gun robh a' 'Bhirlinn' 'na cuideachadh, co-dhiù shìos fo rùm, gun do thachair e), ach cha b' urra dha idir a thomhas gun canadh Alba fad dà cheud bliadhna 'cha ghabh' ri gach nì a b' fheàrr 's a bu chudromaiche mun ìomhaigheachd chultaraich sin – an litreachas agus na h-òrain a tha air an glasadh suas anns an taigh-ulaidh ris an can sinn a' Ghàidhlig.

RONALD BLACK

Sharing the honour:
Mac Mhgr Alastair and the Lowlands

I take my title, 'Sharing the Honour', from Alastair's introduction to his epoch-making book *Aiseirigh na Seann Chànain Albannaich* of 1751. Writing in English, even though all the poems in the book are in Gaelic only, he begins by saying that he hopes the poems will entertain those who understand them, and raise in others a desire to learn the language, provided they can be persuaded that such poems will make the effort worth while. He goes on to talk about his idea of publishing a historical anthology of Gaelic verse with critical observations and English translations. He says: 'If such a series can be made out, besides the general agreeableness of the thing itself, nothing perhaps will better contribute to discover the progress of genius, through all its different degrees of improvement, from extreme simplicity, to whatever height we shall happen upon examination to find it, amongst this people . . . An agreeable inquiry, surely! and one would think not displeasing, even to the inhabitants of the lowlands of Scotland, who have always shared with them the honour of every gallant action, and are now first invited to a participation of their reputation for arts.'

Note that the title of the book means not 'The Resurrection of the Ancient Gaelic Tongue' but 'The Resurrection of the Ancient Scottish Tongue'. The title contains the word *aiseirigh*, resurrection, literally 'second rising' or 'another rising'. The appeal of the contents is to Jacobite and free-thinking sentiment. Highlanders and Lowlanders have fought together, Alastair says, not just at Prestonpans, at Falkirk and at Culloden, but in 'every gallant action' – including by implication Sheriffmuir, Worcester, Inverkeithing, Flodden, Bannockburn, Stirling Bridge and many another battle in between.

The *Aiseirigh* is the first book of secular Gaelic verse or prose ever published, and the Lowlander is invited to share in the celebration. The author hopes that collections of this kind, as well as the brotherly love of shared political goals and military service, will whet the Lowland appetite for learning the Gaelic language. The three principal aims of the Scottish Jacobites were the revocation of the Treaty of Union, the reinstatement of the Stuart dynasty, and religious freedom. Alastair was here adding to these a cultural aim: that the new independent Scotland thus created should be a united bilingual or trilingual nation, with equality for Gaelic and English, or indeed for Gaelic, English and Scots. This remains a valid cultural aspiration to this day, as reflected in the Gaelic Bill which becomes law next month, although I have to say that I despair at the countless negative twists and turns that the cultural history of Scotland has taken since the defeat of Alastair's party at Culloden.

But what I want to do in this paper is try to trace the steps by which this cultural aspiration was reached in Alastair's mind.

Alastair was the son of a minister, Mgr Alastair. He was born about 1698 and grew up in the manse at Dalilea by the side of Loch Shiel in Moidart. He will have received a trilingual education, in Gaelic, English and Latin, in his father's study, and a thoroughgoing Gaelic-medium education, as we would call it nowadays, in the ceilidhhouses of the district. Then he was packed off to Glasgow University. There is no record of his matriculation or graduation; all we know is that he attended classes there, which is quite normal for the time. The late Rev. T. M. Murchison pointed to the fact that he set two of his songs, 'Òran a' Gheamhraidh' ('The Song of Winter') and 'Allt an t-Siùcair' ('The Sugar Burn'), to the airs 'Tweedside' and 'The Lass o' Patie's Mill', which, in 1822 and for long before, were played by the chimes on Wednesdays and Thursdays respectively in the Tolbooth Steeple at Glasgow Cross, a few hundred yards from the Old College in the High Street. 'May we not think of him,' mused Murchison, 'sitting uncomfortably on a hard bench in a dull classroom, while the professor drearily discoursed in Latin about Aristotle and the rest, letting his mind wander to his beloved Highlands and Allt an t-Siùcair, as the chimes of "The Lass o' Patie's Mill" tinkled faintly through the window?'

What would he have read in those years around 1712? Martin Martin, *A Description of the Western Islands of Scotland*, 1703, would have showed him that there was a great curiosity among the savants of the new United Kingdom to know more about the islands, especially in so far as the Highlanders might possess the key to health. James Watson, *A Choice Collection of Comic and Serious Scots Poems*, 1706, showed him that the traditional poetry of ordinary people was thought to be worthy of preservation by collecting and printing. Edward Lhuyd, *Archaeologia Britannica*, 1707, demonstrated scientifically that there was a distinct family of Celtic languages, of which Scottish Gaelic, Irish, Manx, Welsh, Cornish and Breton were all thriving. Alexander Pope, *The Rape of the Lock*, 1712, showed that poetic satire could be amusing, incisive, elegant and in print, all at the same time.

There's a tradition that Alastair's university career was ended by an early marriage, but the only marriage of his for which we have clear evidence, to Jane MacDonald from Glen Etive, appears to have taken place in or around 1727. Probably there was some kind of amorous escapade in Glasgow for which he got into trouble. It seems more likely to me that what put an end to his studies was that well-known event of 6 September 1715, the raising of the Jacobite standard on the Braes of Mar, leading to the battle of Sheriffmuir on 13 November. If I'm correct in putting Alastair's birth in 1698, Alastair would have passed his seventeenth birthday, and would have been quite old enough to buckle on a sword and join his father and his elder brother Aonghas Beag in Clanranald's regiment. In two early poems, 'Dìomoladh Chabair Féidh' ('The Dispraise of Cabar Féidh') and 'Moladh an Leoghainn' ('The Praise of the Lion'), there are three quite detailed references to the events of Sheriffmuir, and what's more, in Alastair's memoirs of 1745 there are two references to the battle in the first person plural. 'As we enter'd this pavilion we were most chearfully welcom'd by the Duke of Athole to whom some of us had been known in the year 1715.' And later, when speaking of Dunblane: 'It was in this neighbourhood that many of our fathers and severalls of us now with the Prince fought for the same cause just thirty years ago at the battle of Sheriffmuir.'

Sheriffmuir was a disastrous battle for the Clanranald, and its fallout was to shape the rest of Alastair's life. The chief, Allan, was killed and his lands forfeited. Allan is believed to have wanted Alastair to study law with a view to his succeeding Farquhar MacCulloch, the notary who did the legal business of the estate. Allan's successor, Ronald, being in exile, had an even greater need of lawyers. He died at St Germains in 1725, and was succeeded by his cousin Donald MacDonald of Benbecula, who was also a first cousin of Mgr Alastair. Alastair clearly did receive some legal training, as we have at least one Clanranald legal document written in his hand. Probably he spent time gaining experience in the writing chamber of some Edinburgh lawyer or other during the years following the '15. Surviving letters show that during the 1720s he acted for Allan's widow Penelope in the complex matter of negotiating with the Government for the restoration of the forfeited Clanranald estate. This would have involved a great deal of travelling between Benbecula, South Uist, Moidart, Inverness, Edinburgh and perhaps also London. One nineteenth-century source, John Reid, has it that he acted as ground-officer in Canna in or before 1725, and if that is true, he held the post under the Forfeited Estates Commissioners.

All this experience put Alastair right at the cusp of cultural change. He had attended a Lowland university during the decade following the Union, when Lowland Scots were beginning to forge a new political and cultural identity. And we can see in retrospect that it was the big battle of Sheriffmuir, not the small battle of Culloden thirty years later, that shattered all the old certainties of life in the Highlands. It's clear that Alastair never saw himself as a traditional poet whose task was to praise famous men and remind them of their obligations to society. It was only in the '40s when he became a leading Jacobite propagandist that he praised people at all, usually Prince Charles. He preferred to praise almost anything except famous men – women, MacCrimmon's pipes, a pet dove. In 'Guidhe no Ùrnaigh an Ùghdair don Cheòlraidh' ('The Author's Prayer or Petition to the Muses') he devotes a stanza to each of the nine muses – 'the nine daughters of mighty Jupiter / And of gentle Mnemosyne' – and throws in one each to Apollo and Minerva as well. The gods and goddesses of Greece and Rome – this was new in Gaelic. And his elegy to the dove stands as an indictment of the panegyric tradition, whose prime purpose was to re-enact ritu-alistic formulae:

> It's not that no coffin or linen shroud covers your corpse
> Under grave-slab in soil
> That, though it's harsh, I'm today thoroughly mourning
> But that you've been killed by a dog.

In other words death itself is what matters and not the minutiae of exequies. So Alastair moves towards the notion of a new Gaelic poetry motivated by genuine thought and emotion rather than coldly calculated aims and social objectives. There's an intellectualisation going on here, too, for this is surely a private poetry of the individual rather than a public message to be distributed to the people via the medium of song. He says:

> Don't give me work that rattles in the ear
> And is empty of intellect.

But this is ultimately negative. It's clearer at this stage what Alastair *doesn't* want to do than what he *does*, and he is frustrated:

> I lack polished language, though abundant is my desire –
> I'm empty of skill:
> Art without schooling's a thing without substance
> Even on a subject like honey.

So amidst all this introspection, Alastair looks at what Lowland poets are doing. Indeed, in the first stanza of 'Mìomholadh Mòraig' ('The Dispraise of Morag') he names one of them. But before I cite the stanza, I must tell you what had happened. Alastair had made a big song of praise to a woman, Morag, praising her from head to toe. He had said at the end that it was Morag he was thinking of when he and Jane were making love. Jane took this badly, as you would expect, and at the beginning of 'Mìomholadh Mòraig' the voice we hear is Jane's:

> You black, brazen Moidart man
> Of cutting words,
> Stop your ridicule and wheedling
> Adze-mockery.
> Cease deriding me at once
> Or I'll contact Allan the Bard

> And every poet who takes my case
>   In Edinburgh:
> They will make you burst
> And rot completely from your bones
> Into a foul hairless leper,
>   Bald and disgusting.
> That's the prize you'll have
> For that love affair of yours
> And for your vacuous mocking praise,
>   You wide-mouthed lout.

'Allan the Bard' is certainly Allan Ramsay. On another occasion we find Alastair taking a notion to a love-song entitled 'SONG. Tune – Throw the Wood Laddie' in volume 1 (1724) of Ramsay's immensely popular *Tea-Table Miscellany*. Ramsay begins:

> As early I walk'd,
>   on the first of sweet May,
>   Beneath a steep mountain,
>   Beneath a clear fountain,
>   I heard a grave lute
> soft melody play,
>   Whilst the Echo resounded
> the dolorous lay.

Alastair sets 'Òran an t-Samhraidh' ('The Song of Summer') to the tune 'Through the Wood, Laddie', so it's in the same metre. It starts:

> When I awoke in the morning
>   With the dew on the wood.
>   On the brightest of mornings
>   In a dark little hollow,
>   I heard a pipe chanter
>   Melodiously playing,
>   While the echoing rocks
>   Responded 'Bròn Binn'.

This is virtually a translation of Ramsay – the lute becomes a whistle, but the echo and the dolorous lay are there. 'Bròn Binn' ('Sweet Sorrow') is the title of a Gaelic ballad about King Arthur. So Alastair is delving back into Gaelic tradition to produce his translation of Ramsay. It's enough to get him going: the rest of the song is entirely independent of Ramsay. So we can say that his 'Song of Summer' was made in 1724 or after, and we know that his song to winter was made in 1743. Nobody had made songs to summer or winter in Gaelic before – as we will see later, the inspiration was clearly James Thomson, who had published 'Winter' in 1726 and 'Summer' in 1727.

As we have seen, Alastair's marriage to Jane appears to have taken place in 1727. Their son Ronald, whom we now know as Raghnall Dubh, was born in 1728, and from 1729 we find Alastair working in various places in Moidart and Ardnamurchan as a schoolmaster and catechist for the Society in Scotland for the Propagation of Christian Knowledge (SSPCK). He needed a steady income, and at first, thanks to King George's Royal Bounty, the money was quite good: £16 per annum, rising to £18 in 1732 before it began to fall again.

What this means in modern terms is that Alastair had become an English teacher. At the time of its founding in 1709 the aim of the SSPCK was to root out the Gaelic language, and to that end it had directed that all instruction in its schools should be in English. It soon became apparent however that the result of this policy was that pupils were learning enormous passages of scripture in English by heart without having the slightest idea what they meant. Many schoolmasters naturally spoke Gaelic in the course of instruction, and the more committed among them sensibly introduced the reading of the Gaelic Bible, psalms and catechism as a halfway stage to the learning of English. This situation began to be regularised in 1723 with the suggestion that pupils be required to prove their understanding of English texts by translating them into Gaelic. Two years later, in 1725, the necessity of publishing a Gaelic–English vocabulary began to be understood, and it was decided that the job should be done by substituting Gaelic words for Latin in James McEwing's *The New Vocabularie for the Use of Schools*, and that the Presbytery of Lorn be asked to appoint one of their number to do it.

It's obvious that Alastair did not disagree with the sensible methods now being adopted to achieve the policy of teaching English in Highland schools, because he it was who emerged in due course as the author of the book called in Gaelic *Leabhar a Theagasc Ainminnin* ('A Book for Teaching Names') and in English *A Galick and English Vocabulary*, which they eventually published in 1741. The economic benefits that a knowledge of English could bring would have been obvious. All of the schools in which he taught were within twenty miles of Strontian, where the York Building Company had been mining for lead since the acquisition of the land by Sir Alexander Murray of Stanhope in 1724. By 1733 the mines were being managed by the celebrated English letter-writer Captain Burt, who for many years was involved in that other great enterprise of the day in the Highlands, the building of roads. The best proof that Alastair's attitude to economic development and the teaching of English was entirely positive lies in the following poem in English, which was published in or around 1751 from the papers of the late Alexander Robertson of Struan:

MacDonald the Bard's Salutation to General Wade.

Hail! Fav'rite of Great-Britain's Throne,
Prime Executor of her Law!
Whose Skill and foreward Zeal alone
Could Fierceness to Submission draw.

Thro' rugged Rocks you forc'd a Way,
Where Trade and Commerce now are found,
The Indigent look brisk and gay,
Since Plenty does thro' you abound.

The steepest Mountain opes her Womb,
To let her Sons and Hero meet;
Who could have dream'd it was her Doom,
E'er to have vy'd with London Street.

As Dòmhnall Uilleam Stiùbhart has pointed out, 'MacDonald the Bard' could only be
Mac Mhgr Alastair himself. If it be argued that this is a Whig poem, the counter-argument
is that there was no greater Jacobite in this period than Alexander Robertson of Struan
himself. The reality of life in the Western and Central Highlands in the decade from 1735
to 1745 consisted of a genuine acceptance of economic progress, a big outward show
of conformity to the status quo, and hard work behind the scenes to achieve what we
would now call 'regime change'. So, as I have shown in my study 'Mac Mhaighstir Alastair
in Rannoch', on his way home from the meetings in Edinburgh on 16 and 20 November
1738 at which he handed over his manuscript of the *Vocabulary* to the SSPCK and was
awarded £10 for his trouble, it's highly likely that he spent some time in the congenial
company of Struan Robertson himself. I also speculated that Alastair went to those meetings in Edinburgh convinced that the *Vocabulary* represented a change of policy by the
SSPCK, and that the Society would now be willing to publish Gaelic texts such as 'The
Seven Wise Masters', a manuscript of which he had also brought with him, as models
of good Gaelic style for the proper teaching of the language in its schools. It's clear to
us now that the Society's purpose in commissioning and publishing the *Vocabulary* was
simply to ease the children's transition to English, but Alastair would have seen it as a
step forward for Gaelic too, and as I pointed out in that paper, it's not in the nature of
the Gaelic activist to rest content with a single concession. I concluded: 'It would have
been made very clear to him by the Society that the change of policy had nothing to do
with teaching the graces of the Gaelic language. In disgust, perhaps, he would have found
other uses for the manuscript. Exactly six-and-a-half years later he rose in armed rebellion against everything that the SSPCK stood for.'

On this same trip to Edinburgh Alastair would have bought, or been given by the author, a copy of the *Essay on the Antiquities of Great Britain and Ireland* which had just been published by the Rev. David Malcolme, minister of Duddingston. Malcolme, who was very interested in Gaelic, sought in this book to demonstrate the antiquity of the Celtic languages, and to justify the biblical legend of the Creation by showing that there was a connection between them and the language of Darien. This, following on the heels of his work on the vocabulary, inspired Alastair to produce 'Moladh an Ùghdair don t-Seann Chànain Glàidhlig' ('The Author's Praise for the Old Gaelic Language'), in which he says, among much else,

> She yet survives,
>   Nor will her speech be lost to us
> Despite the guile
>   And great ill-will of Lowlanders.

> She's what all Scotland spoke,
>   Including Lowland peasants,
> Our nobles, our princes
>   And, uninhibited, our dukes.

> In the council chamber of the King
>   When his court sat down to judge,
> It's polished Gaelic that unravelled
>   The knot of every case.

> She it is that was spoken
>   By famous Malcolm Canmore,
> By every commoner and noble
>   In Scotland, great and small.

> Lowlanders spoke her and Gaels,
>   The laity and clergy,
> Every man and woman
>   Who could move a tongue in mouth . . .

> She's what Adam spoke
>   In Paradise itself,
> And Gaelic was fluent
>   From Eve's lovely mouth.

The result's plain to see:
Defective, inadequate, gapped
Is the voice of each tongue
That speaks language but she . . .

She has no need of loans
And asks them for nothing –
What a beautiful grandmother,
Full of hundreds of virtues!

She herself is always
Rich, opulent, complete,
Her treasure houses full
Of admirable words . . .

The tuneful, luxurious language
Of glorious good taste
Spoken by the many descendants
Of Scota and Gaidheal Glas.

And, according to Mr Malcolm,
An author much to be praised,
She's the golden root and primer
Of the speech of every nation.

This poem is Alastair's 'mission statement'. He puts it at the start of the *Aiseirigh*, and it chimes with the ideas in his introduction of Gaelic as the common inheritance of Lowland and Highland Scotland, a national treasure preserved by the Gael and now ready to be given back to the nation as a whole. I find the image of the 'beautiful grandmother' particularly compelling. Of course Alastair could be unsubtle at times. Here, for the first time, he invites the Lowlander to share the glories of the Gaelic language, but at the same time he can't refrain from using that phrase which has since become so famous, *mì-rùn mór nan Gall*, 'the great ill-will of Lowlanders'. It's the kind of inconsistency which was part of the man's complex character, but it has to be said that it reflects a problem that still exists today, the jostling together of contrary moods. Gregory Smith called it the Caledonian antisyzygy. Another example of it is Alastair's description of Gaelic as having 'no need of loans', because right down to 1747 he was making songs full of English loan-words. Why does he do this? Well, 'The Song of Winter' is speckled with English words like 'planet', 'globe', 'sign', 'tropic' and 'hymns', and as Jack MacQueen has pointed out, these words were all James Thomson's

favourites in the *Seasons*. Homage to Thomson? But in 'Òran Bachail' ('Drinking Song')
Alastair says:

> Is tu chuireadh an *curaids* san t-sluagh
> 'N àm cogadh ri aodann nan ruag.

('You'd put courage in the host / When battling in the face of assaults.') And there
are some pretty outrageous examples in his 'Òran do Raghnall Òg Mac Mhic Ailein'
('Song to Young Ronald of Clanranald'), which was a plea to young Clanranald in
exile in France – yes, it had happened again – to pull some strings and find him a
job following the amnesty of June 1747. He says among other things:

> Leoghann guineach calma luaineach
> Tuilbheum sgrios-mharbhach san ruaig thu,
> Beithir bheumannach 'n àm fuathais
> *Phas* a *chùrs'* an *colaist* cruadail.

('You're a wounding lion, brave and restless, / A death-dealing torrent in the pursuit,
/ A smiting dragon in time of terror / Who's *passed* his *course* in *college* of toughness.')
Having praised Ronald, the poet pours out his personal misery:

> 'S ged a tha mi ann am' dhùthaich
> Is beag an-seo their *how do you do* rium;
> Is buileach a chaill mi mo chùrsa,
> Mi gun *phump* gun chairt gun stiùir orm.

('And though I'm in my native district / Few here will say *how do you do* to me; / I
have completely lost my *course*, / I have no *pump* or chart or rudder.') There's no
obvious reason why he should use so much English. Pending a full study of the issue
I will content myself with saying this: Alastair thought using a lot of English was a
good thing, but others would have thought it a bad thing, and there is not one word
of English in 'Birlinn Chlann Raghnaill' ('Clanranald's Galley'), his longest and most
important poem, which was made in the '50s.

That is not to say that there is no English influence in the 'Birlinn', but it's an
influence that pertains to literary theory. In Thomas Blackwell's influential *Enquiry into
the Life and Writings of Homer* (1736), the author had laid down a definition of epic
poetry. It requires great wars, he says, the marvellous and the wonderful, but not
comedy or polished language. 'A Poet describes nothing so happily, as what he has
seen; nor talks masterly, but in his native Language, and proper Idiom; nor mimicks
truly other Manners, than those whose Originals he has practised and known . . . Is what

we call *Heroism* indeed any thing else, than *A disinterested Love* of Mankind and our Country, unawed by *Dangers*, and unwearied by *Toils*? If it is not, the social Passions, and noblest affections must prevail in an *Epic-Poem*.'

The 'Birlinn', which Alastair seems to have begun in Canna when he got a job as factor there about 1750, is such a poem. In a little over 600 lines he describes how the galley is blessed and rowed to a sailing place, how the crew are deployed, how they sail from South Uist on St Brigid's day (1 February), and how they survive a great storm to arrive safely at Carrickfergus in Ireland. Most of it was recited rather than sung, and the metre varies from section to section. The poem operates at the level of allegory as well as of factual description, and is notable for the growing list of its sources of inspiration. The more of these that come to light, the better we see how Alastair created a coherent new vision out of fragments of the old. This is how he made his case for the unity of the Gael and the primacy of the people over their leaders. He provides enough clues to show that the 'Birlinn' is an allegory of the Clan-ranald ship of state, a microcosm of the Gael and of Scotland, being navigated by its heroic crew through the dangerous waters of the '45. As the storm rises to a crescendo all the most disgusting creatures of the deep rise to the surface and surround the ship; they are described in five quatrains, beginning:

> All the sea becomes a vile
> Discoloured porridge,
> The blood and gore of lamed beasts turns it
> A foul dull red.

The scene described here is the carnage inflicted on Sir John Cope's army at Preston-pans. But the beasts around the ship become more numerous, aggressive, noisy, terri-fying. This is Culloden, informed I think by a classic little piece of Jacobite writing in English, *Alexis*, written in 1746 by the Rev. Robert Forbes from materials supplied by Alexander MacDonald of Kingsburgh. 'Alexis' is Prince Charles, and 'Sea-Monsters' are defined as 'Ships of War'. Flora MacDonald declares: '*Providence*, I hope, will carry *Us* safely, and preserve *Us* from the *Sea-Monsters* which swim round this Island, and would be greedy of such a Prey as the great *Alexis*.' And the author says: 'Upon their setting out a thick *Mist* descends, by which Means they get safely through the *Sea-Monsters*, who would have been ready to devour them.'

A couple of stanzas later in the 'Birlinn' Alastair begins to speak of 'Our being blinded by spindrift', 'Bullets of fire', 'The smell and smoke of the reefing sail / Completely choking us', 'war', 'Earth, fire, rain and elements / Raised against us', and finally 'peace'. This is no ship: the reef of a sail does not catch fire. It is Culloden. It's what makes the 'Birlinn' epic poetry, for it concerns heroes surviving overwhelming odds to make history, and is consciously made from existing oral elements, transcended by one individual's powerful imagination and personal experience of war. John MacDonald, tacksman of Ardnabee in Glen Garry, put his finger on Alastair's ultimate source of inspiration when he said to him:

> You have surpassed even Homer
> Great musician though he was in Greek.

The 'Birlinn' may thus be seen as the middle link of the chain that connects Homer, Blackwell, James Macpherson and Elias Lönnrot. Macpherson certainly heard it performed in Badenoch ceilidh-houses during his teenage years; it is unlikely that he saw it in writing until it was published by Raghnall Dubh in 1776, in the anthology which his father had promised. Nothing as radical was attempted again in Gaelic verse until in the 1930s Sorley MacLean blended the vocabulary of Free Presbyterian theology with echoes of John Donne and traditional Gaelic song to pour out personal passion in 'Dàin do Eimhir' ('Poems to Eimhir') and political anger in 'An Cuiltheann' ('The Cuillin').

Alastair Mac Mhgr Alastair changed Gaelic verse for ever. In all sorts of ways which I haven't mentioned here, he had prescribed the norms, styles and functions of a new verse for the post-Culloden era. He did this by absorbing influences from the rest of Scotland and beyond. This made him alive to what was best and worst in his own tradition. What was best he utilised to the full. But I'll end with this thought. In his early life of travelling with Lady Clanranald to cities like Edinburgh and London, in his teaching career as a young married man, and in those amazing nine months when he marched to Derby with the Jacobite army and took part as an officer in the last three battles ever fought in Britain, he lived at the interface between the worlds of Gaelic and English. He must have had some sense of what Scotland was going to be like in the future. I've heard it said recently that after Culloden Scotland took on the Gaelic cultural identity. In fact, what happened was that Scotland cherry-picked some parts of the Gaelic cultural identity – the bagpipe, tartan, Highland dress, militarism, whisky, loyalty to a clan, heather as a national symbol. When he wrote of 'sharing the honour', Alastair was clearly foreseeing something like this happening (and I believe that through the 'Birlinn' he indirectly helped it to happen), but he couldn't possibly have guessed that for two hundred years Scotland would say 'no thanks' to what was best and most important about the Gaelic cultural identity – the literature and songs that are locked up in the treasure-house which we call the Gaelic language.

CHRISTOPHER MACLACHLAN

Literary Edinburgh in the time
of Alexander Macdonald

The first thing to try to establish is what the time of Alexander Macdonald's Edinburgh was. For this I rely chiefly on the biographical section of the introduction to Derick S. Thomson's *Alasdair Mac Mhaighstir Alasdair: Selected Poems* (Scottish Gaelic Texts Society, 1996). Professor Thomson seems to offer a well-balanced account of the life of a poet about whose biography there remain a number of obscurities, beginning with his date of birth. Professor Thomson says we do not know the year of birth of any of the family of MacDonald's father, and by process of conjecture, based on dates that are known in the lives of Alexander and his brothers, settles on 'the mid-1690s or slightly earlier' for the birth of the poet. This allows for the strong possibility that he took part in the 1715 Jacobite rising. There is some evidence that before this he had been at university in Glasgow, and that goes along with other evidence that he had some legal training.

The period from 1715 to 1725 is the one of least certainty in MacDonald's life and it is possible that during this time he had some contact with Edinburgh. In his article on the poet in this volume Ronald Black says that the poet 'probably spent time gaining experience in the writing chamber of some Edinburgh lawyer or other during the years following the '15'. It is however to a later period that firm evidence that MacDonald was in the city belongs. 'We know', says Professor Thomson, 'that he visited Edinburgh in 1738, in 1745 and in the years from 1747 to 1751' and he goes on to speculate that the influence of certain Scottish poets on his work shows that MacDonald was in touch with literary circles there. However strong these literary contacts were during the earlier visits, they surely cannot have been the result of prolonged stays in the capital since from 1732 to the ominous year of 1745 Alexander MacDonald was a schoolteacher in Ardnamurchan. This period covers the publication in 1741 of his Gaelic–English *Vocabulary*. The 1738 visit to Edinburgh was occasioned by this work, but he was not in the city when the book was printed, since the first edition contains an apology for mistakes resulting from the 'Author's absence from the Press, and the Difficulty of reading his Manuscript' (quoted in Thomson, p.18).

There seems no doubt that MacDonald took part in the '45 and was probably involved throughout. Presumably he accompanied the Prince to Edinburgh, but it was

hardly an opportunity for literary discussions. After Culloden the poet seems, naturally enough, to have been very downhearted, and his whereabouts have not been easy
to trace, but a few years later he began a series of visits to the Reverend (later Bishop)
Robert Forbes of the Scottish Episcopal Church, who lived in Leith, the port of
Edinburgh. These visits took place in 1747, 1748 and 1751. During this time MacDonald
appears to have been resident on the island of Canna, probably until 1751.

This of course is the year of publication in Edinburgh of his volume of Gaelic
poems, the first book of secular Scottish Gaelic literature to be published. No doubt
when he visited Robert Forbes in April 1751 his presence in Edinburgh had something to do with his new book, and perhaps some of the earlier visits had a similar
purpose. After 1751, however, his movements are again a puzzle, for which the best
clues seem to be in his late poems. Professor Thomson suggests he spent time on
the Glenuig estate of the chief of Clanranald, then in Knoydart, Morar and Arisaig,
where he died around 1770. There seems to be no evidence that he returned to Edinburgh after 1751, during the last twenty years of his life.

I have sketched the biography of Alexander MacDonald here, such as it is, not
just for the benefit of those who may not know it but also as the basis for choosing
the period for the focus of this paper. Though the evidence for visits to Edinburgh
in the 1720s is vague it is enough to suggest that that decade must be taken into
account, notwithstanding the fact that the earliest known visit is in 1738. This was
made in connection with the *Vocabulary* of 1741, but despite this and the probable
presence in Edinburgh in 1745, it is in the later period around 1750 that we can be
surest that Alexander MacDonald could have had sustained contact with literary Edinburgh. The Edinburgh of Alexander MacDonald seems therefore to belong to roughly
two periods, the 1720s and the years around 1750.

To begin with the later period, it has to be made clear that the Edinburgh of 1750
was not the fully fledged city of the Enlightenment admired today. Work on the New
Town would not begin for another decade and the people of Edinburgh were still
living in the crowded Old Town along the ridge running down from the castle to the
Canongate and on to Holyrood. This was a city of some thirty thousand people in
1752. It was a centre of law, religion and government and had a printing and publishing
industry to match. A directory of Edinburgh in 1752 lists no fewer than 56 booksellers, including bookbinders and printers, in the city. The same directory lists 164
alesellers and 33 brewers and distillers.

A name missing from the list of booksellers is Allan Ramsay, who retired from
the business in 1740. Ramsay was still alive when Alexander MacDonald made his
recorded visits to Edinburgh and would not die until 1758, but his active career as a
poet belonged more to the earlier period of MacDonald's contact with Edinburgh,
the 1720s. Ramsay made his name with his anthologies of Scottish poetry, *The Ever
Green*, first published in 1724, and *The Tea Table Miscellany*, of which the first of five

volumes also appeared in 1724. His own poems were published in various forms, both single and collected works, in the same period, and his verse drama, later converted into a ballad opera, *The Gentle Shepherd*, appeared in a series of forms between 1725 and 1729. The last volume of *The Tea Table Miscellany* was published in 1737, the year of Ramsay's *Collection of Scots Proverbs*, his last major publication. In the later period of Alexander MacDonald's connection with Edinburgh around 1750 he would know of Ramsay as the grand old man of Scots poetry. One can assume he had heard of Ramsay (as Ronald Black shows elsewhere in this volume, MacDonald imitates Ramsay's verse on at least one occasion), but whether he was ever in Ramsay's shop in the 1720s or met him elsewhere is a matter for conjecture. It is not unlikely, given Ramsay's reputation and his evident pleasure in meeting other poets and discussing poetry with them, what is nowadays known as networking. The evidence for this networking is the many references to other poets and the verse about them and to them, in the form of epistles, in Ramsay's work. There is however no reference to Alexander MacDonald in Ramsay.

Ramsay's career and reputation would have had an influence on MacDonald, as it did on other poets. Allan Ramsay came from a rural middle-class background, with no more than an elementary education and with few social advantages. His relatively humble origins were surely an inspiration to later poets and they mark a move towards a more middle-class literary world. Ramsay began his life in Edinburgh as a wig-maker and barber and gradually built up his literary interests into a flourishing career as bookseller and even librarian, establishing one of the first lending libraries in Britain. In this he shows the connection between literature and commerce. He was a writer who was involved in the book trade himself, and so not abashed by the money-making side of books. While building up his bookselling business his own verse won increasing attention, until he had built up enough of a reputation to begin publishing his own work. At the same time he collected and published older Scots poetry in *The Ever Green*, an action that both showed his dedication to the tradition of Scots verse and his own assumption of the authority to hand on that tradition.

Ramsay's career surely presented an attractive model for any poet in Scotland in the first half of the eighteenth century, a time when the older conventions of patronage were dying out and a new social and economic literary world was coming into being. English poets continued to struggle with the moribund system of court and aristocratic patronage, hankering after government sinecures and chafing at the apparent need to flatter noblemen. Leading English writers such as Pope and Swift distrusted the commerce of publishing as it was developing at this time. They denounced those who made a living by the pen as hack-writers, the mercenary scribblers of the proverbial Grub Street, despite the fact that increasingly even the best writers were coming more and more to depend for their incomes on deals made with printers and publishers. Ramsay's career has a much more modern appearance than that of his leading English contemporaries. He grafted his creative work, with its very evident flourishes towards Augustan values, on to his living in the book trade. He was a poet with a day job and showed that this was no dirty compromise but a viable way for a man to be a poet and make ends meet. It was to be the model that his Scots successors, Robert Fergusson and Robert Burns, would quite conspicuously follow, and the latter in turn would make it the default mode for Scottish poets down to this day. Thanks to the powerful image of Burns as both working man and poet we Scots tend not to have a snobbish view of what poets must do to sustain themselves, but Burns follows Ramsay in this. I suggest that in this respect Ramsay also had an influence on Alexander MacDonald.

Another sort of influence surely comes from the kind of poetry Ramsay was famous for. Perhaps it would be better to say 'kinds of poetry' since there is a great range of types of poetry in his work, but almost all of it has a public dimension. Ramsay is a community writer. This is partly because of his neo-classical Augustan ambitions, the aspiration to become a Scottish Horace, whose poetry addresses national concerns and is meant to be read by all thinking men and women, not just a literary coterie. Even in his verse epistles, where one might expect Ramsay to be private, the thought and expression is aimed beyond the individual addressee to a wider possible readership. And Ramsay is not afraid to tackle controversy and politics in his writing, though he tries to do so with humour, and sometimes he is covert and devious. Nevertheless he gives the impression of being an engaged writer, ready to comment on contemporary life and to voice opinions that are lively and frankly individual. His verse epistles, though modelled on those of Horace, are nevertheless made topical in their allusions to the local and contemporary.

At the same time he is always aware of tradition and his poetic forebears. His anthologising makes this unmistakable but in his original poems, too, he shows debts in style, metrics and language to previous poets. This gives him the stature he needs to convey his own ideas and it lends authority to his voice. Yet at the same time the gestures to the past are reminders that much of the tradition of Scots poetry is in the past, that it is in danger of being forgotten and that the reader owes in turn a debt to Ramsay for keeping it alive. Again Ramsay seems to mark a very modern development in literary culture in his utilisation of older poetic traditions. There is a complex paradox in our modern way of viewing the past as always on the verge of disappearing and in need of revival, which justifies both our imitating and transforming it and our pride in what is new as more vital than what has gone before. For Scottish poetry Ramsay is a key figure in articulating the modern system of using the traditional and the historic as a complex form of validation of the contemporary.

The interplay between old and new is very much the dynamic of eighteenth-century Gaelic poetry, including Alexander MacDonald's, and in this there is a parallel with the cultural situation of Scots poetry, if not all poetry, in the same period. Ramsay is at the forefront of the continuous debate throughout that century about the relation of the old and new, a debate whose continuity has been obscured by the conventional division of eighteenth-century literary history into a neo-classical beginning and a Romantic end. Both neo-classicism and Romanticism are fundamentally about the relation of past and present, tradition and innovation. In the middle of the century the eighteenth-century entanglement of past and present, tradition and innovation, would impinge on Gaelic and Scottish literature in the Ossianic controversy. Ramsay's own work as a pasticheur of older poetry, in a poem like *The Vision*, written in Ramsay's idea of mediaeval Scots, and his work as an imitator of older poetry, in for example his added cantos to *Christis Kirk on the Green*, are forerunners of Macpherson's Ossian, and open the way for the exploitation of older texts and styles. Ramsay's imitations and his high-handed editing of older poems confront readers with issues to do with authenticity and accuracy in ways that become more acute as the century goes on. He raises the questions, even if he does not satisfactorily answer them, of how the literature of the past is to be used and what the responsible way of doing this might be.

It is easier to speak of Ramsay's possible influence on a Highland poet like Alexander MacDonald in these general terms than in more specific ways, and there is no real sign that Ramsay himself had any knowledge of Gaelic poetry. While some echoes of Ramsay have been found in MacDonald's verse, there are no Gaelic echoes in Ramsay's and very little Highland influence at all. *The Ever Green* contains only poems in Scots, and several of these evince scathing attitudes to Highlanders, for example, 'Donald Ower's Epitaph' (Ramsay's title) by William Dunbar, a diatribe against leniency towards a Highland rebel. If, however, MacDonald read Ramsay's preface to this collection, he might have been encouraged by praise of Scottish poetry set in its native land:

When these good old bards wrote, we had not yet made use of imported trimming upon our clothes, nor of foreign embroidery in our writings. Their poetry is the product of their own country, not pilfered and spoiled in the transportation from abroad. Their images are native, and their landscapes domestic . . . We are not carried to Greece or Italy for a shade, a stream, or a breeze. The groves rise in our own valleys, the rivers flow from our own fountains, and the winds blow upon our own hills.

This is all very well, but though the implication is that the valleys, fountains and hills may be found throughout Scotland, in practice the poems in the collection are largely confined to the southern part of the country. The scope of *The Tea Table Miscellany* is almost equally confined. The songs it contains are almost all from the Lowlands and Borders. The only obviously Jacobite song, despite the strong suspicion of Ramsay's own leanings to the Stuart cause, is a version of 'The Blackbird' (discussed elsewhere in this volume by Murray Pittock). The first edition did contain a version of 'The

Highland Laddie', and later editions added a companion piece, 'The Highland Lassie', but these comparisons of Lowlanders and Highlanders as lovers are evidently from a Lowland point of view, though it might just be argued that they are harbingers of later, positive views of Highlanders as Scottish icons.

There is, however, one major poem in which Allan Ramsay does at least cross the Highland line, and that is 'Tartana, or the Plaid' (1718), a work of 368 lines in pentameter couplets. It is a plea to the ladies of Scotland not to give up wearing the tartan plaid. There is perhaps a political angle to this, coming relatively soon after the defeat of the 1715 Jacobite rebellion. The poem certainly considers the wearing of tartan as a sign of national pride and it must be one of the earliest long poems in praise of tartan as a symbol of Scottishness. It is however an uneven work in style and structure. Ramsay does not solve the problems of writing a long poem on a theme that does not lend itself to extended narrative and 'Tartana', like its subject, often seems a patchwork, combining, none too successfully, paragraphs on various aspects of its subject. The tone is also variable, twisting between conventional praise, social comment that verges on satire and neo-classical, even baroque, mythologising. One suspects that a major influence on Ramsay's poem was Pope's *The Rape of the Lock*, with its attention to women and their fashions, but the mock-heroic approach of the English poem is not very helpful to Ramsay. Where Pope wished to make amusing satire out of the superficialities of dress and appearance, hinting at the moral gap between the trivial elegance of the court and the business of government, Ramsay's aim was instead to assert the value of the tartan plaid, finding greatness in the ordinary. What Ramsay set himself to do has more resemblance to William Cowper's much later poem in praise of the sofa, *The Task* (1785), but Ramsay lacks Cowper's resources of gentle irony and a positive view of small things derived from the mid-century rise of sentimentalism. For Ramsay, a long poem still has to have epic qualities, however out of place they may seem in a discussion of ladies' fashion. Hence the appearance in the poem of a passage of over twenty lines in praise of Scottish soldiers wearing tartan, and even carrying tartan standards. This passage comes before Ramsay turns to the female wearers of the plaid.

But 'Tartana' is never entirely clear about its Highland connections. It opens by invoking as muses the spirits of the Tweed, the Clyde and the 'gentle Tay', nowhere further north, and then rapidly returns to 'Edina's streets'. The poem never seems entirely comfortable with the Highland origin of tartan. The society beauties whose example as wearers of the plaid Ramsay commends are named in heroic neo-classical fashion like minor deities and some clearly have Highland names: Campbella, Stuarta, Fergusia, Keitha. These however are outnumbered by those with Lowland-sounding names: Pringella, Ramseia, Hepburna, Humea, Hamilla and Maxella. Incidentally, it might be supposed that Tartana is one of these names, a personification of tartan itself, and I have a nineteenth-century edition of Ramsay's works whose frontispiece is an engraving by J. C. Armytage of a picture by A. Johnston entitled 'Tartana' showing a pretty girl in a fine silk gown with her head and shoulders covered by a tartan shawl, standing against a distant prospect of Edinburgh Castle, but the poem itself uses the word 'tartana' to refer to the shawl, not its wearer. Possibly Ramsay added a third syllable to the word 'tartan' for metrical reasons, converting a word with a trochaic or even spondaic rhythm into something more convenient for iambic verse.

The uncertainties of tone and attitude come to a head towards the end of the poem when Ramsay offers a mythical account of the origin of tartan. He tells the tale of how 'am'rous Jove' came down from Olympus 'beauty-hunting' and found Iris, the goddess of the rainbow, sleeping 'beneath a fir-tree in Glentanar's groves' (Ramsay's footnote refers to Glen Tanar as a 'large wood in the north of Scotland'; it is in fact to the south of the River Dee between Ballater and Aboyne). Jove grants Iris a wish in return for her favours:

> 'Make me a Goddess,' cry'd the Scotian Maid,
> 'Nor let hard Fate bereave me of my Plaid.'
> 'Be thou the Hand-maid to my mighty Queen,'
> Said Jove, 'and to the World be often seen
> With the celestial Bow, and thus appear
> Clad with these radiant Colours as thy Wear.'
> (lines 321–6)

This unsteady mixture of the Scottish and the Classical exemplifies the spirit of Ramsay's 'Tartana'. Though he may be said to conform to the letter of the preface to *The Ever Green* in setting his myth in Scotland, carrying Jove and Iris there from Greece does not seem in keeping with the spirit of his own preface. 'Tartana' is surely a significant gesture towards the Highlands but not an altogether convincing one.

Assuming, then, that Alexander MacDonald knew of the writings and reputation of Allan Ramsay – and it would be hard to doubt this – it seems fair to say that they could have had an influence on the Gaelic poet's ideas about poetry and the poet, just as they did on Scots poets like Fergusson and Burns. This would be an important result of MacDonald's contacts with Edinburgh. It is difficult, however, to find other Edinburgh poets in his time who might have had an influence on him. Ramsay's first notable successor, Robert Fergusson, was only born in 1750 and published nothing before MacDonald's death. The most significant Scottish poet other than Ramsay in the second quarter of the century is James Thomson and his *Seasons* are accepted as influences on MacDonald's poems, but Thomson of course emigrated to London at an early age and is in no sense an Edinburgh poet. Nevertheless one supposes that it was probably on his visits to Edinburgh that MacDonald learned about Thomson's poetry.

We must however not allow ourselves to forget that for the eighteenth century
what we now think of as creative writing was not the only kind that was regarded as
literature. Indeed, literary Edinburgh in the eighteenth century prided itself on many
forms of writing other than poetry. I therefore turn to consider the activities of some
of the leading writers, in the broad sense, of the period when Alexander MacDonald
was in Edinburgh, but I have to say straight away that generally speaking he was too
soon for the best work of most of them.

To begin with the most obvious example, and that of the leading Scottish writer
of his time, perhaps of the century: David Hume does not reach the height of his
fame until after 1750. Hume was in France, writing his *Treatise of Human Nature*, from
1734 until 1737, whence he returned not to Scotland but to London. The *Treatise* was
published there in 1739, but not with the success Hume had hoped for. 'It fell *dead-
born from the Press*', he later wrote. By this time Hume was back in Scotland and beginning work on his essays, which began to be published in 1740 and 1741. These would
bring him a more popular reputation than the philosophical *Treatise*. Nevertheless,
after failing to be appointed a professor of philosophy at Edinburgh University Hume
left Scotland again in 1745 and did not return to Edinburgh until 1751. He then became
much more a fixture of the literary scene than ever before. In 1752 he was appointed
Keeper of the Advocates' Library and used his time there, until 1757, to do the research
for his *History of England*, the work, published in six volumes between 1754 and 1762,
which more than any other made his name in his own time. He would become known
in the eighteenth century as Hume the historian.

If Alexander MacDonald heard of Hume in the 1740s and later he must have had
a different impression of him from that which we have today. The Hume of the
essays is a writer on a number of rather abstract issues, applying his sceptical and
detached mind to economics, politics, religion and the development of society, including
literature and culture. The essays are highly intellectual and, though they give the reader
many illustrative examples from history and literature, especially the classics, their point
is often general and theoretical. The reader must make the applications, which in fact
I think Hume intended, to contemporary society, especially Scottish society. Throughout
the essays there runs a theme of social improvement and the mechanisms of progress:
one representative essay title is 'Of the Rise and Progress of the Arts and Sciences'
and another is 'Idea of a Perfect Commonwealth'. In modern parlance, Hume was
acting as a guru, and was surrounded by a number of others in what we might today
call a think-tank, exploring the concept of progress and, implicitly, how to bring it
about, not least in Scotland. During the 1750s Hume was involved with the leading
intellectual club in eighteenth-century Edinburgh, the Select Society, which brought
together most of the major figures of the Scottish Enlightenment. It was Allan Ramsay's
son Allan, the painter, who suggested the society, which met for the first time in 1754.
Founder members included Adam Smith, Adam Fergusson, Alexander Carlyle, Hugh

Blair, William Robertson, David Hume and Henry Home, Lord Kames. Eventually the membership swelled, reaching 135 in 1759, and the society, grown too big for its own good, began to decline, but not before it had spawned the Edinburgh Society for Encouraging Arts, Sciences, Manufactures and Agriculture in Scotland, which offered prizes and medals for new ideas. This indicates that the Select Society was not just for blue-skies thinking but saw the need to encourage practical developments and the application of ideas to industry and other forms of social activity. The Select Society also brought into being the first *Edinburgh Review*, though it ran to only two numbers in 1755 and 1756. Still, it did contain work by Adam Smith, who had been elected Professor of Logic at Glasgow University in 1751 and whose first major publication, his *Theory of Moral Sentiments*, would appear in 1759; but it would be another seventeen years until *The Wealth of Nations* was published.

Of the other founding members of the Select Society, Adam Fergusson succeeded Hume as Keeper of the Advocates' Library in 1757. A Gaelic speaker, he had been a chaplain to the Black Watch between 1747 and 1754. His major work, the *Essay on the History of Civil Society*, appeared in 1767. It furthers the aim of the Scottish Enlightenment to lay open the means by which social progress happens. William Robertson's *History of Scotland* was published in 1759, an obvious counterpart to Hume's *History of England*. Both works explore history to reveal the springs of action in society. But for MacDonald it could only have been the foreshadowing of these works in earlier debates that could have influenced him. Work on literary theory was also too late for him, Hugh Blair's *Lectures on Rhetoric and Belles Lettres*, for example, achieving publication only in 1783. Although Edinburgh in the time of Alexander MacDonald was certainly the seed-bed of the Scottish Enlightenment it had hardly begun to bloom, let alone fruit, in his time.

There is perhaps one exception to this and that is a figure I have only mentioned in passing: Henry Home, in 1752 made a Law Lord as Lord Kames. Perhaps MacDonald's own involvement in the law might have brought Kames to his attention more than some of the other figures I have mentioned. Born in 1696, Kames was of an earlier generation than the others. If indeed Alexander MacDonald had some legal education he may have known, or known of, Kames's first book, *Remarkable Decisions of the Court of Session, from 1716 to 1728*, published in 1728, which soon became a standard legal work. Yet Kames's non-legal writings, like those of Hume, Smith, Robertson and the rest, also belong to the mid-century and later. In 1751 he published *Essays on the Principles of Morality and Religion*, one of the earliest works dealing with key areas of Enlightenment thinking, and although he is not the most rigorous thinker of the Scottish Enlightenment Kames is in some ways the most typical, an accessible generalist who embodies the curiosity and intellectual restlessness of his time and place. His writings range from the *Elements of Criticism* of 1762, a solid contribution to literary aesthetics, to *The Gentleman Farmer, being an attempt to improve Agriculture, by subjecting it to the test of rational principles* (1776). As well as a lawyer and philosopher, Kames was also an agricultural improver. He reminds us again that the Edinburgh circle of writers and thinkers was keenly interested in the practical effects of what they thought and wrote.

Edinburgh in the time of Alexander MacDonald is a topic that needs attention but it is a difficult, not to say impossible, task. Apart from the guesswork about all save a handful of the poet's visits to Edinburgh, and the guesswork as to why he was there when we know he was, the period around 1750, when we are sure he did visit the capital, is not the highest one for literary activity. He came to Edinburgh more or less in the gap between Ramsay and Fergusson, and at a point where the great figures of the Enlightenment were preparing themselves for the outburst of activity which would secure their fame and that of their city as a 'hotbed of genius'. Perhaps something of this expectation of great things to come affected MacDonald but that is yet another speculative thought amongst the many one has to resort to in discussing this topic.

Bibliography

Gilhooley, J., *A Directory of Edinburgh in 1752* (Edinburgh: Edinburgh University Press, 1988).

Mossner, Ernest Campbell, *The Life of David Hume* (Oxford: Clarendon Press, 1970).

Ramsay, Allan, *Works*, edited by Burns Martin, John W. Oliver, Alexander M. Kinghorn and Alexander Law (Edinburgh: Scottish Text Society, 1944–74).

Ross, Ian Simpson, *Lord Kames and the Scotland of his Day* (Oxford: Clarendon Press, 1972).

Thomson, Derick S., *Alasdair Mac Mhaighstir Alasdair: Selected Poems* (Edinburgh: Scottish Gaelic Texts Society/Scottish Academic Press, 1996).

NEIL MACGREGOR

Orm a Laigheas Gach Seanchas:
The Gaelic songs of John Roy Stuart

First of all, a question: does the name John Roy Stuart mean anything to you? Don't worry if it doesn't, because the first time I saw it I'd never heard of him. This was twenty odd years ago, in the Macgregor family tree. According to the parish records of Abernethy, in Strathspey, John McGregor, miller in the Garlyne, on 27 December 1773, married Janet, lawful daughter to Alexander Stewart in Lynebeg. According to my great-uncle, 'A Stuart of the house of John Roy Stuart, a descendant of Robert III.'

If I'd asked the question a hundred years ago, nearly everyone – at least in the Highlands – would have heard about him. He was so well known – unfortunately some writers would say, 'I need not tell or . . . ' and not tell you the story. It was the same in John Roy's home country of Strathspey. One man I knew in Nethy Bridge, Lewis Grant, had grown up in Tulloch at the back of the Abernethy forest, before the First World War. He told me about John Roy's cave: 'Aye, I've been in John Roy's cave up on Craiggowrie . . . it was down in a hollow, and he had it kind of built up in stones right round and heather on the floor for a bed, for all I know! Oh, it was going for a long time, there was a lot of students used to come up there and stop in it . . . then they went up through the hill an' that, they were great hill boys. There wasna so much aboot it, after the [First] war. It was aal before the war, it was a great attraction, and the lads came wanting to find out about that. But the war put a feenish to aal that.' If I were writing a summary of his life, it could go something like this: 'Iain Ruadh Stiubhart, born 1700 at Knock of Kincardine, Strathspey, son of a tacksman and grandson of a baron. Served in the British Army, in the Scots Greys, c.1727–c.1737. Arrested as a Jacobite spy and escaped to France. Served in the French Army in 1744–5 (against the British) and again in 1747–8. Colonel of his own regiment in the Jacobite army of 1745. Died in France c.1748, or maybe in 1752. A versatile, skilled composer of Gaelic songs and particularly noted for his songs of the '45.' There are probably thirteen or fourteen of his songs surviving, some so far unpublished. I have been working on him, on and off, for twenty years, and have gathered together as much as I can find of his life and songs for the Gaelic Society of Inverness. The results will appear in the next volume of the *Transactions* (Vol. LXIII). It is not short, but each time I warned Hugh Barron that it had grown, all he said was, 'It's all good stuff, keep it coming.'

With John Roy, the facts are only half the story. Like Rob Roy MacGregor, he has always attracted stories, and he still survives in oral tradition in Strathspey. Son of a tacksman, yes – his father was Donald Stuart, tacksman on the Gordon lands of Kincardine. But only one generation before, this had been the Barony of Kincardine, a Stuart property since 1400, when it was gifted by Robert III to Walter Stuart. Walter's father, Alexander, of royal blood, is remembered as the Wolf of Badenoch. The barony was more stolen than lost, and John Roy had a full measure of family pride.

John Roy's mother was Barbara Shaw, from Guislich in Rothiemurchus. According to local tradition she was fifty-three or fifty-five when he was born. The Rose MS, compiled *c*.1820, says that she was a native of Glenlyon and was sixty the night he was born: 'take care of the boy', it says, 'he would be a great man and crown the kings of three nations.' He received a good education, first in Inverness, and then abroad, it seems, in France or Spain. As the family was Episcopalian or Catholic, this would not have been unusual. He was quick, intelligent and gifted. Jim Collie, who farmed in Rothiemurchus, told me that John Roy could speak five languages, and W. G. Stewart, from Connage, noted that he could write in English, Latin and Gaelic.

However, he grew into a difficult teenager. The youngest in the family, he got bored quickly. Drummond Norie described him thus: 'A youth of spirit, fond of daredevil escapades, and always ready to crack a head, or a bottle, kiss a pretty girl or chaff an ugly one.' Kincardine lies on the rievers' road, Rathad nam Mèirleach, and the Lochaber men were still on the go in the early 1700s. John Roy tried his hand at cattle-lifting too, along with some of his friends. Fortunately, their neighbours were tolerant. When he plotted to kidnap a guest of the Laird of Grant, he was deterred, but seemingly not punished.

His talent for composing songs soon became obvious. Often, the subject was his own mishaps. If you went out to a funeral wake, got drunk, started a fight and got chucked out into the cold, you might want to forget all about it. Not John Roy. He sat down and composed 'Òran a' Bhranndaidh', while still slightly under the influence. Folk liked it, and in 1859, Donald Shaw reckoned it was his most popular song in the district. Here's a taste of it:

> Mìle marbhphaisg air a' ghòraich!
> Is mairg a dh'òladh branndaidh!
> Lìonaidh e làn gaoith is bòst sinn.
> Is mòr a bhios de chainnt uim';
> Is ionann sin is mar dh'èirich dhòmhsa.
> Rinn mi òl sa ghleann seo.
> Is ann a leig e air mo bhuaireadh,
> Is bhuail e anns a' cheann mi.

*

Ciamar dh'fhaodainn gun dol thairis?
Lìon a' chaile ghòrach
Trì dramachan gun fharraid
Thairis air a' chòir dhomh;
'S cha bhuidheach tha mi do na balaich
Lìon iad làn an stòip dhomh.
Fhuair mi siud gu m' chur am chabhaig
Agus glainne beòrach!

*

Ach ged bhithinn-sa 'n dèidh caithris,
Teas is fallas dannsa,
A dhaoine! A bheil sibhs' am barail,
Ged dh'òlainn galan branndaidh,
Gu bheil de dhaoine anns a' bhaile
Na chuireadh thairis mi do m' an-toil?
Ach 's èiginn dhomh aideachadh a-nis
Gun robh misg orm aon uair!

('Òran a' Bhranndaidh', pp.7–11, Stanzas 1, 3 & 9)

A thousand curses on the folly!
Woe to him who would drink brandy!
It fills us with wind and boastfulness.
And there will be much said of it;
That's just what happened to me.
In this glen I took to drinking.
It tempted me,
And it struck me on the head.

*

What could I do but go under?
The foolish girl poured out three drams
More than I should have had.
I didn't ask for them;
And I am not thankful to the lads
Who filled the stoup right up for me.
I got all that to get me going
And then a bumper of beer!

*

But although I had come from a wake,
The heat and the sweat of the dancing,
Man! Do you think,
Although I were to drink a gallon of brandy,
That there are enough men in the toun
To put me over against my will?
Now, however, I have to confess
That I was drunk once!

Despite some of his comments in 'Òran a' Bhranndaidh', he got on well with women, and enjoyed their company. Some, like Màiri Ghrannd, he worshipped from a distance. To her, he composed quite a racy song of love. Here's a couple of its ten verses:

Och 's och mar tha mi fèin,
'S bochd 's tinn tha mi nochd,
Chan eil fios aig neach fon ghrèin
[C'ait a bhuile mo chreach tu goirte; ?]
Is bochd an galar tha mi tàrmach',
D'fhàg e mi gu h-iomlan loit;
Lot e mo chridhe is m' àirnibh,
'S chan eil earrainn slàn am chorp.

*

Aghaidh sholais air a' ghruagaich,
Falt na chuachaibh air dhreach theud;
Mala chaol gun chealg gun ghruaimean
Is a dà ghruaidh co dearg ri cèir;
Sùil chorrach ghorm mar an [criostal ?],
Fàile [muste ?] teachd o beul;
Uchd sòlais nan tùr geal bàna
Air a' mhnaoi as àillt' fon ghrèin.

('Màiri Grant', pp.18–22, Stanzas 2 & 5)

Alas and alack as I am now,
Sick and ill am I tonight,
No-one under the sun knows
[Where my soul's wounds are; ?]
Wretched is the illness that I suffer,
It has left me deeply hurt;
My heart and my kidneys are pierced through,

And there is no part unbroken in my body.

*

The maiden has a pleasant face,
Curled hair in shape of melodious strings;
Slender brow without malice or gloom
And her two cheeks as red as waxen candle;
Sharp blue eye as clear as [crystal ?],
Scent of [musk ?] comes from her mouth;
Delectable breast of the pure white towers
On the most beautiful woman under the sun.

In tradition and in printed sources, you hear about children he fathered in Strathspey. Certainly, in one case he mentions being up before the Session, and had to leave Strathspey. He composed a song to his sweetheart there. According to the Rose MS her child grew up to serve in the British Army in the '45.

Bheir mo shoraidh 's mo bheannachd
Dh'fhios na caileig as bòidhche;
Thoir do làmh 's do ghealladh
Gum bi thu 'd charaid re d'bheò dhi.

Labhraidh mise mar shanntaicheas,
'S a h-ainm cha chuir mi san òran;
Tha i shìos anns a' ghiuthais
Am bun na bruthaich a' còmhnaidh.

*

Ach 's ann leam gum bu bheud e
'S mo chreach lèir mar a thachair:
'S ann tha mise 'n Dùn Èideann
'S tusa 'n Srath Spè le mo phàisde;
Gar am faic mi thu 'm-bliadhna,
Gun glèidh an Rìgh rium mo shlàinte –
Cha bhi mo chaileag gun tochradh
'S òr an Cofar na Spàinte.

Ma gheobh mise Coimisean,
Cha mhist' is' air mo làimh-sa;

71

B'olc dhomh nam bu mhiste
'S bu sheachd miosa mur b'fheàirrde;
Caileag bhochd rinn mo bhuaireadh
'S a chuir mi 'm fuath air a càirdean,
Nan dèanainn a trèigsinn,
Bu mhairg tè bheireadh gràdh dhomh.
            ('Òran do Leannan', pp.24–8, Stanzas 1, 2, 12 & 13)

*Take my greetings and my blessing
To the most beautiful girl;
Give your hand and your promise
You will be a friend all your life.*

*I will speak as I wish,
And I won't put her name in song;
She is down in the pinewood
Living at the foot of the bank.*

*

*But for me, what has happened
Is my distress and my complete ruin:
I am here in Edinburgh
And you in Strathspey with my child;
If I do not see you this year,
May the Lord preserve my health –
My girl shall not be without a dowry
And gold from the Spanish Treasury.*

*If I can get a commission,
She will not be the worse for my hand;
It would be ill of me [if she were worse off ?]
And seven times worse [if she were not better off; ?]
The poor girl who tempted me
And so I put hatred among her relations,
If I were to forsake her,
Woe to any one who would love me.*

He got his commission, not in the King of Spain's but in the Scots Greys, a lowland
cavalry regiment. Here he rose to the rank of quartermaster and lieutenant, and became
a sound professional soldier. At some point he tried to get into the Black Watch, who

were certainly more Gàidhealach, and had been recruiting in Strathspey. He didn't get in. Dr Forsyth, minister in Abernethy, mentions a song on the subject – but it seems that that song has now been lost.

In 1736 or 1737 he was arrested as a Jacobite spy, and was put in Inverness jail. The Stuarts of Kincardine were strongly Jacobite anyway, and John Roy more so than most of them. He may well have witnessed the end of the '15, as on the night of 11 March 1716 the remains of the Jacobite army had passed through Kincardine on their way to Badenoch.

However, he wasn't a prisoner for long, and a few days after escaping, he was at the house of the Sheriff, Lord Lovat, as an honoured guest. When Lord Lovat came to trial in 1747, his servants' recollections of those days became important evidence for the prosecution. Not only had they captured seditious Jacobite verses, but, even worse, they had done so in Gaelic.

John Roy seems to have spent some time in Atholl before leaving for the Continent, and an exchange of letters with Lady Lovat still survives. With her, he corresponded in Gaelic, and with Lord Lovat, in French. From 1737 or thereabouts until 1745, John Roy was in Europe, as part of the Jacobite Court, and latterly as an officer in the Scottish brigade of the French Army. Along with his nephew Dòmhnall Breac, he fought against the British and their allies at Fontenoy, in May 1745. Here, too, the Black Watch were blooded, and Dr Forsyth recorded a typical John Roy escapade. Several of his friends from Strathspey were in the Black Watch, so, the night before battle, he crossed the lines for a ceilidh with them.

There are two main sources for this period of his life: one is the Letter Book of his cousin, Bailie John Stewart, who was a merchant in Inverness, and the other is the Stuart Papers, a collection of Jacobite correspondence now in Windsor Castle.

We now come to the events for which John Roy is principally remembered – the '45. Of his work at this time, there are three songs on Culloden and its aftermath – and a number of shorter songs and rhymes composed while he was on the run. There is also a song from early on in the campaign which may well be his work. Two versions survive, one more Spéach than the other, which is credited to a Glengairn bard. The Spéach version is attributed to him, and the style and language fit. King George is described as 'an collach musach laithach romach', the bristly lazy hairy boar. The opening verses, however, are pastoral, and give a good picture of shielings – ruighean – in the hills. The hills at the back of Nethy are still called 'the Càrns'.

Ho, mo nighean, 's tu mo chridh',
Dhut bu dligheach bhith 'do dheann,
Bhith cur ri gnìomh 's a' triall 's a' dìreadh
Air an ruighe anns a' ghleann,
Tional dhachaigh dhuinn [meanbh-bheathach ?]

Bhios gu h-anmoch air gach càrn,
Bleoghain a' chrodh-laoidh 's nan gamhnach
Nis bhon 's e ar samhradh th'ann.

Gu dearbh cha tèid mi fhèin ri aonach
Dh'iarraidh chruidh na laogh na mheann,
'S chan eil iùl agam air meanbh-chrodh
Bhios gu h-anmoch feadh nan càrn;
'S cha mhò thèid mi 'na bhuaile,
Gogan is buarach nam làimh:
'S nach do shlànaich mi 'n leth-bhliadhna,
B'olc an ciall duibh mo chur ann.

('Òran Eadar E Fhein Agus Leanabh Nighean',
pp.46–50, Stanzas 1 & 2)

Ho my girl, you are my heart's delight,
For you it's right to be in haste
To set in order, travel and ascend
On to the shieling in the glen,
To gather in for us [small livestock ?]
Which wander late on every carn,
Milking the cows with calf, and yearlings,
Now that summer is here.

I'll certainly not go off to the hill
In search of cows, calves and kids,
And I cannot track the sheep and goats
Which wander late among the carns;
Nor will I go to the fold,
Coggie and cow-fetter in my hand:
Since I have not reached my half-year,
'Twould not make sense to send me there.

Now it is my turn to say 'we need not tell . . .' about John Roy, but for reasons of
space, as his actions in the '45 are fortunately quite well documented. In the summer
of 1745 he was still serving in the French Army at Ghent. A letter from the Prince,
who was now in Scotland, summoned him to the cause and he met up with the
Jacobite army at Blair Atholl. Having raised his own regiment in Strathspey, Perthshire
and Edinburgh, he served throughout the campaign. For a professional soldier,
raising and running a regiment posed no great problems. As the army kept on the

move, his skills as a quartermaster were especially useful. He had a talent for guerrilla warfare, which is still praised in Strathspey to this day. His useful views on military strategy often went unheard.

What about the songs? The Gaelic songs of the '45 have sometimes, in the past, been ignored by historians of the period, but for the Gaels they were and are the historical record. Every mood and need is covered – celebration and sadness, praise and hatred, hard news, propaganda and politics. There are two major Gaelic poets of the '45 – Mac Mhaighstir Alasdair and Iain Ruadh Stiùbhart. Both fought in the campaign, Alasdair as a captain and John Roy as a colonel. Each, however, has his own style and particular interests. Put them together, and you have a fairly complete view of Bliadhna Theàrlaich and its aftermath.

While Alasdair certainly served in the campaign, his main purpose was as propagandist-in-chief to the Jacobite cause. His songs tackle the big issues, but we don't learn much about what he himself was doing, or of the campaign. John Roy, on the other hand, was a professional soldier with a strong interest in military strategy. From him we get a practical, personal view. His first-hand account of Culloden tells us more than any military history could.

On the main issues, they both reflect the general mood. Early in 1744, the Prince left Italy for France, to make plans. John Roy wrote: 'I cannot express the joy I felt . . . ' And when the news of the Prince reached Mac Mhaighstir Alasdair, he composed 'Òran don Phrionnsa': 'O hi ri ri, tha e tighinn'. Both show the justice of the cause – Mac Mhaighstir Alasdair in 'Òran don Phrionnsa': 'Mac an rìgh dhlighich tha uainn [the son of the rightful king who is from us]' and John Roy in 'Òran Eile':

> 'S bidh sinn uile fa-dheòidh,
> Araon sean is òg,
> Fon rìgh dhligheach don còir dhuinn gèilleadh.
>
> ('Òran Eile air Latha Chùil Lodair', pp.65–73, Stanza 45)

> *And we will all be at last,*
> *Young and old alike,*
> *As lieges under the rightful king.*

However, while both praise the chiefs and clans, they do so in different ways. Mac Mhaighstir Alasdair, in 'Brosnachadh do na Gàidheil' and 'Òran nam Fineachan Gaelach', praises them to encourage them to rise in support of the cause. He uses the conditional tense, telling of what they would or could do. John Roy, in 'Òran Eile', uses the same imagery to tell us what they actually did on the battlefield. Here he praises Captain Robert McGillevray, who fell at Culloden:

Chaill sinn Raibeart an àigh,
'S cha bu sgrubaire e
Measg chaigneachadh lann is bhèigneid.

Fhuaras teisteas o d' nàmh
Gum bu deas do dhà làimh,
'S gun do sheas thu ri bàs gun ghèilleadh.

('Òran Eile air Latha Chùil Lodair', Stanzas 30 &31)

We lost Robert, whom fortune favoured,
Not niggardly was he
Amid the clashing of swords and bayonets.

Testimony was got from your foe
That your two hands were skilled in action,
And you looked death in the face without yielding.

John Roy was sometimes described as being too proud and impetuous. Very occasionally he was criticised for being too cautious. But he also had the reputation of being a good professional soldier, trustworthy and reliable. In his third, and least known, song on Culloden, 'Latha Chùil Lodair nan Sìol', he describes the opening of battle as he himself saw it from the Jacobite front line. There is a degree of confidence, and some unkind words for the enemy. Also, a hint of what was to come:

Chuir iad an òrdugh blàir,
Thug sinn uille dhaibh hosà;
Thug sinn cuireadh dhan a' ghràisg
Iad a mheàrrsal leth an rathaid dhuinn.

Cha bu dàna leis a'ghràisg:
Sheas iad shìos aig taobh na pàirc;
Cha digeadh iad a-nìos 'nar dail
Ged thàmhadh sinn fhathast ann.

Thug an Comanndair an sin dhuinn gaoir:
'Bidh sinn caillt' le uisg' is gaoth;
Bithibh unnt', a luchd mo ghaoil!
Chan fhaod sinn bhith feitheamh orr'.'

They formed up in battle order,
We gave them all a huzza;
We dared those scrapings of the barrel
To come and meet us half way.

The low rabble were not bold:
They stood down east beside the park;
They would not have come up to meet us
Were we to be stopping there yet.

The commander then gave us a cry:
'Lost will we be in the wind and rain;
Up and at them, my dear friends!
No longer may we wait for them.'

Very quickly, a dangerous situation becomes a disaster:

Bha iomadh anacothrom eil' ann:
Uisg' is gaoth gar dèanamh dall,
Canan a-null 's a-nall,
Gearradh [runne(?)] 's gan sgathadh dhuinn.

Ged bha na laoich ghast' neo-mhùcht',
Dol an adhbhar ceart a' Chrùin,
Bu mhò 's [moir (?)] air fear mu thriùir
'S gur fùdar bhathas a' caitheamh orr'.
            ('Latha Chùil Lodair nan Sìol', pp.75–9, Stanzas 1, 2, 3, 5 & 6)

There was much further hardship:
Wind and rain blinding us,
Cannon fire over and at us,
Cutting and chopping right through us.

Although the braw heroes were resolute,
Striving in the just cause of the crown,
'Twas more than [one man in three ?]
Who was wasted by powder and shot.

In his song 'Latha Chùil Lodair', composed while he was on the run in Strathspey, his despair at the turn of events is obvious:

Cha do shaoil mi le m'shùilean
Gum faicinn gach cùis mar a tha.

I never thought that my own eyes
Would see things as they stand.

And he draws comparison with 'a' Chomhachag', the Owl of Strone, subject of a Gaelic song from one hundred years before:

Tha ar cinn fon a' choille,
'S èiginn beanntan is gleanntan thoirt oirnn,
Sinn gun sùgradh, gun mhacnas,
Gun èibhneas, gun aitneas, gun cheòl;
Air bheag bìdh no teineShort of food and fire's warmth
Air na stùcan an laigheadh an ceò,
Sinn mar Chomhachaig eile
Ag èisdeachd ri deireas gach lò.

('Latha Chùil Lodair', pp.85–90, Stanzas 7 & 12)

We are now outlaws,
We must make for the hills and glens,
Without sport or enjoyment,
Without joy, music or pleasure;
On the rough hills where the mist lies,
We are as another owl
Hearing each day of disaster.

Over the next few months John Roy had plenty time to think over what had befallen the Jacobites. In 'Òran Eile' he notes that the choice of battlefield, 'lom an t-slèibhe', the bare moorland slope, had done them no favours. Then there was the weather. 'As an adhar thàinig trian ar lèiridh', he said: 'from the skies came a third of our torment'. But he also seems to have been among those who believed a rumour that swept the army in the immediate aftermath of Culloden. Lord George Murray, it seemed, had turned traitor. In hindsight, this may tell us more about the mood in the Jacobite army than historical truth. As for the Prince's misguided Irish advisers, they seem to have escaped any blame.

However, he reserved his real hatred for the Duke of Cumberland. The two were certainly known to each other and the Duke is reported to have had a great respect for John Roy's abilities in battle, having noticed him in the French ranks at Fontenoy. In the closing stages of 'Òran Eile' John Roy curses him in a truly magnificent and horrible manner:

'S gum bi Uilleam Mac Dheors'
Mar chraoibh gun duilleach fo leòn,
Gun mheur gun mheangan gun mheòirean gèige.

Guma lom bhios do leac,
Gun bhean gun bhràthair gun mhac,
Gun fhuaim clàrsaich, gun lasair chèire.

Gun solas, sonas no seanns,
Ach dòlas, donas is plàigh,
Mar bha air ginealach Chlann na h-Èipheit.

'S chì sinn fhathast do cheann
Dol anns an adhar ri crann,
'S eòin an adhair ga theann-reubadh.
('Òran Eile air Latha Chùil Lodair', pp.65–73, Stanzas 41–44)

And may William son of George
Be as a tree without leaves, afflicted,
Lacking branch, bough and twig.

May your hearth be bare,
Without wife, brother or son,
Without music of the harp or light of waxen candle.

Without joy, pleasure or luck,
But grief, misfortune and plague,
As befell the offspring of the Children of Egypt.

And we shall yet see your head
Swinging to and fro on the gallows,
While the birds of the air peck it eagerly.

Having attended the last gathering of Jacobite leaders at Loch Arkaig in May 1746, John Roy spent the summer on the run in his native Strathspey. As was his way, he composed songs not only about Culloden, but also about his many escapes from the redcoats. Strathspey, as Grant territory, for the most part, was nominally on the Government side, but local loyalties ran deep. Tales of his exploits have been collected over the last two hundred years, and others remain in oral tradition to this day. Folk still visit Uamh Iain Ruaidh, John Roy's Cave, upon the face of Craiggowrie. I recorded the following story from Jim Collie, who farmed Lower Tullochgrue in Rothiemurchus. John Roy had heard from the Prince, who was in hiding at Ben Alder: 'This word came to his ears . . . when he was in Nethy, so he decided now to get away and join the Prince – well, that's to be a problem, you see, because the redcoats were hot in the area, and the Campbells too, in redcoat clothing. Anyway, he was to get a safe journey, there was two men of Moidart were sent down, and two of Cluny's, to take him through Rothiemurchus and Badenoch . . . to get him safely conducted up to Ben Alder. On the way through, above Tullochgrue, a place up there – it's on Tullochgrue ground, I'll show you on the way up – they went into this house, and they were taken in there, because there was gleaners in the fields, aye, in September, and they appeared just as the gleaners, there was a crafty old woman there and she knew fine they were so-and-so . . . so anyway she put a big shawl on Roy, while he was gleaning there, he was tired, and his compatriots, they were gleaning away with sickles until about four o'clock . . . and in the meantime there was govermnent troops seen going into some of the buildings, so the lady went up to consult them, and they were looking for Roy and company, so she declared no such persons had passed this way. They were in another field, across the moor. She very craftily concealed them, kept them there till evening, till the redcoats cleared out . . . So, anyway, Roy, he was conducted from up the back of Loch an Eilein, Loch Gamhainn way, up the Thieves' Road, right through Badenoch, through into Laggan . . . it's a true story that, because it was passed down from the old Collies.'

He escaped to France with the Prince and rejoined his old regiment. Meanwhile, government agents in Scotland continued to report his presence there. One had even spoken to him on the road to Crieff. Some of his letters survive from this time. It seems that the failure of the '45 had left him broken and angry. For the first time he began to question the wisdom and authority of the Jacobite leadership. According to letters written by his wife in France, John Roy died in the early spring of 1748. Or maybe not. The minister of Abernethy, writing in the 1790s, stated that John Roy Stuart died in 1752. As far as I know, his burial place is not known.

Most of John Roy's surviving songs are political or personal, but there are also two formal songs. Both are elegant and well conceived, showing the breadth of his knowledge and education. One is an elegy to Lady MacIntosh and the other is in praise of Grant of Rothiemurchus. In the opening lines of this John Roy himself appears as 'Am Fear Ruadh', the Red-haired One. According to a local tradition noted in the 1860s, John Roy was a keen fisherman, and here he adopts the usual model to create a hunting and fishing song:

> Fhuair thu urram nan crìochan s'
> Airson iasgair is sealgair, Is ma fhuair, gur tu a b'fhiach e,
> Airson do ghnìomh anns an àm ud;

Bu leat tacar na h-abhna,
Is càch nan laighe ga dearmad;
Is cha bhiodh miann air na mnathan,
Bhon as tu dam b'aithne a mharbhadh.
('Òran do Mhac Ailpein an Dùin', pp.12–14, Stanza 3)

You were esteemed in these bounds
As a fisher and hunter,
Indeed, you were worthy of that
On account of your actions at that time;
You won the river's store
While others lay forgetful;
And the women would want for nought,
For you knew how to make the kill.

The lands of MacIntosh of Moy lie between those of the Grants and Inverness, so the family was well known to John Roy. Unfortunately, around the 1730s, there were two Ladies MacIntosh, both of whom had Menzies connections, so it's not easy to tell which is the subject of the elegy. John Roy's song is an elegant jewel in five verses. A writer in the *Celtic Monthly* for October 1916 noted that it was somewhat in the English, rather than the Gaelic, style of the period. The second verse is typical of it:

Mar choinneal chèir 's i lasadh treun,
Mar eàrr na grèin ro nòin,
Bha reul na mais' fo shiantaibh deas
A-nis thug frasan mòr,
Oir bhris na tuinn 's na tobair bhuinn,
'S le mulad dhrùidh na neòil:
'S e lagaich sinn 's ar n-aigne tinn,
'S gun ruith ar cinn le deòir.
('Cumha do Bhaintighearna Mhic an Tòisich', pp.15–17, Stanza 2)

Like a waxen candle burning strong,
Like the sun's ray before noon,
The elements were favourable to the graceful star
Where now rain down great showers,
Since the waves and the wells of the deep burst out,
And the clouds poured down their grief:
It drained our strength while our spirits were low,
And our heads were running with tears.

As I said earlier, John Roy Stuart is one of a select band of characters in Scottish history who became legends in their own lifetime and remained so. Wallace, Bruce, Rob Roy MacGregor – and John Roy Stuart. 'Orm a laigheas gach seanchas,' he says in the song to his sweetheart; 'I am the subject of every story,' and it's true. And the stories travelled, just as his songs did.

Here, for example, we have one of his escapades while he was on the run after Culloden. Two versions of the story exist: one published in recent years in the *Stewart Magazine* in Australia, having come down through oral tradition; the other was collected by James Hogg around two hundred years ago.

First, the *Stewart Magazine*'s version of events. The story was written down by the Rev. W. G. Shaw, who had heard it as a child at the house of John Shaw of the Balloch, in Glen Isla. It takes place at Inchrory, up in the turn of Glen A'an, above where Tomintoul would later be built. Shaws had lived at Inchrory until the Gordons took it back for a deer forest in about 1845. The Gordons gave them instead a newly cleared and almost empty Kincardine, ancestral home of John Roy Stuart. On 25 March 1846, the *Inverness Courier* reported proudly how upwards of thirty small farms and crofts there had been replaced by two farms. According to local tradition, the Shaws of Inchrory had taken an active part in these clearances. Here's the story:

> John Roy Stuart was surprised in the house of Inchrory, whilst his friends were in concealment among the neighbouring hills. Holding up his bonnet at the corner of an aumry, which was visible from the window, the party which consisted of five dragoons, discharged their carbines at it, fancying that it was his head. John Roy, who had left the door ajar, slew the first two who attempted to enter, one after the other, with sweeps of his broadsword. Another he cut down a few yards from the door. When John Roy's companions made their appearance the other two took to flight, pursued by the Jacobite Colonel, kilted as he was, on the horse of one of the dead dragoons. The fugitives, however, escaped.

James Hogg most probably heard the story on his Highland tour of 1801. On 22 July 1802, he wrote to Sir Walter Scott, telling how, the previous year, 'I took another journey through the eastern parts of the Grampian Hills, penetrating as far as the sources of the Dee, where I beheld large tracts of fine pasture countries . . . ' He certainly visited Glen More forest and reached Loch A'an, in the heart of the Cairngorms. While he looked at the country with the professional eye of a sheep farmer, he was also after material for his 'Jacobite Relics'. In the same letter he admits to Scott that he used 'a little colouring' on what he found, but his version of the story is still very interesting. He published it under the title of 'A Story of the Forty-Six'. It contains everything in the Rev. Shaw's version and a lot more. He gives us a rough date, 'one day in July 1746', which would certainly fit. Inchcroy, he calls the house, but that's pretty close to Inchrory. Mrs Shaw and her three daughters are alone there, as the laird is in hiding. Enter 'a tall raw-boned Highlander', claiming to be a Sergeant Campbell, there to search the house for rebels – and he knows where they are hiding. An English officer – Cornet Letham, of Cobham's Dragoons – and five dragoons now enter the house and Mrs Shaw turns to them for aid. However, the Highland sergeant claims precedence. Letham takes hold of him, but the 'tall red-haired loon' fells him with one blow. Five pistols are immediately drawn . . . but the door to the room is so narrow that only two dragoons can enter at one time, and they're not keen to, as the Highlander has both pistol and sword. Two of them head round to shoot him through the window. He puts up his bonnet and they fire at it. Got him! He then goes for the other three dragoons, fells two of them before they reach the outer door and the third after a short pursuit. The remaining two are now off on horseback, but the Highlander – named by Hogg as John Roy Stuart – goes after them on the officer's horse, bloody sword in hand. They escape, but John Roy's companions, and the two hidden in the house, are all safe.

While Hogg has altered the place-names and has added a postscript to give the story a setting, most of what happens here sounds like typical John Roy Stuart. Many other stories show him in the same light and his skill, intelligence, bravery and daring are still talked of today. As Alasdair Grant, who farms Ballinluig, near Grantown, told me: 'See. I maintain myself, they're all on about *Bonnie* Prince Charlie, but I think he was a bloody idiot. See, that John Roy Stuart had been fighting on the Continent for a lifetime and he advocated guerrilla warfare . . . long before Culloden, when they were in the district, that was his policy.' I have heard it said that John Roy Stuart was the model for the character of Alan Breck in *Kidnapped*. We know that Stevenson read Hogg, and if stories such as the above gave him ideas . . .

We have John Roy the soldier, brave, proud, practical, respected by all, friend and foe. We also have John Roy Stuart the bard. Sorley MacLean had great respect for John Roy's abilities and placed him on a level with the great Lochaber bard Iain Lom. Their work, he said, combines a 'pregnant simplicity' with a masterly use of rhythm, form and language, giving their songs a hard razor-sharp edge. Praise indeed.

Notes

Page references are to the long article *John Roy Stuart – Jacobite Bard of Strathspey* by Neil MacGregor, published in *The Transactions of the Gaelic Society of Inverness* Vol. LXIII (2002–4), Inverness, 2006. In that article the unmodernised texts of these poems are printed in full.

MURRAY PITTOCK

The Jacobite song:
was there a Scottish *aisling*?

There remain many key questions concerning the Jacobite song: its transmission, its survival, the relationships between its texts, its connexions to broadside ballads and chapbooks and so on. These problems have been addressed to some extent in the recent edition of James Hogg's *Jacobite Relics* of 1819–21 (a work which established the Anglophone Jacobite song canon) and elsewhere.[1] The question this essay addresses is one which is both fugitive and controversial: the question of whether there was a Scottish *aisling*. The enquiry which follows is of necessity provisional: nonetheless it intends to challenge the existing boundaries of the *aisling* subgenre, and to recognize the importance of the permeability of the form as well as its fixity. While criticism of Anglophone literatures has long recognized the instability and variation in the development and inflection of genre, the *aisling* has been tethered to the tenets of essentialist nationalism in a paradigm which, deriving ultimately from Daniel Corkery, was refined by Gerard Murphy in the first (1939) issue of *Eigse*. This essay will conclude with evidence that their claims are misplaced, and that a broader reading of literary dialogues within and across cultures better reflects the evidence we have available: it will suggest that such dialogue was in itself driven by the need to express local cultural and political values hedged about by external forces as Corkery and others argued, but that the act of translation or incorporation was one of reinforcement, not dilution.

The *aisling*, or dream vision, poem is the mainstay of Irish Jacobite poetry in Gaelic: among its chief exponents are Aodhogan O Rathaille (1671–1729) and Eoghan Ruadh O Suilleabhain (1748–84). Daniel Corkery defines it thus in *The Hidden Ireland*:

> . . . a typical example would run somewhat like this: The poet, weak with thinking on the woe that has overtaken the Gael, falls into a deep slumber. In his dreaming a figure of radiant beauty draws near. She is so bright, so stately, the poet imagines her one of the immortals. Is she Deirdre? . . . or is she Helen? or Venus? He questions her, and learns that she is Erin; and her sorrow, he is told, is for her true master who is in exile beyond the seas . . . the poem ends with a promise of speedy redemption on the return of the King's son.[2]

Unsurprisingly, given the underpinning paradigm of Corkery's book (the survival of a nation under occupation, conceived in essentialist terms), one of Corkery's chief points is that the woman/nation in the *aisling* is a demonstration of primary nationalism and secondary Jacobitism in the Irish situation, whereas in Scottish Jacobite writing the converse is true: 'the place that the Stuarts themselves occupy in the Scottish poems is occupied in the Irish poems by Ireland herself' (Corkery, 134). The *aisling* thus becomes part of the unveiling of nationality by the Gaelic tradition, which transfers its more contingent allegiances from the Stuarts to Daniel O'Connell, while 'the transformation of the "allegorical lady" into the "poor old woman" of nationalist Ireland can be traced through the moveable feast of the *aisling*'s politics'.[3] Fifteen years after Corkery's book, Gerard Murphy provided an anthropology of the form, identifying *aislingi* of love and prophecy from the eighth and ninth centuries, with an allegorical political form which grew to full strength in the eighteenth, which, in its combination of the beloved and the supernatural visitant from earlier traditions with the allegorized nation, created the image of the 'speir-bhean', sky-woman: a supernatural manifestation of the state of the nation, and an avatar of its deliverance. She has various names, among them Caitlin Ni Uallachain and Roisin Dubh.[4]

Despite the doubts which have grown round Corkery's definition of authentic Irishness as persisting only in the redoubts of Gaelic Munster (his particular version of 'The West's Awake'), most subsequent critics seem to endorse his view of the *aisling*. Some commentators have traced it back much earlier, yet even in its early manifestations have seen it as symbolizing 'the Sovereignty of Ireland . . . the earth mother embodied in the land'.[5] It is seen as distinctively Irish, and also as contingently related to the Jacobite song but more centrally a work of self-definition, flexibly transferred to new messianic deliverers and new versions of the feminized nation, as it was to older ones, such as the O Neill (Williams and Ford, 217–18). Central to the special status of the *aisling* in these terms is that it is uniquely Irish, and that there are no Scottish *aislingi*, neither Gaelic nor Anglophone, although there are English-language variants of the form claimed for Ireland: a fact which will be important to the case advanced below (Zimmerman, 90).

What the *aisling* is is thus a question of definition, of how narrowly the form is circumscribed. The central Irish political function argued for by Corkery, Murphy and others in the case of the later *aisling*, and its inextricable relationship to earlier exemplars, firmly places it as the anterior prop to the sacrificial matriarchalism of twentieth-century blood sacrifice nationalism, a credit note from literary history to the linguistic currency of physical force Republicanism. The insistence that the *aisling* is really only Irish confers national particularism on a form which in its broadest terms (those of dream-vision) is widespread in European literature. Since the *aisling* was valorized by Corkery, it has become a defining genre of Irish Gaelic dispossession: this is the role that it fulfils, for example, in the influential collection *An Duanaire: Poems of the*

Dispossessed (ed. Sean O Tuama), which first appeared in 1981. It seems that no matter how much revisionists may undermine Corkery's mythologized history, the status of the *aisling* as a pure guarantor of its reality remains an unaltered assumption of the literary history of the period. The pure Irish form was truly national and nationalist; Scotland, which did not use this form, was neither. Some recent Irish commentators (for example Vincent Morley) have sought to stress the lack of a national conscious-ness in Scottish Gaelic poetry of the period, whether rightly or wrongly is an issue for another paper (there is of course clear pro-Scottish and anti-English sentiment in the poetry of Aonghas MacDhomhnuill, Alasdair Mac Mhaighstir Alasdair, Rob Donn and Uilleam Ros, to mention no more; see also John Macinnes' essay in *The Middle Ages in the Highlands* (1981), cited below. As MacMhaighstir Alasdair put it, 'the inhabitants of the lowlands of Scotland . . . have always shared . . . the honour of every gallant action' with the Gael). The trouble, however, with the narrow defini-tion of the *aisling* adopted in much of the existing criticism is that, in Bourdieu's terms, such critics 'can only register, unaware, the effects of those authors they do not know on the authors they claim to analyse'.[6] Examination of some of these authors follows in an argument which states, cautiously and provisionally, that we may be missing important dimensions in the relationship between Scottish and Irish writing in adopting too narrow a definition of the *aisling*, and too narrow a defin-ition of its relation to Jacobitism, to bilingualism and to Scottish–Irish literary rela-tions in general.

For example, it is not the case that the explicitly Jacobite *aisling* belongs to the Jaco-bite period alone, and was thereafter rapidly transformed into a more realistic poli-tics in Ireland. The Jacobite *aisling* endured 'until as late as 1840', when it can still be found calling 'To banish the foreign hosts of Calvin' and to bring back 'James, the lawful monarch'.[7] The adaptability of the *aisling* (heard in Kerry by Corkery as late as 1915) certainly did not lead to the end of its Jacobite version before 1798, or before the age of Young Ireland either (Zimmerman, 90). Nor are all agreed that knowledge of the form was limited to Ireland: Seamus Heaney has argued that an Anglophone Scottish writer such as Burns knew exactly what he was doing in a poem such as 'The Vision': 'this is Burns' *aisling*, and its transcultural allegiance to the Gaelic heritage of Scotland is made clear by his calling each section of it a *duan*.'[8] Not only is the *aisling* presented here by Heaney as a form known outside Irish culture: it is implicitly itself a Scottish form. Burns' familiarity with *duan* and *aisling* alike is part of the same 'trans-cultural allegiance'. Colm O Baoill mentions Iain Dubh's (*c*.1665–*c*.1725) Jacobite vision poem 'Am Bruadar' of 1715 (which John MacInnes suggests has *aisling* qualities) in the context of both Burns' poem and Allan Ramsay's *A Vision* of 1724. William Gillies cites another example (one might also catch echoes of the tone in Uilleam Ros's 'Feasgar Luain'/'Monday Evening' and elsewhere), and Macinnes also draws attention to the links between 'saviour figure, prophet and fairy hill' in Scotland: links very much those made in Irish *aislingi*.[9] What Heaney identifies as 'transcultural allegiance' I elsewhere define as part of 'altermentality', the process whereby the dispossessed become more open to one another's mutual traditions, and to external traditions, in order to sustain their ability to defend and express their own cultural and political agenda in the face of a unitary language and the centripetal cultural forces: in this case, those of eighteenth-century Britain.

These Scottish songs are not exactly in the Irish mould, but this rather begs the question that genre should be consistent, and the Scottish tradition dependent, whereas the very nature of genre's presence in national literature is that it is inflected to meet the needs of local conditions. How many seventeenth- and eighteenth-century English odes which claim to be are truly 'Pindaric' (Norman MacLean has said that 'the Great Ode was "the free verse" of the neoclassical period',[10] and why do we interpret the Doric as Scots, except on the basis that it was the only successful espousal of realist pastoral using native speech? The Doric of Theocritus could as easily have been Northumbrian dialect if history and status had been different: the very word we owe to Ramsay and Ramsay's inflection of the pastoral towards Scottish language and cultural politics in order to preserve their ability to express themselves in their own tongue without having to rely on a limited range of forms. In Scottish language poetry, too, we see a tantalizing closeness to the themes of the *aisling*: and, just as importantly, such writing shows a clearly marked confluence with Irish models, Irish and Scottish versions alike existing of a number of the songs, not least those which portray the nation as an abandoned or bereft woman.

'The White Cockade' (Hogg I: XVIII, very similar to Kinsley, 306) was a Jacobite song in both Scotland and Ireland: it refers, of course, in its most familiar versions, to a woman who promises to sacrifice all her material gain to follow her lost love. In Scotland it was very popular as an Anglophone song, and the air is recorded a number of times throughout the eighteenth century (Pittock (2002–3), II: 490). It was also the title of Uilleam Ros's elegy on Charles Edward in Gaelic. In Ireland, it was also a popular air;[11] it was played at Fontenoy and was otherwise used to enlist recruits in the Irish Brigades. It was also 'a favourite tune among the old Jacobite natives, especially in Munster', where it was played on the harp or pipes. It was also known as a song in Irish Gaelic.[12] By the 1780s, a version known as 'The Green Cockade' was in circulation in Ireland in the patriot cause, and although this might seem to bear out the idea that the Jacobite rhetoric was a flag of convenience for the nationalist reality, it is interesting to note that 'The White Cockade' itself also retained an association with Irish radicalism, as when the MP Arthur Cole-Hamilton 'threw his glass' at a blind fiddler in Belfast for playing the song in 1793.[13] As one political song has it, 'We are the British Orange Boys which never were afraid,/To . . . burn a white cockade' (Zimmerman, 301).

Similarly, a song such as 'It was a' for our Rightfu King' (Hogg I: XV) has a dual inheritance in Scottish and Irish (not to mention English) tradition. It first appears as a broadside ballad in London in 1690, where a soldier is leaving his beloved to fight for his king in Ireland (the name of the king is uncertain, which is why the ballad is probably Jacobite – what incentive otherwise would there be not to declare one's loyalty explicitly?). It certainly appears to display such politics in the only other English version known to me, '*Molly Mog* of the *Rose*' in *Mist's Weekly Journal.*[14] In 1746, it appears as a chapbook, 'Molly Stewart', which Burns subsequently reworked into the song we know; but it also appears as a 'slip-song' where it is the woman who speaks, mourning her abandonment, and as a later variant, which mourns the loss of Lord Lewis Gordon. Here and elsewhere 'Molly Stewart' and Scotland seem to be equated (Pittock (2002–3), 11: 433–4).

'Molly Stewart' also has a strong presence in the Gaelic tradition. In Sileas Na Ceapaich's 'Do Righ Seamus' ('To King James'), Scotland is '*Mo Mhali Bheag O*'/'My Little Mollie O') in the refrain. There was also a Gaelic oral version, '*Mhali bheag og*', which John MacDonald of Kingsburgh learnt from a Breadalbane man in 1738. Similarly, Ewen MacLachlan remembered in Old Aberdeen in 1820, hearing a song of the same title in the Lochaber of his youth.[15] A Scots version of *Bonny Mally Stewart* was published at Stirling as late as 1823: the 'a' possibly betraying a link to the form of a Gaelic original. Mac Mhaighstir Alasdair's 'Òran Luaidh No Fucaidh' ('A Waulking Song' – Campbell, 144ff.) may be related. As Niall Mackenzie argues in his recent article on the 'poetical performance' of Lord Lovat and John Roy Stewart in 1736, the feminization of nationality in Jacobite culture is both a profoundly deep and varied phenomenon, and one which, except in the case of the explicit *aisling*, has 'received little comment' (apart from one 1996 article by Mairin Nic Eoin). The *aisling* dimensions of MacMhaighstir Alasdair's 'Morag' are a case in point.[16]

The characterization of the nation as female, then, and longing for the return of a male deliverer, is known in Scottish Jacobite poetry. More than that, it is common: how common can be obscured by the fact that in Scottish song the woman often speaks in her own voice, rather than being the object celebrated as a personification of the beloved nation by a male poet. Songs such as 'Somebody', 'Lewie Gordon', 'To daunton me' and of course 'Charlie is my Darling' and 'O my bonny Highland Laddie' (Hogg, *Relics* II: XXII, XLI, XLVI, XLIX, LX) are all examples of this.

It is not surprising that Scottish and Irish Jacobite songs should follow similar forms. As Michael Enright pointed out in a 1976 article in *Scottish Historical Review*, the idea that the king was married to the nation was present in Scotland as well as in Ireland.[17] It was equally clear in both traditions that the rule of the just king was associated with fertility and prosperity, while under an unjust one 'the soil and the elements will rebel against him. There will be infertility of women and cattle, crop-failure, dearth of fish, defeat in battle, plagues . . . The relationship between a king and his territory may be viewed in sexual terms.'[18] The plague of 1645 and the War of Montrose, King William's ill years in the 1690s and the poor harvest of 1744 are only three of the specific events in Scottish history which are associated with a resurgence of Stuart royalist feeling, and which fulfil these traditional signs of loss or abandonment. The trope is more generally present in Jacobite song. In Irish tradition, the true king should 'have a perfect body, free from blemish or disability' (Kelly, 19), and the same was true in Welsh tribal law.[19] It is intriguingly possible that the many idealized (if one compares contemporary French portraits) images of 'Bonnie Prince Charlie' may serve a similar function in Scotland: the representation of the heir as flawless, fair and almost childishly beautiful. For example, Antonio David's (or his studio's) 1729–32 portrait of Charles (National Portrait Gallery 434) and Louise Gabriel Blanchet's 1738 portrait (NPG 5517) arguably continue to underpin later Scottish representation in both paint and print into the 1750s, while on the Continent the images of 1740 and 1744 following Domenico Dupra (NPG D16608, D19272) or the 1748 painting by Maurice Quentin De La Tour (Scottish National Portrait Gallery) show a wilier, haughtier and more mature figure. In this role (*Tearlach Ruadh*) he was a fit 'harvest husband' to the land, for the idea of the king marrying the land, ancient practice in Connacht, was also found in Wales – interestingly, the yellow beak of the blackbird (see below), and its association with dispossession, is a possible comparator.[20] Enright argues that the same conception of kingship was present in Scotland, and indeed the kinds of muted reproach to James VI's absence in England in poems such as Drummond of Hawthornden's 'Forth Feasting' from *The Muses' Welcome* (1617) can be seen as bearing witness to this, characterizing the land as they do in the guise of an abandoned woman.[21] In other words, the high likelihood is that the women portrayed in Scottish Jacobite songs are explicitly allegorical representations of the nation in just the same manner as the *speir-bhean* of the *aisling*.

It is clear that this confluence of Scottish and Irish tradition and expectation in the representation of national selves was established and understood in the eighteenth century, across both Scots/English and Irish and Scottish Gaelic. MacMhaigstir Alasdair uses at least ten airs from the Anglophone tradition, and his incorporation of influences from Gavin Douglas, James Thomson and Allan Ramsay ('*Ailean Bard*') in his work is perhaps part of a project to strengthen Gaelic cultural expression by appropriation of a wider Scottish tradition. Carolan produced variations and part-imitations of at least three airs from the Scottish language tradition, including the Jacobite 'Cock Up Your Beaver' (Hogg II: LXIV), while as Eamonn O Ciardha points out, Anglophone Jacobite airs were in circulation in Ireland; Sean Clarach Mac Domhnaill even translated one Scottish Jacobite song into Irish Gaelic.[22] The United Irish (UI) use of 'popular Gaelic tunes' and iconization of Carolan is thus rather more complex than it appears, as we have already seen in the case of 'The White Cockade': there is an increasingly clear link between Jacobite and Jacobin language of opposition, and in Ireland this is often expressed in English, the UI hybridizing Gaelic to Anglophone traditions as MacMhaighstir Alasdair had done in reverse. The UI also used

Anglophone Jacobite rhetoric originally designed to aver the bastardy of George II, and even so mild a use of the Jacobite song tradition as John Gay's led to the banning of *The Beggar's Opera* in 1793.[23] The tropes return and cross traditions: William Farquharson, coming late to Culloden, breaks his fiddle in grief; John Macpherson, hanged in Ireland, plays his bagpipes on the way to the gallows as James Macpherson, hanged at Banff, played his fiddle and 'brak it ower a stane'; Moore's Minstrel Boy breaks his harp. The restrung harp of the UI is the reawakened nation, and the harp's role in national renewal and a display of male love for their nation/queen is of course obviously present in Hogg's *The Queen's Wake*, just as the image of the Aeolian harp bequeathed by Macpherson to the English Romantics is a sign of the absence of virility, the palsied, broken or dead fingers of the bard being useless members which cannot enable the loved instrument to sound at human hands. The crossovers between the traditions are remarkable: nor is Macpherson's 'cloud of years' so different from the 'Magic Mist' of Eoghan Rua O Suilleabhain.

None of these manifold similarities does, however, provide unambiguous evidence of the presence of a Scottish *aisling* unless we allow for the kind of inflection of genre typical of literary self-definition. There does remain, however, a very important case in point, which exists in distinct Irish and Scottish versions: 'The Blackbird', a version of which appears in Hogg's *Relics* (I: XXXIII), but is better known in other sets (v. Pittock (1994), 48). In this song, a more conventional *aisling* situation is presented: the poet comes across a 'fair maiden' ('the grieving figure of Erin' as Boyan Coleborne calls it in *Field Day* I: 474n.) lamenting the loss of her 'blackbird', the king, who will return from oversea. Like some Irish *aislingi* (but unlike Scottish Anglophone Jacobite song), it places the Jacobite cause in its international context, by mentioning France and Spain. Like all similar songs, it hopes for a messianic royal return (or she will go to him, which is more unconventional). This is to happen in the spring, in tune with the restoration as an image of fertility.

'The Blackbird' as a title is traditionally taken as referring to the dark hair of James VIII and III. Peter Davidson identified a version referring to Charles II, published as a broadside in 1651.[24] Cornelius O'Callaghan, attesting in 1870 to its popularity in Ireland, recalls that the song 'was a favourite tune among the old Jacobite natives, especially in Munster' (O'Callaghan, 605; cf. O Ciardha, 50). *Field Day*, which identifies 'The Blackbird' as using the 'conventional device' of *aisling* poetry, relates the Irish set to its Scottish antecedents (I: 474n., 476, 492). But things are more complicated than this.

The epithet 'The Blackbird's Son' is used to describe Fionn MacCumhail's sword in Irish Gaelic poetry. The association of Jacobite warriors with the Fianna was established (it occurs, for example, in Donnchadh Ban Mac an T-Saoir/Duncan Ban MacIntyre's writing (Anja Gunderloch has suggested an ironic use of the sword as heroic Fenian weapon in Donnchadh's writing) and in Liam Inglis' comparison of the wild goose Ulysses Browne to Fionn (Campbell, 210–11, 214–15; O Ciardha, 339)), and 'Blackbird speech' was a term used in Irish Gaelic writing to describe the Fenian swords.²⁵ Much later, Francis Ledwidge would call the men of 1916 Blackbirds.

A 'large number of Irish political broadside ballads celebrate heroes under the guise of birds' (Zimmerman, 56), and this of course brings to mind James' appearance as 'The Bonny Moorhen' and in other guises. More specifically, *londubh*, 'blackbird', is the Irish term for a Jacobite, a rapparee or more generally a hero: entirely suitably applied then, in both Gaelic and English, to the returning Stuart. An Irish version of 'The Blackbird' in English is known from 1718, and the song continued in persistent circulation. In 1848, John Mitchel appeared as 'The Blackbird'; in 1881, Parnell was celebrated as 'The Blackbird of Avondale'. Perhaps most interestingly of all, in the 1840s 'The Blackbird' (in its Irish set) was printed alongside 'My Name is Duncan Campbell' in a Glasgow broadside designed to attack anti-Irish prejudice and to point out the commonality of the sea-divided Gael: 'For I'm from Argyllshire in the Highlands so braw,/But I ne'er took it ill when called Erin-go-bragh'.²⁶ The continuity is striking on every level: in 1919, Sinn Fein put out a pamphlet which gave 'the names of thirteen men and women' who have been arrested for 'disloyal songs and expressions' and 'seditious choruses' by the oppressive British government (Zimmerman, 57, 72, 119–26, 240, 277). The circumstances to which Sinn Fein were objecting were precisely those of the Jacobite period, and it is no surprise, therefore, that the obliquity with which sedition represented itself took similar forms. The avian connexions of birdic nationalism are almost entirely unexplored: but, like the sword of Allan Breck, they have their own song.

'The Blackbird', then, fulfils most of the fundamental features of the *aisling*. It is known both in Scottish and Irish versions, it has clear links to Gaelic tradition, and, like the *aisling*, it practises political continuity by shifting its subject across time:

> Once on a morning of sweet recreation,
> I heard a young maiden a-making her moan,
> With such sighing and sobbing and sad lamentation,
> Crying, 'My blackbird most royal has flown!
>
> In England my blackbird and I were together,
> Where he was still gentle and generous of heart,
> O woe to the time that they sent him thither,
> And now they have forced him to dwell far apart.
>
> In Scotland, he's deemed and highly esteemed,
> In England he's known as a stranger to be;
> But his fame shall remain in France and in Spain,
> Good luck to my blackbird, wherever he be!

Whether it is the blackbird, the wren, the moorhen or the wild goose who has been made a 'stranger to be' by the strangers, the consequences of political dissent remain the same across the centuries: diaspora of space through exile, or of time through death. Located in the *aisling* or 'the blackbird', the methodology of representation is the same. Was there a Scottish *aisling*? Nearly: and for those who think that is not enough, one may ask whether Aristotle would think *Macbeth* a tragedy or Pindar recognize himself in Cowley's verse. The application of the gendered nation to the song of vision and loss across the languages and cultures of Scotland and Ireland in the eighteenth century deserves both more liberal and more detailed consideration than that offered by a paradigm which has subjected the intriguing polyphony of eighteenth-century Scottish and Irish literature to a monolingual essentialist nationalism rooted in one interpretation of the history of Munster in the century before the West awoke.

Notes

[1]   James Hogg, *The Jacobite Relics of Scotland*, ed. Murray G. H. Pittock (Edinburgh: Edinburgh University Press, 2 vols, 2002–3); v. also Murray G. H. Pittock, *Poetry and Jacobite Politics in Eighteenth-Century Britain and Ireland* (Cambridge: Cambridge University Press, 1994); William Donaldson, *The Jacobite Song* (Aberdeen: Aberdeen University Press, 1988).

[2]   Daniel Corkery, *The Hidden Ireland* (Dublin: M.H. Gill & Son, 2nd ed, 1925), 129.

[3]   Murray G. H. Pittock, *Poetry and Jacobite Politics in Eighteenth-Century Britain and Ireland* (Cambridge: Cambridge University Press, 1994), 191; Georges-Denis Zimmerman, *Songs of Irish Rebellion* (Dublin: Allen Figgis, 1967), 56.

[4]   Gerard Murphy, 'Notes on *Aisling* Poetry', *Eigse* 1 (1939), 40–50; Seamus Deane et al. (eds), *The Field Day Anthology of Irish Writing* (Derry: Field Day, 5 vols, 1991), I: 275–6.

[5]   J. E. Caerwyn Williams and Patrick K. Ford, *The Irish Literary Tradition* (Cardiff: U. Wales Press, 1992 (1958)), 218.

[6]   Alastair MacMhaighstir Alasdair, introduction to *Aiseirigh na Seann Chanain Albannaich* (1751), tr. Ronald Black; Pierre Bourdieu, 'Flaubert's Point of View', in Randall Johnson (ed. & tr.), *The Field of Cultural Production* (New York: Columbia University Press, 1993 (1988)), 197; v. Marshall Brown, 'Passion and Love: Anacreontic Song and the Roots of Romantic Lyric', *English Literary History* 66: 2 (1999), 373–404 (390) for a fuller citation.

[7] Pittock (1994), 190; Diarmuid O Mathuna, 'A Late *Aisling*', *The O Mahony Journal* 14 (1990), 15–21.

[8] Seamus Heaney, 'Burns's Art Speech' in Robert Crawford (ed.), *Robert Burns and Cultural Authority* (Edinburgh: Edinburgh University Press, 1997), 216–33 (231).

[9] Ian Dubh: *Orain*, ed. Colm O Baoill (Aberdeen: An Clo Gaidhealeach, 1994), 28–9, 55n. I am indebted to Dr Niall Mackenzie for bringing this point to my attention. V. also John Macinnes, 'Gaelic Poetry and Historical Tradition', in Loraine Maclean (ed.), *The Middle Ages in the Highlands* (Inverness: Inverness Field Club, 1981), 142–63 (154, 162); William Gillies, 'Gaelic Songs of the 'Forty-Five', *Scottish Studies* 30 (1991), 19–58; Derick S. Thomson (ed.), *Gaelic Poetry in the Eighteenth Century* (Aberdeen: Association for Scottish Literary Studies, 1993), 147ff.

[10] Cited in Stuart Curran, *Poetic Form and British Romanticism* (New York and Oxford: Oxford University Press, 1986), 65.

[11] John Lorne Carnpbell (ed.), *Highland Songs of the Forty-Five* (Edinburgh: John Grant, 1933), 286ff; Colm O Lochlainn (ed.), *Irish Street Ballads* (Dublin and London: Constable & Co., 1939), 22.

[12] John Cornelius O'Callaghan, *The Irish Brigades in the Service of France* (Glasgow: Cameron and Ferguson, 1870), 355, 605; Joep Leerssen, *Mere Irish and Fior-Ghael* (Amsterdam and Philadelphia: John Benjamines, 1986), 213.

[13] Kevin Whelan, 'The United Irishmen, the Enlightenment and Popular Culture', in David Dickson et al *The United Irishmen* (Dublin: Lilliput, 1993), 269–96 (283).

[14] John Gay, *Poetry and Prose*, ed. Vinton A. Dearing and Charles E. Beckwith (Oxford: Clarendon Press, 2 vols., 1974) I: 294.

[15] NLS MS 893 pp. 93, 95.

[16] Kirkpatrick Sharpe Collection 3:49, John Rylands Library, University of Manchester; Niall Mackenzie, 'The "Poetical Performance" Between John Roy Stewart and Lord Lovat (1736)', *Eigse* XXXIV (2004), 127–40 (134–7). See Mairin Nic Eoin, 'Secrets and Disguises? Caitlin Ni Uallachain and Other Female Personages in Eighteenth-Century Irish Political Verse', *Eighteenth-Century Ireland* 11 (1996), 7–45.

[17] Michael J. Enright, 'King James and His Island: an Archaic Kingship Belief, *Scottish Historical Review* 55 (1976), 29–40.

[18] Fergus Kelly, *A Guide to Early Irish Law* (Dublin: Institute for Advanced Studies, 1988), 18.

[19] T. P. Ellis, *Welsh Tribal Law and Custom in the Middle Ages* (Oxford: Clarendon Press, 2 vols, 1926), I: 29.

[20] Proinsias MacCana, *Celtic Mythology* (Feltham: Neymes Books, 1983 (1968)), 117; Robi Chapman Stacey, 'King, Queen and *Edling* in the Laws of Gower', in T. M. Charles-

Edwards, Morfydd E. Owen and Paul Russell (eds), *The Welsh King and his Court* (Cardiff: University of Wales Press, 2000), 29–62 (36). For the tradition of the blackbird's yellow beak representing its having 'come down in the world', v. Alexander Rober Forbes, *Gaelic Names of Beasts* (Edinburgh: Oliver and Boyd, 1905), 246. I am indebted to Dr Niall Mackenzie for this point.

21 Murray Pittock, 'From Edinburgh to London: Scottish Court Culture and 1603', in Eveline Cruickshanks (ed.), *The Stuart Courts* (Stroud: Sutton, 2000), 13–28.

22 Alastair MacMhaighstir Alasdair, *Selected Poems*, ed. Derick S. Thomson (Edinburgh: Scottish Academic Press/Scottish Gaelic Texts Society, 1996), 6–7, 25; Donal O'Sullivan, *Carolan: The Life, Times, and Music of an Irish Harper* (London: Routledge and Kegan Paul, 2 vols., 1958), I: 277–8; II: 69; Eamonn O Ciardha, *Ireland and the Jacobite Cause, 1685–1766: A fatal attachment* (Dublin: Four Courts, 2002), 47, plate 28 (Royal Irish Academy MS23 E.1 p. 5).

23 Kevin Whelan, *Fellowship of Freedom: The United Irishmen and 1798* (Cork: Cork University Press, 1998), 26, 37; Howard Mumford Jones, *The Harp That Once: A Chronicle of the Life of Thomas Moore* (New York: Russell & Russell, 1970 (1937), 38.

24 British Library c.20 fol. 14 (32); Peter Davidson (ed.), *Poetry and Revolution: an Anthology of British and Irish Verse, 1625–1660*, (Oxford: Clarendon Press, 1998), no. 329.

25 Sean O Tuama (ed.), *An Duanaire: Poems of the Dispossessed* (Dublin: Dolmen Press, 1981), 43, 49; Anja Gunderloch, 'Donnchadh Ban's *Òran do Bhlar na h-Eaglaise Brice*: Literary Allusion and Political Comment', *Scottish Gaelic Studies* XX (2000), 97–116.

26 National Library of Scotland L.C. 1270 (003).

This essay was first published in substantially similar form as 'The Jacobite Song: Was There a Scottish *Aisling*?' in *Review of Scottish Culture* 19 (2007), 45–53, and is reproduced here by kind permission of the editor.

DONALD E. MEEK

Evangelicalism, Ossianism and the Enlightenment: the many masks of Dugald Buchanan

Currently, I am in the final stages of a new edition of the verse of the eighteenth-century Gaelic poet Dugald Buchanan (1716–68), who was a schoolmaster in the Loch Rannoch area of Perthshire from the early 1750s to the time of his death. I have had an interest in Buchanan since my boyhood days in Tiree; his hymns and religious songs were known throughout the Gaelic area, and not least in the islands. However, my real enthusiasm for the man and his work was sparked when I was a student at Glasgow University. I once wrote a very long essay on Alexander MacDonald and Dugald Buchanan, and that kindled my academic study of Buchanan. On a sleepy afternoon in Glasgow University Library, when preparing the essay, I decided to do some original 'sleuthing' about Buchanan's poetry. This diversion from my normal postprandial lethargy was stimulated by a curious ambivalence which I detected in the standard edition of Buchanan, namely Donald MacLean's edition of 1913 (MacLean 1913). To put matters at their simplest, I found one picture of Buchanan in the introduction to MacLean's book, and another picture in the notes at the back. The Buchanan presented in the introduction was the 'sublime' spiritual bard of the Highlands; while the Buchanan at the back of the book, carefully and warily tucked into the notes, was a poet who was apparently heavily influenced by English-language poets of the seventeenth century and the early eighteenth. While acknowledging 'fairly free translation' of the English poets by Buchanan, the notes were somewhat defensive, and I decided to take a closer look at the evidence. When I pulled out the dusty English texts from the depths (or should it be the heights?) of Glasgow University Library, what I saw suggested to me that a little bit of Puritan plagiarism might have been going on. At an early stage of my enquiry, in a mood of youthful scepticism, I wondered whether MacLean's emphasis on 'sublime grandeur' might be the very necessary counterbalance to excessive 'borrowing', since it pulled attention away from the poet's use of 'sources'. At any rate, it seemed to me that there was something here which was worth investigating much further. That investigation has been, as I say, at the back of my mind over the years, but there have been occasional bursts of activity which have taken it to the forefront of my thoughts. I discussed Buchanan in *Gairm* in the late 1980s (Meek 1989), showing in some detail how he was deeply indebted to the English poets, and I have discussed his use of the natural world in *Scottish Gaelic Studies*, 17 (Meek

97

1996). In the present paper, I will try to remove the many masks which have obscured Dugald Buchanan – some cleverly designed by himself, and others constructed by his admirers – and I will endeavour to place him in his *real* context as a poet, prose-writer and man of letters.

Although I have used the term 'context' in the singular, I wish to provide several contexts for the reassessment of Buchanan. First, I want to deal with the biographical context, that is Buchanan's life story – 'the invention of the biographical Buchanan'; then I want to look at the literary context; and thereafter I want to cast a glimpse at Buchanan in the context of 'Ossian' and the Scottish Enlightenment. Finally, I wish to say a little about the later 'myth' of Dugald Buchanan, and the 'sublime spirituality' which is ascribed to him in the process of elevating him, rightly or wrongly, to the position of Gaelic Scotland's spiritual poet *par excellence*.

The biographical Buchanan

At the outset, I will offer only a summary of Buchanan's life, as popularly conceived, since a full account would provide a paper in itself, and, in any case, I intend to write a book (in English) to complement my Gaelic edition of his hymns. Here, I want to draw attention to new (rather than old) evidence which substantially alters the traditional picture of Buchanan.

The popular biography is based partly on Buchanan's spiritual autobiography, which was written by the poet himself in English (not Gaelic!), and first published in 1836 (Buchanan 1836), almost seventy years after his death. The traditional picture goes something like this: Buchanan was born in Ardoch, Strathyre, in the parish of Balquidder, Perthshire, in 1716. Influenced by godly parents and particularly his mother, he was initially a tutor in the area before setting out to learn his trade as a joiner in Kippen, Stirling and Dumbarton. He lived a somewhat dissolute life as a teenager, and was lucky to escape alive from brawls and mishaps. In the early 1740s, he began to be seriously concerned about the state of his soul, and to attend communion services in different parts of Perthshire and the Lowlands; for instance, he attended the Cambuslang communion of 1742. By 1744, after an agonising period under conviction of sin, Buchanan had experienced evangelical conversion, and thereafter he gradually achieved assurance of faith. In the 1750s he was given a job as a schoolmaster in the forfeited estate of Strowan, and was settled as a schoolmaster at Drumcastle, and had moved to the new village of Kinloch Rannoch by the mid-1760s. He had a great influence in civilising the area, which was a stronghold of Highland cattle reiving and banditry, and, of course, a hotbed of Jacobite insurrection. He was an exemplary schoolmaster, and also a fine preacher. Reputedly, the people wanted him to become a minister, but his way was blocked for some unknown reason. He was, of course, a great poet, a sacred bard who published his small collection of verse in 1767, the same year as the

New Testament in Scottish Gaelic was published. Buchanan was in Edinburgh at the time, supervising the printing of that very same Gaelic New Testament. His little volume of Gaelic hymns – only eight in number – was printed and published by Balfour, Auld and Smellie, printers to the University of Edinburgh, who also printed and published the Gaelic New Testament. While in Edinburgh, Buchanan allegedly met David Hume, the philosopher, and debated great issues with him. Buchanan died early in June 1768, having contracted a fever which was doing the rounds in Kinloch Rannoch. He was buried in the graveyard of Little Leny, just outside Callander.

That, broadly, is the standard biographical outline of Dugald Buchanan, and it has been reinforced by Presbyterian hagiographical trends in the last quarter of the nineteenth century (Sinclair 1885) and the early twentieth century (MacLean 1913), with no small amount of repetition. The detail can now be modified substantially in the light of my research, but that is not my concern at present. Suffice it to say that the traditional picture is perplexing and opaque in some respects, but that much fresh detail can be recovered (Meek, forthcoming a, b).

The evidence confirms certain aspects of the traditional view, though not all of it. Buchanan was certainly a lowly schoolmaster – and it was indeed a lowly calling. One wonders how he managed to stick it out. He was underpaid seriously by both the Forfeited Estates and the Society in Scotland for the Propagation of Christian Knowledge (SSPCK), who were anything but generous to him. For a brief period at the end of the 1750s, he apparently left his Drumcastle school and returned to work on his father's farm in Ardoch, because he could not survive on his diminishing salary, which had become ever more elusive. He returned to his post largely because of encouragement from friends in Edinburgh, and the promise of enhanced pay, which does not seem to have materialised. Edinburgh was to become even more important in Buchanan's life. The poverty-stricken pedagogue was also a very brilliant scholar, deeply versed in the biblical languages, who, in preference to all Gaelic ministers, schoolmasters and amanuenses, went to Edinburgh to supervise the printing of the Gaelic New Testament. By the time he had returned to his school in Kinloch Rannoch, the SSPCK had discontinued his salary, but he did the society the favour of dying before matters became much more difficult for him or for it. The SSPCK's grudging attitude to Buchanan does nothing to redeem its image. The role of the Commissioners for the Forfeited Estates is hardly more distinguished. Their civilising intent is counterbalanced by their own practical incivility. Buchanan appears to have fallen victim to the territorialism and penny-pinching niggardliness of both bodies. Initially hand-picked by William Ramsay, then factor of the Strowan estate, as an exemplary schoolmaster for the Rannoch area and supported initially by Ramsay as a patron, he soon encountered the rough realities of serving institutions with their own expanding agendas, but with diminishing resources and little respect for individuals. It is not a new problem.

The essence of the traditional picture of Buchanan is, nevertheless, that of a child of nature who becomes a child of God, and then, out of his deep spiritual experience, composes great poetry. It is a romantic portrait at its heart – that of a spiritual 'Rabbie Burns', in effect – and it is at this point that the popular image becomes vulnerable, and begins to fall apart. There is very little in this picture which illumines, or considers in any depth, the mental world of Dugald Buchanan, and especially the formative influences on his early education. The educational and psychological 'force fields' in which he operated are not delineated in their totality. We know from his autobiography that he was educated in the local SSPCK school in Ardoch, and that he was able to take advantage of books in the households in which he worked as a boy tutor before setting out to learn his trade. But what happened after that? Here the new evidence takes us in unexpected directions.

Buchanan, the college student

A recently discovered piece of information sheds significant light on Buchanan's educational background and linguistic interests. I owe this material to Dr Donald William Stewart, who has given me invaluable help as my research assistant on the Buchanan project. A decade and more after my first attempts to provide new perspectives on Buchanan's verse, I now find – very happily – that there is a body of material in MS archives and elsewhere that confirms and supplements my earlier impression that there is an 'alternative' Dugald Buchanan out there, waiting to be discovered. The 'alternative' Buchanan is, however, a very complex individual, and very different from the Buchanan of popular romantic spirituality.

The first piece of 'new' evidence relating to his education takes us to Glasgow, and to the Divinity College. It is to be found in a letter from the Rev. John MacLaurin in Glasgow, writing to his brother, Colin MacLaurin, the noted mathematician, in 1740 (Mills 1982, 83):

> In Company where the Conversation turn'd on the most eminent young men about our Divinity hall now, I have heard one Mr Buchanan who has Irish, from Balquidder or Bupridir [?] commended as of that number. This made me take pains this day, both forenoon & afternoon, to meet with Persons who could give me the best Account of him; I did not find the person I wanted in the forenoon, but in the evening I return'd a visit I was owing to the Master of College whom I have heard Speak of him formerly, & after Speaking about the Scarcity of Probationers now & the Talk that was some time ago about licensing some of our best young men; He confirm'd the Accounts I had heard of Mr Buchanan before, as one of our best Students; & particularly as one well skilled

100

in the learn'd Languages & its Divinity. Meantime I have heard oftner
than once that he is reckon'd what they call, too monkish & retir'd.

Here, then, is remarkable evidence that Dugald Buchanan was in the Divinity College
in Glasgow around 1740, and that he was particularly highly regarded there for his
special skill in biblical languages. Being sought out by the MacLaurin family is in itself
an indication of his remarkably high standing in academic circles. We may assume
that Buchanan was hoping to enter the ministry, but there is a note of caution at the
end of the extract – he is 'reckon'd . . . too monkish & retir'd'. Buchanan never
became a minister, but his skill in biblical languages explains very neatly why he was
supervising the printing of the Gaelic New Testament in Edinburgh in 1765–7, and
raises the further question of the extent to which he may have been involved in its
actual translation. I have long suspected that he may have given very considerable
assistance to the man who is normally given all the credit for the translation, namely
the Rev. James Stewart of Killin. Suffice it to say that there is clear evidence in SSPCK
Minutes that Dugald Buchanan was, in fact, the first person to translate any portion
of the New Testament into Scottish Gaelic – but that is another story, and one which
has lain concealed for more than two centuries, in favour of ministerial interests, one
suspects. Schoolmasters were not allowed to rise above their station.

So Dugald Buchanan was in Divinity College in Glasgow, intending to enter the
ministry of the national church. He did not do so, and it is possible that he never
graduated from the Divinity College, though we cannot be sure about that. What went
wrong? The answer to that question may lie in the phrase that MacLaurin applied to
Buchanan – 'monkish & retir'd'. It is clear that Buchanan became absorbed with the
state of his own soul in the years between 1740 and 1742, which was a time of considerable evangelical activity in Lowland Scotland. In that context, he is likely to have
changed from a fairly liberal theological position to that of a profound and deeply
'concerned' evangelical. His spiritual quest is set out in detail in his autobiography,
which is a kind of spiritual diary (Buchanan 1836). This remarkable piece of work is
very low on biographical detail from the period around 1740 – the year in which
Buchanan is known to have been in college. In fact, Buchanan does not even as much
as hint in his autobiography that he was ever in college or in Glasgow. Indeed, he
gives us the impression that he knew very little about theology prior to a gradual
dawning of spiritual reality in the 1740s. His autobiography concludes around 1750,
and has nothing to say about the Rannoch years. That is understandable, but reference to Glasgow is conspicuous by its absence.

The silence of Buchanan's autobiography about his Glasgow sojourn could have
been an attempt to blot out the 'bad' years of his spiritual pilgrimage – 'bad', that is,
from an evangelical perspective which would not have had a high regard for training
in a divinity college, particularly since the college in question was then tainted with

Deist teaching. There may also have been an element of shame in having failed to 'make the grade', and in having become, in effect, what the Scots call a 'stickit minister'. We must note, however, that we are now unable to see to what extent the diary was edited, either by Buchanan himself or by his family, before it was published in 1836; I am not aware that the original manuscript version survives. Even so, there is a consistency in the existing narrative, and that consistency seems to have no place whatsoever for the aspiring candidate for the ministry or for the brilliant young scholar. Here we encounter the spiritual 'wretch', the 'vile worm' of Puritan discourse, replete with all the trappings of human depravity. The keynotes of Buchanan's autobiography are his great sinfulness, his self-abasement, his agonising conversion, and his no less agonising search for assurance. Buchanan devotes most detail to spiritual 'high points' or 'connecting nodes' in his life, among them his presence at Cambuslang in 1742 when the great contemporary evangelist, George Whitefield, was preaching (Buchanan 1836, 100–104):

> At this time I was hearing a great noise about the great work of God at Cambuslang, in consequence of which I went there, and was greatly comforted to hear the people speaking of their experience to one another. On the Sabbath there was a great multitude gathered together. Such a sight I never saw before. Mr Whitefield lectured from Matt. xiv, and there was uncommon concern among the people. But although I heard great threatenings denounced against sinners of all descriptions, yet I was not in the least affected thereby, and saw that unless the Spirit of God wrought upon me, it was beyond the reach of any mortal to do it.

Buchanan, it should be noted, is not chronicling the 'revival' at Cambuslang with complete approval. It has generated 'great noise', and 'great threatenings' are being uttered, but he claims not to have been 'in the least affected thereby'. His spiritual paradigm belongs elsewhere, and not with the 'new evangelicalism' of 'noisy revivalism' which was at the heart of the Great Awakening on both sides of the Atlantic, so well bridged by the ocean-commuting Whitefield.

The Bunyanesque Buchanan

Buchanan is being honest between the lines, so to speak, but is the tale of a painful spiritual quest, and the tussle with the 'Spirit of God', itself entirely true to Buchanan? Do we have the 'real' Buchanan there? Is anybody else 'speaking' in, or behind, his paragraphs? It is, in fact, very evident that his (?) autobiography is not a wholly original work. It is, in fact, closely modelled on the seventeenth-century Puritan classic by John Bunyan, *Grace Abounding to the Chief of Sinners*, first published in 1666

(Stachniewski and Pacheco 1998). The modelling is so close in places that even some supposedly personal incidents in Buchanan's pre-conversion narrative can be paralleled in Bunyan's book, including a narrow escape from drowning. There is, of course, much self-expression and originality. For example, in addition to his picture of Whitefield at Cambuslang, Buchanan gives some very interesting glimpses of evangelical communion services on the southern edges of Perthshire. This is a foretaste of the kind of evangelicalism that was to sweep into the Highlands in the course of the next half-century.

Buchanan's taste for Puritan classics, and his evident urge to possess the Puritan conversion paradigm as his own, is also significant. In 1750, the year in which Buchanan's diary ends, the first Gaelic translation of a Puritan work was published – a translation of Richard Baxter's *Call to the Unconverted* by the Rev. Alexander MacFarlane, minister of Kilninver and later of Arrochar. Buchanan, of course, knew MacFarlane well. MacFarlane had been approached by the SSPCK about 1755 as their prime candidate to translate the New Testament into Gaelic. When MacFarlane had difficulty in carrying out the intended commission, Buchanan offered to be his amanuensis for three to four months – and, in an attempt to clear the impasse, he even produced his own Gaelic translation of the Second Epistle of Peter!

Buchanan is thus matching the mood of the age, and 'reinventing' himself as a Puritan evangelical. And Puritan evangelicalism – which placed great emphasis on unworthiness and the despairing quest for assurance – became, in due time, a major part of Highland Presbyterianism. Bunyan, in translation, became a naturalised Highlander, able to speak to Highland spiritual experience and to provide a 'morphology' for abasement and conversion. When Bunyan became Buchanan's alter ego, it was a foretaste – indeed, quite literally, the shape – of things to come. Buchanan, in exchange, became a naturalised Bunyan. This is an outstanding example of what psychologists would call the 'shared biography' – shared, that is, with a purpose. As Stachniewski and Pacheco (1998, xxvii–xxviii) point out, the narratising of spiritual experience was crucial to the quest for assurance of salvation, in that it helped to confirm the possible possession of that assurance.

Whether Buchanan would ever have wanted to have his autobiography published, we do not know. The work may have been intended as nothing more than an exercise in spiritual creativity, following prominent exemplars – although that may imply an element of creative duplicity. Psychologically, it can be seen as Buchanan's attempt to understand himself, to explain his feelings, and to cast an anchor in firm ground, relative to the immensely strong spiritual 'force fields' affecting the southern edges of the Highlands. In Bunyan, he found a spiritual 'soul friend', who held the key to inner turmoils. It needs perhaps to be emphasised that Buchanan's work was written in English; the bilingual Buchanan could write in English as easily as he could in Gaelic. He was completely and effortlessly fluent in both languages. It is fascinating

to note that, in the manner of the Puritan classics, his autobiography was itself translated into Gaelic, apparently by John MacKenzie, and published in its Gaelic version
in 1844.

Buchanan, the borrower

Like his prose, Buchanan's poetic adventures depended to a considerable extent on
borrowing from English models. His closest 'soul friends' were almost inevitably
English and English-writing divines. We have already noticed the tendency towards
imitation in his debt to Bunyan. The phrase that I have used of his autobiography –
'an exercise in spiritual creativity, following prominent exemplars' – can be applied
with equal force to his poetry. Here, as in the case of the autobiography, we also seem
to lose the 'real' Buchanan behind the mask of imitation. Buchanan was very well
aware of the riches of English verse, as of English prose, and, as I have demonstrated elsewhere, several of his published body of eight Gaelic poems draw extensively on the works of Isaac Watts, Edward Young, Robert Blair and James Thomson.
Buchanan, however, was attracted particularly strongly to Watts (Watson 1999, 133–170),
and especially to his *Horae Lyricae* (1706).

The overall position is roughly as follows: three of the eight poems owe much to
Watts, and one of the three ('Mòrachd Dhè' ['The Greatness of God']) contains close
translations of verses in Watts' poem, 'The Creator and Creatures'. Of the remaining
five, one (his 'epic' on the Day of Judgement) draws on Young, and, of course, the
New Testament itself; one ('An Claigeann' ['The Skull']) draws on Blair; and one ('An
Geamhradh' ['Winter']) owes its starting-point to Thomson's poem of that name
(Meek 1989, 1996). This leaves two which show less dependence on external sources.
As in the case of the autobiography, there is much in the poems as a whole that is
original (and brilliantly so, especially in Buchanan's cleverly controlled use of language),
but the debt to external models is abundantly clear.

This debt becomes even clearer when we look at the manuscript versions of some
of his poems, preserved in the collections of McLagan and McNicol. The relevant
poems, in their manuscript forms, carry additional evidence of their origins as imitations or translations of Watts (and Buchanan himself must surely have been involved
in making these texts available to the transcribers). Thus, the poem which is called
'Mòrachd Dhè' at the very outset of the printed book is called 'An Cruthadair agus
na Creutiribh' ('The Creator and the Creatures') in the manuscripts in both the
McLagan and the McNicol collections, a title which reflects the close connection
between Buchanan's poem and Watts' piece. It looks as if an earlier title could have
been expunged prior to printing.

To make matters even more fascinating and perplexing, another poem, entitled 'Ma
thimchioll Morthachd Dhe' ('Concerning the Greatness of God'), is contained in the

McLagan MSS. It shows all the marks of having been composed by a man who knew precisely the same selection of Watts' poetry as Dugald Buchanan used in his Wattsian imitations. The composer even knew Buchanan's style and his distinctive register. We can therefore conclude safely that this is undoubtedly another hymn by Dugald Buchanan, but one which has remained unpublished – and forgotten hitherto. It was, presumably, rejected (by himself?) from the printed canon – but why, particularly given its unquestioned excellence? Was part of its title 'switched' to the printed poem to give the latter an element of disguise at the last minute? In taking his texts to print, did Buchanan have to cover his tracks, and disguise his debt to Watts? We may note that there is ample evidence in the manuscripts to show that Buchanan, in all probability, adjusted actual words and phrases in the earlier versions of his Gaelic hymns, in order (one supposes) to correspond less literally to Watts (Meek, forthcoming c). If Buchanan was acting in this way, where does that leave our view of Buchanan's intentions and his integrity?

The bilingual Buchanan

In answering that question, we need to acknowledge, first, that Buchanan functioned in a bilingual context, and that the models for Protestant spiritual verse, as for prose, lay largely outside the Highlands. There was a tradition of Protestant spiritual verse within the Highlands, and Buchanan knew of that too and he utilised it, but he would have been greatly tempted to look elsewhere for fresh ideas. English material was readily accessible to him, and the body of printed religious books was infinitely larger in English than in Gaelic. As a man brought up on the southern edge of the Highlands – on the frontier with the Lowlands – Buchanan would have been well aware of the riches to be found in the Saxon tongue.

Indeed, it is worth observing that Buchanan's first attempts at verse were apparently in English, not Gaelic. Because of the desire of earlier editors to present us with a solely Gaelic Buchanan, this important point is skilfully overlooked. The full text of his autobiography as published in 1836 contains a poem composed in English apparently around 1750 (Buchanan 1836, 221–223). I say 'apparently' because we cannot be sure when Buchanan actually placed the poem in the context of his autobiography. It is immediately evident that this poem is likewise indebted to the work of Isaac Watts; the tell-tale evidence lies in the style, and also in the metre, which is one which was regularly used by Watts. This form of metre was carried over into Buchanan's Gaelic poetry, and enhanced by providing some of the metrical adornments characteristic of Gaelic verse. Watts helped Buchanan to find his poetic 'voice' – and, to judge by the manuscript evidence, Buchanan gradually gained the confidence to expunge the more egregious signs of earlier Wattsian scaffolding.

Second, we need to bear in mind the very nature of the poetic art in the eighteenth century – and by that I mean the poetic art as practised not only in the Highlands, but also throughout Britain. In the Gaelic-speaking Highlands, as elsewhere, there was a highly, and very respectably, imitative dimension to the poetic craft of the time. In the Gaelic context, we can think readily of Alexander MacDonald, and his equally unacknowledged debts to James Thomson's *Seasons* and to Allan Ramsay's *Tea Table Miscellany* (Thomson 1974, 160–162). Again, if we set Buchanan in the British context, we find that he is by no means unique in borrowing, translating and modifying other poets' ideas and words as part of his poetic method. Thus, the Augustan school of eighteenth-century poets in Wales borrowed extensively from English literature, and there we can find a direct parallel to Buchanan. The Welsh poet Goronwy Owen, from Anglesey, similarly composed a Welsh poem on the Day of Judgement, and, like Buchanan, he had read and used Edward Young's poem on 'The Last Day'. The Welsh literary critic Saunders Lewis writes of Goronwy Owen as follows in his major study, *A School of Welsh Augustans* (Lewis 1969, 102):

> We may conclude then that Goronwy Owen had read Young's poem. He could hardly avoid doing so, for Young's fame in the forties and fifties [i.e. the 1740s and 1750s] challenged even that of Pope. But the tedious moralising of Young's thousand odd lines appealed little to a poet like Goronwy, who so passionately sought precision; and the indebtedness of the Welshman may be dismissed as insignificant.

Perhaps the indebtedness of Dugald Buchanan to Young is equally insignificant! Like Goronwy Owen, Buchanan disliked Young's diffuse style, and preferred 'precision' – the Welshman and the Gael were Augustans both. In the relationship of Buchanan and Owen to Young, we have an example of what would be called today 'intertextuality', functioning in a bilingual context. Patterns of literary indebtedness spread like a fishnet – even like an internet! – in this period, and show little respect for cultural boundaries.

Buchanan, man of the Enlightenment

Dugald Buchanan, I would thus argue, is very much a man of the eighteenth century, responding to literature and culture in the wider British context, as other poets did, and showing a marked interest in literature of many kinds. To clinch the argument, I would like to place him, finally, in the context of the Scottish Enlightenment. This gives us a remarkable glimpse of his Gaelic interests beyond the composition of Christian verse and prose, and it alters significantly the conventional picture of this complex man.

Again, the evidence is found in another letter (SRO GD 18/4529), and once again I owe this wholly to Dr Donald William Stewart. On this occasion, Dugald Buchanan himself is writing in 1767 to no less a figure than Sir James Clerk of Penicuik, and asking for support, not for his hymns, but for the compilation of a Gaelic dictionary:

> Some time in harvest last the Society for propagating Christian Knowledge proposed to me that while I was correcting the Galic New Testament just now in the press that I should arrange all the words in an alphabetical order as they intended to publish a small Dictionary for the use of their schools, I told them that all the words in the old as well as in the New Testament could be comprised in very little room when properly arranged and that such a Dictionary would be very defective even with respect to the Terms used in Divinity so that in my opinion they ought to add all the words in the Common prayer Book the Confession of ffaith & Catechisms with all the Galic words in Llhyd's Archaelogia Britannica and that even with all these materials before a tollerably perfect Dictionary could be made out it would be necessary that the Compiler should travel thro the Isles and western Coasts of Scotland and collect the work of the antient & modern Bards, in which alone he could find the Language in its purity. Whether the necessary expence of travelling which behoved to be very considerable deterred them from coming to any conclusion I know not but I have not heard any more of it since and imagine that this motion like many others that has been made to compose a Dictionary of this Language is crushed in the bud.
>
> One can scarce reflect without indignation on the unworthy treatment that the immortal Llhyd met with in publishing his Dictionary by popular preju-dices and artifice of Book-sellers together with the baseness of subscribers in withdrawing their subscriptions from his second volume which [is: deleted] certainly is a vast loss to posterity. Mr Mcomb shared the same fate after he had been at vast pains in searching out the antiquities of the Scots Nation and Language and printed a specimen of his intended work he was deserted by those that seemed at first to support him so that his work never appeared.
>
> It is pretty curious to observe that in an age where Arts & Sciences are brought to equal if not to exceed antient Greece or Rome to find a political Scheme contrived for / extirpating this antient and very emphatick Language of our great forefathers and neither Historian or Antiquarian endeavouring to transmit the least remains of it to posterity in a Dictionary were it of no more use than to inform them that it was not only the Language of Great Britain but of all the western parts of Europe and help to increase and orna-ment their Librarys . . .
>
> But this is all Digression from my present purpose which was to shew that in collecting the Poems of the antient & modern Bards as the proper materials of a Dictionary many Poems might perhaps be met with worthy of

being transmited [*sic*] to Posterity to inform them of the heroic valour the love of Liberty the tender Passion the natural Description, the sublime Sentiment and uparalelled [*sic*] Hospitality of their great forefathers.

This breath-taking letter places Buchanan in another frame of reference, quite different from that of the hard-worked, underpaid schoolmaster who wrote endless 'petitions' to the tight-fisted Commissioners for the Forfeited Estates and to the SSPCK in an effort to gain his salary, so often in arrears. The man who appears within it is quite different too from the stereotype of the 'hard-hearted Calvinist', hell-bent on destroying Gaelic secular culture (Meek 2002). In this extract, we see Dugald Buchanan as a man who stands back and views the 'big picture'. In calling for comprehensive dictionaries and anthologies of Gaelic songs, he even anticipates the sorts of 'projects' with which we are familiar today. Here we have the scholar, the probing, evidence-gathering, empirically rooted intellectual with a passion for Gaelic lexicography, and also for the preservation of secular Gaelic poetry. He is familiar with the works of earlier and contemporary Gaelic scholars. He knows of Edward Lhwyd, he is familiar with 'Mr Mcomb', i.e. David Malcolme of Duddingston, and (as he shows elsewhere in the letter) he is on terms with Jerome Stone of Dunkeld. He is also impatient with the SSPCK for their stalling tactics and their neglect of the Gaelic language (though we may note that he gives us, in passing, an important glimpse of the Gaelic literary interests of this cross-grained and contradictory body). We may well wonder – again – how such a man, filled with such a lively intellectual spark, could have remained such a long time in their excruciating service as the undervalued and poorly remunerated schoolmaster of Drumcastle and Kinloch Rannoch.

The 'sublime' Buchanan

In his letter to Clerk of Penicuik, the leading antiquary of the Scottish Enlightenment, Buchanan is far from presenting himself as the agonising Puritan portrayed in his Diary. Rather, he is very much a man of the contemporary Enlightenment, and concerns himself solely with Gaelic cultural matters. This, one imagines, is a picture much closer to the Buchanan who was in divinity hall in Glasgow in 1740. He is even under the spell of 'the sublime', and his references to 'antient & modern Bards' and the 'great forefathers' of Highlanders put it beyond any reasonable doubt that he had an awareness of the contemporary Ossianic debate, stimulated by the 'translations' of James Macpherson which appeared in 1760–3 (Meek 2004). Buchanan, like others of his day, believed that one could find 'sublime Sentiment' in secular Gaelic poetry.

There are interesting questions which deserve to be asked in this context. One of these is the extent to which the Enlightenment may have had a progressively 'enlightening' influence on Buchanan himself, by steering him away from his earlier spiritual introversion and narrowness, which is evident in the 1740s, and leading him into a broader interaction with Gaelic culture. Did it give him a new field of vision? Did his commitment to Gaelic benefit from the Enlightenment, and particularly from the pro-Gaelic influences of the Ossianic controversy? A strong Gaelic consciousness is evident in his letter to Clerk, and even a sense of pride in Gaelic secular culture. The man who was so evidently a follower of English models in prose and verse acknowledges, in 1767, the importance of Gaelic verse as a repository of 'sublime Sentiment'.

It is highly likely that Buchanan's winter sojourns in Edinburgh to supervise the printing of the Scottish Gaelic New Testament widened his horizons, and provided congenial companionship of a kind not readily available in the fastnesses of Rannoch. This context is surely also relevant to the publication of his little book of Gaelic hymns, which also appeared in 1767. The first hymn in the collection is the one to which I have already alluded, 'Mòrachd Dhè' – a title which was apparently not its original one, but which can be translated 'the greatness of God', or perhaps even 'the sublimity of God'. Were Buchanan's hymns intended, in part at least, as a response to the humanist emphasis which was a part of the Scottish Enlightenment, at least that part of it represented by David Hume? Was Hume's scepticism among the key considerations that goaded him into printing – in Edinburgh – verse which might otherwise have had its existence solely in oral transmission and in manuscript? Is it possible that Buchanan was engaging, not so much in a display of originality, as in an oblique dialogue with prevailing Enlightenment emphases which were perhaps (in his view) in danger of extolling too greatly the rational mind of mere human beings, and the greatness of the natural world, at the expense of special revelation from God himself? Who, or what, is God, and how should we respond to him? That is the interrogative heartbeat of Buchanan's collection of hymns.

The God portrayed in the very first verse of 'Mòrachd Dhè' is one who is above and beyond human reason, and whose existence is therefore not jeopardised by the scepticism of David Hume or others of his kind – a minority within the Enlightenment, it has to be said. Given his awareness of men like Clerk of Penicuik and his undoubted sympathy with Enlightenment ideals, it is entirely feasible to suppose that, as tradition relates, Buchanan met David Hume and debated some important issues with him. There was much to talk about between great men with great minds – and Buchanan was assuredly one such.

It is interesting that Buchanan himself was destined to be portrayed in nineteenth-century criticism as a poet of 'sublime' spirituality. The reverend gentlemen who edited his literary remains after 1800 used one of the key words of the Scottish Enlightenment – the word 'sublime' – consistently to describe the sentiments of his verse. His poem on the Day of Judgement, which shows the whole physical world as accountable before God, was reckoned by the anonymous writer of the 1836 preface to his Diary to be 'the sublimest composition ever written in the Gaelic language'. I referred

109

at the beginning of this paper to the 'sublime grandeur' which Professor MacLean detected in his verse in 1913. The 1946 popular edition of his hymns, published by Alexander MacLaren and almost certainly taking its cue from the earlier work of Professor Donald MacLean, declared (Buchanan 1946, [ii]):

> Buchanan is the most sublime of all the Gaelic bards. These songs though numbering only eight in all, are Gaelic classics, and have had an immense influence by their force, fervour and virile power on the religious life and thought of the Highland people for nearly two hundred years.

Conclusion

Buchanan's verse certainly has a fair amount of spiritual grandeur at its heart, and that may make it 'sublime' to ecclesiastical critics intent on finding a 'spiritual Ossian' in the Highlands. However, simply to accept Buchanan and his poetry as both are presented in the printed reconstructions of a much later day, and to turn him into an iconic Presbyterian saint, beloved by Free Church professors like Donald MacLean, is to miss the point – badly. 'Sublime' is hardly the most appropriate adjective, if used beyond its eighteenth-century context; it represents only one dimension of the man, and it hides too much. The greatest tribute we can pay Buchanan is not to dress him up in another set of masks, but to try to get behind the masks which he himself uses to define the reality of his own existence.

As the fresh evidence unearthed by Dr Donald William Stewart indicates, and as my own literary and historical analyses have (I hope) shown, Buchanan was a highly complex individual, and an equally complex man of letters with a wide range of interests, styles and 'voices'. He was sophisticated and 'genre-aware', to a remarkable degree, and he 'reinvented' (as we would say today) his persona as he applied his mind to imitating in Gaelic the 'good literature' available in English. Intertextuality – which we think we have discovered! – was no new concept to the humble, hard-pressed schoolmaster at Kinloch Rannoch. He was delighted to imitate English literary models, and to provide the Gaels with the equivalent of Watts' hymns – in Gaelic. These English literary models had helped him to 'make sense of himself', and through them he found 'his' voice(s). He may have wished others to make similar discoveries, and to share the excitement of venturing intellectually beyond the Highland line. His sophistication in so doing may even give the impression that he is out-Wattsing Watts!

Buchanan, then, was assuredly no 'child of nature', and no pure prophet sent directly by God to minister to the Gaelic people. Nor was he a model of 'sublime spirituality' or of Puritan plagiarism. He was a man of his age, a man of feeling – for words, and for 'good' literature in both Gaelic and English. He combined 'narrower' spiritual interests with 'broader' cultural pursuits, and conformed to different moulds and models at different stages. He went beyond the Highland line, as required, and laid hold on the 'other', and gladly made it his own. He appears to have experimented freely with, and to have responded with alacrity and pleasure to, some of the major spiritual, literary and cultural movements of his time. Although grimly fated to teach at an SSPCK school in Rannoch for most of his life, he was no parochial school-master. Rather, he was, in the final assessment, an 'Enlightenment man', completely in tune with the literary and cultural currents of the wider world, and experimenting with their intellectual benefits.

Mixing and matching, imitating and replicating, was our man's literary calling. The 'real Dugald Buchanan', as a consequence, is discoverable, but also – and paradoxic-ally – very hard to find. We may wish to meet him fully, but, despite our earnest entreaties, he may never allow us to gain access to his innermost recesses. He is too clever for that – and too like ourselves! He is masked in fashionable literary garb, and, just to put us off the scent, he does a quick change each time we knock on the door of his book-lined cottage close to the shadow of Schiehallion.

References

(a) Books and articles

Buchanan, D., 1836. *The Diary of Dugald Buchanan . . . with a Memoir of his Life*. Edinburgh.
Buchanan, D., 1946. *Dàin Spioradail le Dùghall Bochanan*. Glasgow.
Lewis, S., 1969. *A School of Welsh Augustans*. Bath.
MacLean, D. (ed.), 1913. *The Spiritual Songs of Dugald Buchanan*. Edinburgh.
Meek, D. E., 1989. 'Ath-sgrùdadh: Dùghall Bochanan', *Gairm*, 147–148. Glasgow.
Meek, D. E., 1996. 'Images of the Natural World in the Hymnology of Dugald Buchanan and Peter Grant', *Scottish Gaelic Studies*, 17. Aberdeen.
Meek, D. E., 2002. 'The Pulpit and the Pen: Clergy, Orality and Print in the Scottish Gaelic World', in A. Fox and D. Woolf (eds), *The Spoken Word: Oral Culture in Britain, 1500–1850*. Manchester.
Meek, D. E., 2004. 'The Sublime Gael: The Impact of Macpherson's *Ossian* on Literary Creativity and Cultural Perception in Gaelic Scotland', in H. Gaskill (ed.), *The Reception of Ossian in Europe*. London.
Meek, D. E., forthcoming a. *Dùghall Bochanan: Na Laoidhean Spioradail*.

Meek, D. E., forthcoming b. *Sublime Spirit: The Life and Work of Dugald Buchanan.*

Meek, D. E., forthcoming c. 'Beyond the Printed Page: The Revealing Evidence of Manuscript and Oral Versions of the Hymns of Dugald Buchanan'.

Mills, S. (ed.), 1982. *Collected Letters of Colin MacLaurin.* Edinburgh.

Sinclair, A., 1885. *Reminiscences of the Life and Labours of Dugald Buchanan.* Edinburgh.

Stachniewski, J. and Pacheco, A. (eds), 1998. John Bunyan, *Grace Abounding and Other Spiritual Autobiographies.* Oxford.

Thomson, D. S., 1974. *An Introduction to Gaelic Poetry.* London.

Watson, J. R., 1999. *The English Hymn: A Critical and Historical Study.* Oxford.

(b) Manuscripts

Dugald Buchanan to Sir John [*recte* James] Clerk. SRO GD 18/4529. Reproduced here with the kind permission of the late Sir John Clerk of Penicuik, Bt.

McLagan MSS. GU MS Gen. 1042, 4 (a), (b), (c); 20 (a); 21.

McNicol MSS. NLS MSS 14851–14852.

Note: Full references to the MS records of the Forfeited Estates and the SSPCK will be given in Meek, forthcoming a.

Acknowledgements

In addition to my debt to Dr Donald William Stewart, who acted as research assistant for the Buchanan project, I am grateful to those who have listened patiently to different versions of this paper as it has developed, and who have raised questions to stimulate further enquiry. I remember, with pleasure, the particularly valuable comments of Professor Alexander Broadie on aspects of the Enlightenment as they may have impinged on Buchanan.

KENNETH SIMPSON

The place of Macpherson's Ossian
in Scottish literature

In such a conference setting, it is tempting to free some time for exploration of the sublime Ossianic landscape by summarising as follows:

Scotland needs an epic – ideally an ancient epic – to confirm its right to cultural partnership with England. Rousseau's work has initiated the search to find the people who most closely resemble the Noble Savage. Scotland is staking its claim. David Hume writes to John Wilkes, 8 October 1754:

> If your time had permitted, you shoud have gone into the Highlands. You woud there have seen human Nature in the golden Age, or rather, indeed, in the Silver: For the Highlanders have degenerated somewhat from the primitive Simplicity of Mankind. But perhaps you have so corrupted a Taste as to prefer your Iron Age, to be met with in London and the south of England; where Luxury and Vice of every kind so much abound.[1]

James Macpherson has literary ambitions (and, as a boy, has witnessed the pursuit of the Jacobites through his native Badenoch). Macpherson meets John Home on the bowling-green at Moffat, late summer 1759 (entirely by accident, or did the ambitious young poet seek Home out?). The outcome: 'The Death of Oscur'; *Fragments of Ancient Poetry* (1760); *Fingal* (1762); *Temora* (1763). Scots now have an identity: they are pre-eminent in sensibility.

Such a summary, however, under-represents my topic. What follows is an attempt to locate Macpherson's work. Where did he come from, poetically and intellectually? What was his achievement? Who did he influence, and in what ways? What is his legacy?

The interaction of ideas and literary modes and forms always repays attention. This is especially true of the eighteenth century, where the responsiveness of imaginative literature to developments in philosophy is acute. 'The background of ideas' is a misnomer: in this most exciting of centuries ideas impact profoundly on literary forms. And in the case of Scotland another factor is prominent in the equation: awareness of national identity and the need to preserve national culture. Ramsay, Macpherson, Burns, Scott, Hogg – these writers saw themselves as conservators and custodians. Ramsay in his preface to *The Ever Green* (1724) contrasted the 'affected Delicacies and studied Refinements [of] modern Writings' with 'that natural Strength of Thought and Simplicity of Style our Forefathers practised'.[2] With the support of Blair, Macpherson claimed of the *Fragments*: 'tradition, in a country so free from intermixture with foreigners, and among a people so strongly attached to the memory of their ancestors, has preserved many of them in a great measure uncorrupted to this day'.[3] A worrying trend had, it seemed, been reversed.

However, Anglicisation and foreign influence were not the only forces to be countered. Industrialisation was seen as a threat to the survival of culture. Adam Ferguson warned:

> Many mechanical arts, indeed, require no capacity: they succeed best under a total suppression of sentiment and reason; and ignorance is the mother of industry as well as of superstition . . . manufactures, accordingly, prosper most where the mind is least consulted, and where the workshop may, without any great effort of imagination, be considered as an engine, the parts of which are men.[4]

The prime architect of the age of Sensibility is traditionally held to be Rousseau. For J. S. Smart, in his otherwise excellent and largely under-credited *James Macpherson: An Episode in Literature* (1905), it is Rousseau who created the conditions in which Macpherson thrived. Absent from Smart's index is Shaftesbury who in *Characteristics of Men, Manners, Opinions and Times* (1711) (which inspired Pope's 'Essay on Man') had claimed that man possesses a moral sense. Nor is there mention of Francis Hutcheson; Adam Smith is present as testifying to the genuineness of the *Fragments*; Hume is cited in terms of his changing attitude on the question of authenticity. Now while Rousseau's importance is undeniable, account should be taken of the cumulative effect of Hutcheson's recognition of a moral sense, Hume's sceptical critique of reason, and Smith's emphasis on the importance of sympathy.

The outcome is that the characteristics of natural man are identified as melancholy, spontaneous emotion, and benevolence. How do these square with the originals? Smart noted, 'Ossianic legend is free from that strain of overwrought melancholy which Macpherson sustains in unbroken monotone',[5] and he found in the genuine ballads the presence of the grotesque, hyperbole, and jokes, by way of relief. Fiona Stafford cites the account given by Hector MacLean, schoolmaster of Ballygrant, to J. F. Campbell of Islay: 'During the recitation of these tales, the emotions of the reciters are occasionally very strongly excited, and so also are those of the listeners, almost shedding tears at one time, and giving way to loud laughter at another.'[6] Plainly Macpherson has reduced the emotional range of the traditional material in the interests of establishing and sustaining the note of melancholy. 'The Dispraise of Morag', for instance, has no place among his sources of inspiration.

As for the influences on Macpherson, in English poetry Pope's 'Elegy to the Memory of an Unfortunate Lady' is plainly a harbinger of the age of Sensibility. The poem foregrounds tenderness and indicates that intensity of feeling is not given to all; and, anticipating Ossian, the poet ends on a note of awareness of his own mortality: 'Ev'n he, whose soul now melts in mournful lays, / Shall shortly want the gen'rous tear he pays.' In William Collins' 'An Ode on the Popular Superstitions of the Highlands of Scotland, Considered as the Subject of Poetry' (1749), the Highlands are presented as the repository of, in John MacQueen's words, 'internal natural truth, which in a scientific or philosophical sense may not be truth at all, but which convinces the imagination'.[7] Thomas Gray's 'The Bard' (1757) typifies the burgeoning interest in the ethos of primitive society and the role of the bard therein.

As regards Scottish precedents, Macpherson was almost certainly familiar with *The Book of the Dean of Lismore* (James MacGregor) containing material dated 1512. A more immediate prompt was the publication in *The Scots Magazine*, January 1756, of 'Albin and the Daughter of Mey', a translation of a ballad in his collection by Jerome Stone. Fiona Stafford reasonably speculates that, but for his death later that year, Stone 'might well have gone on to publish large collections of imaginative translations of Highland verse, since his accompanying letter reveals a desire to promote Gaelic poetry as the work of "simple and unassisted genius", in accordance with the growing aesthetic demand for "Original Genius"' (*Poems*, xi).

Enter another player, and a major one. The role of John Home in publicising Macpherson's alleged findings and promoting the cause among the literati has been widely acknowledged. Enthusing over 'The Death of Oscur', he encouraged the preparation and publication of *Fragments of Ancient Poetry*. Its preface, written by Blair in consultation with Macpherson, announced 'there is reason to hope that one work of considerable length, and which deserves to be styled an heroic poem, might be recovered and translated, if encouragement were to be given to such an undertaking' (*Poems*, p.6). *Fingal* need not knock at the already-open door.

Commentators have noted that Home would write an Ossianic tragedy, *Rivine, or The Fatal Discovery* (1769). Less attention has been paid to the significant precedent, in diction and themes, established by Home's *Douglas* (1756; published 1757). In the Edinburgh Prologue, Caledonia is compared with ancient Athens in terms of geography; in terms of learning and the arts; and in terms of the noblest passions, such as the victor's pity for the vanquished. There is promise of a Scottish hero to rank with those of the classics: 'This night our scenes no common tear demand, / He comes the hero of your native land!'; and the author guarantees more plays on Scottish heroes if the response is favourable: 'He waits the test of your congenial tears'.[8] This is significant. The tears will be congenial to the audience as well as the author: they will experience the 'joy of grief' that derives from empathising with the suffering; and true sensibility is anything but common – men and women of feeling are an elite, almost a self-appointed elect.

Macpherson's pre-Ossian poems, harbingers curiously omitted from the Gaskill/Stafford edition, are suffused with romantic melancholy. This may be redolent of Young's *Night Thoughts*, Blair's *The Grave*, or Warton's *The Pleasures of Melancholy*; but there are clear echoes of *Douglas* (for instance, Lady Randolph's opening speech) in such lines as these from 'Death', written when Macpherson was twenty:

> Come, melancholy, soul-o'erwhelming power!
> Woe's sable child! sweet meditation come;
> Come, pensive gaited, from thy hermit cell,
> Brood wide o'er life, and all its transient joys.[9]

'To the Memory of an Officer Killed before Quebec' opens:

> Ah me! what sorrow are we born to bear!
> How many causes claim the falling tear!
> In one sad tenor life's dark current flows,
> And every moment has its load of woes
>
> *(Poems*, intro. MacQueen, II, 592)

Bailey Saunders notes that Macpherson probably spent the winter of 1755–6 in Edinburgh.[10] This was when *Douglas* was circulating in manuscript; and he may have witnessed its performance in Canongate Theatre, 14 December 1756. It seems likely that he had read the text in the edition of 1757.

The morose brooding of Home's Lady Randolph anticipates the habitually lugubrious Ossian. Her loss as parent may be equated with both Ossian's lament for the passing of a heroic ethos and Macpherson's sense of the threat to the survival of nationhood and culture. Macpherson's 'On the Death of Marshal Keith' (died 14 October 1758) asserts Scottish pre-eminence in sensibility in terms strikingly similar to those of the Edinburgh Prologue to *Douglas:*

> But Caledonia o'er the rest appears,
> And claims pre-eminence to mother-tears:
> In deeper gloom her tow'ring rocks arise,
> And from her vallies issue doleful sighs.
>
> *(Poems*, intro. MacQueen, II, 588)

The writing of both Home and Macpherson simultaneously exudes patriotism and appeals to it. It is a patriotism that identifies Scotland with purity of feeling and action; the tide of luxury and corruption must be driven back. These lines from Macpherson's 'The Hunter', descriptive of the Scottish capital, pave the way for the identification of the remote Highlands as the site of the natural, uncorrupted state:

> On rocks a city stands, high-tower'd, unwall'd,
> And from its scite the hill of Edin call'd.
> Once the proud seat of royalty and state,
> Of kings and heroes, and of all that's great:
> But these are flown, and Edin's only stores
> Are fops, and scriveners, and English'd whores.
>
> *(Poems*, intro. MacQueen, II, 469)

In an echo of both Ramsay's *The Gentle Shepherd* and Home's *Douglas*, the hunter is found to be heir to a lord and is 'No horrid herdsman, no indecent hind / Of clownish manners or rapacious mind'. (The notion of sensibility as elitist appears in Scottish texts as diverse as the Sylvander–Clarinda correspondence and *The Prime of Miss Jean Brodie* (where it is subtly ironised).) The primitive society of Macpherson and Blair evokes a strictly hierarchical order of response, yet, according to the Preface to *Fragments*, these poems were held to 'abound with those ideas, and paint those manners, that belong to the most early state of society'; and it is asserted that 'these poems are to be ascribed to the bards' *(Poems*, 5).

In assessing Macpherson's achievement, there is no injustice in locating him in the great Scottish tradition of innovation, demonstrating the esemplastic power of the imagination. There is a sense in which the finest Scottish writers cannot leave anything alone: they have a compulsive need to do more than merely tinker. Traditions are not to be deferred to: they are to be adapted, redeployed to meet the expressive needs of the individual vision. Gavin Douglas isn't satisfied with merely translating the whole of *The Aeneid* into Scots: he must add a prologue to each book, thereby offering new perspectives on Virgil's material. In 'Lucky Spence's Last Advice' Allan Ramsay converts the valediction into a vehicle of social criticism. Robert Fergusson uses the flyting technique in 'To the Tron-Kirk Bell' as springboard to trenchant social and religious commentary. Out of his desire to write 'an epic . . . that should equal the *Iliad*,'[11] Burns in 'Tam o' Shanter' employs the trappings of classical epic to celebrate the experiences and responses of the ordinary man, truly 'heroic Tam'. Smollett translates *Gil Blas* by LeSage but makes selective use of features of the picaresque; and in *Humphry Clinker* he offers a quite different take to that of Richardson on the expressive capacity of the epistolary mode.

The Poems of Ossian represent a creative conflation of a range of sources and are a quite remarkable achievement. Fionn is appropriated from the Fenian cycle and becomes a Scot. The Bible influences Macpherson's rhythms and cadences. Histories such as the *Agricola* of Tacitus and Toland's *History of the Druids* are plundered. The *Iliad*, *Odyssey*, and *Aeneid* are vastly influential. Well versed in classical literature, Macpherson imbues his poems with its characteristic features, then astutely claims that, since Ossian could not have known Homer or Aristotle, this both proves the ubiquity of epic and authenticates the poems – a gloriously circular argument.

Macpherson cites the absence of Achilles from the *Iliad* as precedent for those episodes where Fingal is off-stage. Epic similes, apostrophes, and catalogues abound. Implicit throughout is the sense that the nobility of the epic mode is appropriate to the natural nobility of emotion and deed. Macpherson's familiarity with the work of Thomas Blackwell on the epic is evident. Blackwell had written that the age of Homer had 'natural and simple manners; it is irresistible and enchanting; they best shew human Wants and Feelings; they give us back the emotions of an artless mind'.[12] So Macpherson mines the resources of art and artifice to create the illusion of the artless mind. Thus he presents Nature – in both its dimensions – as integral to the heroic ethos. Courtesy of the pervasive melancholic presence of his narrator, he invests epic heroism with the pathos requisite for the age of sensibility. Repetition serves to foreground the values of courage, honour, and fame, the last-named invariably giving rise to a sense of transience; and the rhythmical prose is productive of both sublimity and pathos.

Macpherson's technique is characterised by binaries and patterned alternation. The narrative alternates between account of action (sometimes so vividly rendered as to be relived or virtually present) and anecdote (generally exemplary and pathetic). The moods are alternately celebration and lamentation: achievement is heralded, loss is mourned. Strict chronological order is frequently disrupted, with the effect of drawing the reader into the material of the text to bring to Ossian's sequence a sense of consequence. Stafford comments that '[Macpherson's] audience is forced to share the work of restoration and produce an imaginative experience that is unique to each reader' (*Poems*, xvi). Disruption of regular chronology and plot development; digressive narration; a narrative following the flux of the narrator's consciousness; repetition; a role – a space even – for the reader in the interactive text: where are the parallels to this? In 1759–60 the first two volumes of Sterne's *Tristram Shandy* appeared (and a later volume leaves a space for the reader to draw the Widow Wadman). The privileging of the spatial over the chronological is taken further by Mackenzie in *The Man of Feeling* (1771) where the surviving episodes that comprise the text all play to the sensibility of the reader. Ironically Macpherson (whom I have almost converted into a proto-Postmodernist) believed that he had 'improved' the two-volume *Poems of Ossian* of 1773 by 'arranging the poems in the order of time, so as to form a kind of regular history of the age to which they relate' (*Poems*, xxiii). This may have been to help the reader at the suggestion of Lord Kames, but Gaskill offers an alternative and ingenious explanation:

> It is authorial vanity which is really behind so many of these revisions. Macpherson is tired of being an epigone and is evidently no longer willing to be upstaged by a figure he regards in large part (and in larger part than is warranted) as his own creation. He is jealous of Ossian. Hence the attempt to downplay the blind bard's role as creator of – rather than character in – the poetry. (*Poems*, xxiv)

As for Macpherson's legacy to Scottish literature, it is undeniable that he influenced a host of writers, either positively or by way of reaction. In *Humphry Clinker* (1771) Smollett offers his characteristically distinctive take on the concept of the Noble Savage. Lismahago and Ensign Murphy endure appalling atrocities at the hands of the Miami Indians. The North American Indian rivalled the Highlander as claimant to the title of descendant of the Noble Savage. Plainly Smollett has his doubts. In the same text Jery Melford enthuses:

> These are the lonely hills of Morven, where Fingal and his heroes enjoyed the same pastime: I feel an enthusiastic pleasure when I survey the brown heath that Ossian wont to tread; and hear the wind whistle through the bending grass. When I enter our landlord's hall I look for the suspended harp of that divine bard, and listen in hopes of hearing the aerial sound of his respected spirit – The Poems of Ossian are in every mouth – A famous antiquarian of this country, the laird of Macfarlane . . . can repeat them all in the original Gaelic.[13]

The 'landlord' is Mr Campbell who, as Jery records, has made the Grand Tour and plays expertly on the violin. His vaulted hall daily hosts the traditional bagpiping to which he is averse but on which his clansmen insist as sacred ritual. The tensions between tradition and progress, between natural and civilised states, lie beneath the often-comic veneer of Smollett's novel. Despite earlier enthusiasm for the sublimity of the Highlands, Jery prefers the 'different' wildness of the Southern Uplands' 'fine green swarth, affording pasture to innumerable flocks of sheep'; and, he acknowledges, 'If I was confined to Scotland for life, I would chuse Dumfries as the place of my residence' (p.257).

Jery Melford may be the inspiration for Scott's series of romanticising young hero-visitors, from Edward Waverley to Darsie Latimer, whose romanticising Scott counters with the pragmatic compromises with which *Waverley*, *Rob Roy*, and *Redgauntlet* end (and Effie Deans's son in *Heart of Midlothian* is a variant on the Noble Savage). Equally,

Scott's long poems teem with Ossianic echoes. These lines from *Marmion* (1808) proclaim their inspiration:

> When, musing on companions gone,
> We doubly feel ourselves alone,
> Something, my friend, we yet may gain;
> There is a pleasure in this pain:
> It soothes the love of lonely rest,
> Deep in each gentler heart impress'd.[14]

The poem is characterised by a predominant mood of melancholy, evocative use of landscape, and, by means of man–nature analogies, the confirmation of a close relationship between human and natural worlds; and there is a clear identification of heroism and nationalism. In *The Lady of the Lake*, sections such as those beginning 'Time rolls his ceaseless course', and 'Harp of the North, farewell', bespeak the Ossianic legacy; likewise the alternation between heroic achievement and lamentation. The influence on Beattie's *The Minstrel* is considerable; and Byron composed several Ossianic imitations. As for Burns, a poem such as 'Man was made to Mourn' catches the mood of Macpherson's narrator, while the opening stanzas of 'Lament for James, Earl of Glencairn' are manifestly Ossianic; and James Kinsley in his notes to the Oxford edition cites various clear echoes, perhaps the most striking being the similarity between the lines from 'Open the door to me Oh' – 'The wan moon sets behind the white wave, / And time is setting with me, Oh', and the line from 'Carthon', 'the moon, cold and pale, sinks in the western wave'.[15] I would wish to speculate that the bard, Ossian, inspires Burns to project himself as 'Caledonia's Bard' in various letters.[16] Revealingly, Macpherson's Ossian is cited in Burns's early letter, 15 June 1783, to Murdoch, as one of 'the glorious models after which I endeavour to form my conduct' (*Letters*, ed. Roy, I, 17). Ossian provides Burns with a self-image.

Also, as noted earlier, the elitist nature of sensibility is prominent in the Sylvander–Clarinda letters.[17] The notion that sensibility is the prerogative of people of taste becomes lodged in the Scottish consciousness by the late eighteenth century and helps drive a wedge between polite and popular culture (despite Tom Crawford's convincing case in *Society and the Lyric* for the movement of street ballad to tea-table, and vice versa, earlier in the century).

The line between sensibility and sentimentality is a thin one, and it may be that the direction which some Scottish fiction was to take by the end of the nineteenth century crossed the boundary. There is a sense in which the more extreme Kailyard fictions, with their rural locations, often retrospective vision, repetition of formulae, and small-group focus, inherit Ossianic features but they seriously diminish the scale of deed and emotion of Macpherson's work. Thereby, they establish stereotypes of

Scottishness against which a reaction was inevitable. Hence the 'urban realism' of the past twenty years, until recently so entrenched as to threaten to replace one formula with another. Hence, too, the outburst against 'Scottishness' in *Trainspotting*. Or, rather more subtly, Tom Leonard's response in such poems as 'Paroakial', where he uses Glaswegian patois to argue for a truly international Scottish vision, or 'The Voyeur', in which the limited nature of Scottish perspectives is identified:

> what's your favourite word dearie
> is it wee
> I hope it's wee
> wee's such a nice wee word . . .
> oh my
> a great wee word
> and Scottish
> it makes you proud[18]

Ironically, while Macpherson may have been unwittingly responsible for mapping out a constraining course for Scottish literature, he is undeniably, in company with Burns and Scott, one of the most influential of Scottish writers internationally.

Notes

[1] *The Letters of David Hume*, ed. J. Y. T. Greig (Oxford, 2 vols., 1969), I, 195.
[2] *The Works of Allan Ramsay*, ed. A. M. Kinghorn and A. Law (Edinburgh and London, 1970), IV, 236.
[3] James Macpherson, *The Poems of Ossian and related works*, ed. Howard Gaskill, with an intro. by Fiona Stafford (Edinburgh, 1996), p.5 (hereafter *Poems*).
[4] Adam Ferguson, *On the History of Civil Society* (London and Edinburgh, 1767), 280.
[5] J. S. Smart, *James Macpherson: An Episode in Literature* (London, 1905), 75.
[6] *Poems*, ix; J. F. Campbell, *Popular Tales of the West Highlands*, 1860–2 (London, 2nd edn, 4 vols, 1890), I, iv–v.
[7] John MacQueen, *The Enlightenment and Scottish Literature, vol.1: Progress and Poetry* (Edinburgh, 1982), 68.
[8] John Home, *Douglas*, ed. Gerald D. Parker (Edinburgh, 1972), 21.

9   *Poems of Ossian*, intro. John MacQueen (Edinburgh, 1971), II, 445 (hereafter *Poems*, intro. MacQueen).
10 Bailey Saunders, *The Life and Letters of James Macpherson* (London, 1894), 43.
11 J. DeLancey Ferguson (ed.), *The Letters of Robert Burns* (Oxford, 2nd edn, ed. G. Ross Roy, 1985), I, 439 (hereafter *Letters*, ed. Roy).
12 Thomas Blackwell, *An Enquiry into the Life and Writings of Homer* (London, 2nd edn, 1736), 24.
13 Tobias Smollett, *The Expedition of Humphry Clinker*, ed. Thomas R. Preston (Athens, Georgia, and London, 1990), 233.
14 *Poetical Works of Scott*, ed. J. Logie Robertson (Oxford, 1894), 102.
15 Robert Burns, *The Poems and Songs*, ed. James Kinsley (Oxford, 3 vols, 1968), III, 1427.
16 See *Letters*, ed. Roy, I, 91, 97, 104.
17 See *Letters*, ed. Roy, I, 195, 197, 203.
18 Tom Leonard, *Intimate Voices: Selected Work 1965–1983* (Newcastle upon Tyne, 1984), 23.

MEG BATEMAN

The environmentalism of Donnchadh Bàn: pragmatic or mythic?

This paper is in three parts. As the ground I will look at Donnchadh Bàn's relationship to nature which Iain Crichton Smith and others insist was pragmatic and unromantic; as variation I will consider whether, underlying this apparent pragmatism, there may lie the mythic world view of the pre-Christian Celts; and finally, as *crunn-lùdh*, I will try to link that pre-Christian world view with Romanticism, disparaged as a foreign appliqué to the Celtic tradition. I will make the suggestion that the sensibilities we refer to as Romanticism might even have some genuine Celtic origins.[1] The paper then is a battleground of *isms* – I hope Donnchadh Bàn will nevertheless win through.

A word to the people here who may not have heard of Donnchadh Bàn: Duncan MacIntyre was born in 1724, the son of a crofter, in the Clachan of Druim Liaghart on the shore of Loch Tulla in Argyllshire. His songs give us a wonderful musical metaphor of the contentment of his youth and early manhood, when he worked as a gamekeeper in Mam Lorn and Dalness Forest which took in the spectacular hills of Beinn Dòbhrain and Buachaille Etive Mòr. He describes with endless variation the endless variation of verdant nature and the co-extensive human culture. He married Màiri of Inveroran Inn (which is on the West Highland Way today), who was above his station, and from the internal evidence of his songs (especially 'Cead Deireannach nam Beann', 5568–75) we gather that his drinking led them to impecuniousness which he remedied at the age of forty-three, like many another Highlander at that time, by leaving his job as forester and settling in Edinburgh in the regular employ of the City Guard with a spell as a soldier with the Breadalbane Fencibles. He therefore spent the first forty-three years of his life in Argyllshire and the next forty-five in the Lowlands. Descriptions of his life include his half-hearted fighting on the Hanoverian side at the battle of Falkirk, 1746, from which he ran, abandoning his master's sword, and his later espousal of the Jacobite side, perhaps in the spirit of cultural loyalty. Towards the end of his life he visited Beinn Dòbhrain and was shocked by the changes in land-use and population caused by the Clearances.

With the title of this conference in mind, 'Crossing the Highland Line', an obvious approach for a paper on Donnchadh Bàn would have been to contrast the songs he made as a forester and a praise poet with those he made for the London Highland Society and for the milieu of expatriate Highlanders based in Edinburgh. In these, he takes the self-conscious stance of making songs about those objects by which Lowland culture defined Gaelic culture – the pipes, whisky, Highland dress, etc. However it was our current preoccupation with the environment that prompted me to consider Donnchadh Bàn's conceptualisation of nature and man. Some of you may be squirming at my use of 'conceptualisation' in this context, for it is traditional to portray Donnchadh Bàn as a naive peasant, non-literate and unschooled, whose complexities were metrical rather than conceptual. I am sure I am not alone in refuting any such connection between technological and psychological development. The case need hardly be argued any more. Paul Radin wrote in 1927 in *Primitive Man as Philosopher*:

> It is manifestly unfair to contend that primitive people are deficient either in the power of abstract thought or in the power of arranging these thoughts in a systematic order, or finally, of subjecting them, and their whole environment, to an objective critique. (Segal 2004, 37)

Complexities are further introduced when people are made aware of different value systems, different ways of structuring the world. With his move from the Highlands to the Lowlands, from a kin-based to a money-based society, Donnchadh Bàn witnessed a greater contrast than most of us. The songs he made on his return visit to the Highlands give ample evidence of the clash of these two cultures.

Ùrlar: Donnchadh Bàn's relationship to nature

Even the title of this subsection is misleading because it implies that Donnchadh Bàn and nature were separate entities. Again and again Donnchadh Bàn's songs refute the distinction. Man and nature are one and the same. In 'Òran do Ghleann Urchaidh' it is clear that where nature thrives, so does man; where crops are planted, so too are songs sung; culture simultaneously implies agrarian and human culture. Man's stewardship of nature is natural because man is part of nature. It is what man does, and is no less natural than birds' songs and beavers' dams. In reading 'Moladh Beinn Dòbhrain' we are led to accept the goring of the deer by the hounds as part of a whole. We don't cringe at the demise of the animals that have just been lovingly described because the instinct of the hounds and the skill of the hunter with his ingeniously designed gun are all equally part of nature.

Man and the land belong together. He speaks of Gleann Urchaidh as the place where he belongs and should be buried. In 'Òran nam Balgairean' he sees it as 'mì-nàdarrach' (unnatural) that the glens have become depopulated, and wrong that a man has to leave the place inhabited by his forebears. Throughout the poems Donnchadh Bàn exhibits a passionate love of nature, a love that is not contradicted when part of nature is destroyed by another part so long as the balance is maintained. In 'Cumha

Coire a' Cheathaich' and 'Òran nam Balgairean' the balance is destroyed by a careless forester, waterways become clogged, woodlands mismanaged, the deer retreat, the rent goes up and people move away. Everything fails to prosper. Donnchadh Bàn's editor, Angus MacLeod, describes this as 'but a poet's conceit',[2] but I think there is every reason to take it literally and, as I will explain below, mythically.

Siùbhal: an underlying pre-Christian Celtic world view?

I disagree profoundly with Angus MacLeod's assessment of Donnchadh Bàn. He says:

> We are not satisfied, haunting though the word-music may be. The poet himself does not emerge from the mass of his work with any system of philosophy; he can describe objectively with all the precision of Celtic ornamentation; but he does not play with ideas, nor do we find evidence of 'capacity for pain' in any of his composition. Hence, if in poetry we require sublimity of thought, a philosophy of life or compelling emotion, we shall find Duncan Macintyre wanting. If we look for a revolutionary, a zealot or visionary, we shall be disappointed in the bard of Glenorchy. (MacLeod 1952, xl)

Rev. John Kennedy, also writing of Donnchadh Bàn in the *Celtic Magazine* in 1888, said, '*poeta nascitur non fit* (a poet is born not made) . . . All his inspiration was inborn and not drawn from the works of his predecessors.' Perhaps enthralled by their idea of the peasant poet, both commentators seem to be blind to the ideological systems that shape Donnchadh Bàn's work. Even Iain Crichton Smith, I feel, is guilty of the same, when he says 'In MacIntyre, what we find is a pagan power which has not been philosophised and analysed into mush' (Smith 1988, 6). He is right about its being pagan and not being a mush, but is there not an implication here that the thought is not systematic?

Willie Gillies sounds another note: 'Bardic verse ranked visualising much higher than seeing . . . I am prepared to see "Moladh Beinn Dòbhrain" as a serious and courageous attempt to create a dialectic for the expression of some pretty powerful ideas (Gillies 1977, 45 and 48)'. Gillies suggests that Donnchadh Bàn, in speaking of the deer's rights to the bounds of Beinn Dòbhrain, is making a veiled claim to the people's right to the land and protection of the chief. Gillies makes the connection between this poem and the 'ancient concept of the prince as husband of the land he ruled, which burgeoned and flourished insofar as the king was the rightful king, ruling justly' (Gillies 1977, 45).

I would like to look for further evidence in Donnchadh Bàn's work for this pre-Christian, Indo-European system, where the land, as the female principle of regeneration and destruction, is mated with the male principle of the tribe. The synergy of land and man is therefore represented mythically by the union of goddess and local god (Sjoestedt 1940). Myth need not be taken literally but as a form of knowledge, as an anthropological construct for a people to understand their position in the world.

Personification

Donnchadh Bàn personifies the corrie in 'Òran Coire a' Cheathaich' as a woman, fair-haired ('cùlfhinne'), with green knolls, wearing a substantial cloak ('fallaing dhùinte gu daingean dùbailt') and gay garments, a lush covering of plants filling out her form:

> Tha trusgan faoilidh air cruit an aonaich
> Chuir sult is aoibh air gach taobh a d' chom

> *On moorland contours there is gladsome raiment*
> *that lapped thy bosom in wealth and cheer*
>
> ('Òran Coire a' Cheathaich', 2294–5)

She is a fashionable woman, her coat at Craig Mhòr being of the moss-saxifrage rather than of 'fòlach' (2326–9); her nature is gay ('guanach') and hospitable.

But the mother goddess was changeable and also became a goddess of slaughter, as winter followed summer, famine followed plenty, and all that nature had engendered would be destroyed. Is this duality the basis for Donnchadh Bàn's remark that it would be bliss for young men to stay in the corrie *if it didn't change?*

> Mur dèan e caochladh, b' e an t-aighear saoghalta
> Do ghillean aotrom bhith daonnan ann.

> *unless it changeth it were bliss on earth*
> *for lightsome lads to be always there.*
>
> ('Òran Coire a' Cheathaich', 2300–1)

The land is like the mother who raised him, 'Gum b' ait leinn an tìr sin / On as ì rinn ar n-àrach' ('Òran Dùthcha' 3405–6), helping him to grow healthy and robust:

> Chuidich e gu fàs mi,
> 'S e rinn domh slàint' is fallaineachd

> *It helped me to grow and gave me*
> *robustness and vitality.*
>
> ('Cead Deireannach nam Beann', 5534–5)

It is also the land where he will be buried (for, unlike a human mother, the earth mother gives life and takes it away in a cycle of regeneration and death):

> An t-àit' an còir dhuinn crìochnachadh
> 'S an tiodhlaicear ar cuirp
>
> *the place where 'tis meet our end should come,*
> *and our bodies be interred.*
>
> ('Òran Ghlinn Urchaidh', 2220–1)

The corrie also affords the hunter shelter, the female principle nurturing the male principle:

> An creagan ìosal am bun na frìthe,
> 'San leabaidh dhìona 's mi 'm shìneadh ann
>
> *in the lower crags, in the forest foothills,*
> *in the den of refuge, where I reclined.*
>
> ('Òran Coire a'Cheathaich', 2364–5)

As part of the personification, productive nature is seen as being hospitable. Nature is 'aoigheil' under the rightful ruler for it becomes home to an abundance of life. There is a clear equation in Donnchadh Bàn's thinking between naturalness and hospitality: nature is generous to life, and life, in its turn, is generous/productive. To him, the Highlands after the Clearances are in an unnatural state, because a monoculture of sheep is inhospitable to other species, including man:

> Tha h-uile seòl a b' àbhaist
> Anns a' Ghàidhealtachd air caochladh,
>
> Air cinntinn cho mi-nàdarra
> 'Sna h-àiteachan a bha aoigheil.
>
> *Every practice that prevailed*
> *in Gaeldom has been altered,*
>
> *and become so unnatural*
> *in the places that were hospitable.*
>
> ('Òran nam Balgairean', 5035–8)

It is only in times when man is seen as separate from nature that the Highlands are constructed as an unspoilt wilderness precisely because of the absence of humans.

Is the goddess also the basis for Donnchadh Bàn's belief in the possible recovery of the corrie in 'Cumha Coire a' Cheathaich'? If MacEwan gets the heave, and one of Patrick's line takes over, the corrie will again become fertile and everything will revert to normal. In terms of the myth, the goddess can again be happy if mated to the right ruler:

> Ach mas duine de Shliochd Phàraig
> A thèid a-nis don àite,
> 'S gun cuir e às a làraich
>   An tàcharan a th' ann,
> Bidh 'n coire mar a bhà e,
> Bidh laoidh is aighean dàr' ann . . .

> *But if it be one of Patrick's line*
> *that now goes to the place,*
> *and drives from his position*
>   *the changeling that is there,*
> *the corrie will be as it was:*
> *calves and rutting young hinds will be there . . .*

> Thig gach uile nì g' a àbhaist,
> Le aighear is le àbhachd,
> Nuair gheibh am baran bàirlinn
>   Siud fhàgail gun taing.

> *all will revert to use and wont,*
> *with mirth and jubilation,*
> *when the baron gets a summons*
>   *to quit, and has no choice.*

('Cumha Coire a' Cheathaich', 2550–6, 2562–5)

Personification of animals

The personification of animals is very common in Donnchadh Bàn's songs. Birds, for instance, are described as playing reeds and chanters ('ribheid', 'feadan') and singing various types of human song; the deer are always heavily personified, none more so than the hind in Beinn Dòbhrain, who appears as a giddy, elegant, well-dressed, erratic young woman.

Is this anthropomorphism merely a comical conceit, or does it reflect a blurring of the lines between the human and animal, emphasising their equal rights to be there, in a non-hierarchical view of nature? This would accord with the pre-Christian view of all animals representing life and the respect for animals we see enduring into the early Christian period, e.g. in 'Messe ocus Pangur Bàn' where both the mouse-catching cat and the problem-solving monk are to be praised for their 'craft' (Murphy 1956, 2). We may see here the same understanding which John Scotus Eriugena formulated, of all of creation being part of the emanation of God, rather than the Augustinian system, based on Aristotle, where man is superior to all animals.

Balancing of male and female principle

While Donnchadh Bàn is historically accurate in distinguishing the sheep as the imme-diate cause of the depopulation of Beinn Dòbhrain, he interprets events not in terms of agrarian reform and capitalism but in terms of the earliest Indo-European belief systems. Gilbertus Cambrensis describes an almost identical inaugural rite of a prince, representing the male principle, and a mare, representing the female principle, in twelfth-century Ireland as is known from Hindu description (Ross 1986, 95). The deer, salmon, men and dogs abounding in the corrie may represent the male principle on the female land, with the same elements present as when the Brown Bull of Cuailgne scatters the remains of the White Bull all over the land of Èire, whose name, of course, is the name of a goddess. Their masculinity is emphasised: the salmon is described as wearing armour ('na èideadh colgail bu ghormghlas druim') as he leaps to catch flies with flashes of silver after coming heroically from the stormy ocean, the man is thickly pelleting the deer with lead and the hound is 'blood-thirsty, forceful, valiant, fierce':

> 'S bidh fèidh air ghiùlan le làmhach fùdair
> Cur luaidhe dhùbhghorm gu dlùth nan calg;
> An gunna gleusda 's an cuilean eutrom
> Gu fuileach feumanach treubhach garg

> *Deer will be slung up when blast of powder*
> *Driveth dark-blue lead thick into their pelts;*
> *The gun is ready, and the whelp is nimble,*
> *Blood-thirsty, forceful, valiant, fierce*

> (Òran Coire a' Cheathaich', 2352–5)

Far from this being a show of gratuitous violence, it is a sign of a balance of ener-gies, of nature's ample productivity, her 'hospitality' to all.

Love of nature/the goddess/the deer

Donnchadh Bàn's love of it all could be interpreted in several ways, including love of the goddess, the personification allowing the love to be personal. He refers to the corrie as 'an coire laghach gaolach', the kind, beloved corrie (2455). His criticism of MacEwan's management is expressed as an absence of love, a neglect of a *person*: 'gun duin' aig a bheil càs dheth' (2440). The corrie had gone to ruin because it lacks a man who loves the deer:

> 'S e an coire chaidh an dèislaimh
> On tha e nis gun fhèidh ann,
> Gun duin' aig a bheil spèis dhiubh
> Nì feum air an cùl.

> *How the corrie has gone to ruin,*
> *since now it has no deer,*
> *nor any man who loves them*
> *and is efficient on their trail.*

('Cumha Coire a' Cheathaich', 2486–9)

It is perhaps no coincidence that the locations of MacEwan's neglect – the trees whose tops have been lopped off, and the waterways – are those very sites most sacred in otherworld beliefs where the regenerating powers of the earth/goddess surface in the upper world. Rather than being involved in the manly pursuit of deer stalking, MacEwan collects his rents by wringing the necks of hens. Work with poultry is traditionally women's work. He is manifestly not the perfect partner for the goddess and in consequence the corrie's fertility falters ('Cumha Coire a' Cheathaich'). The male and female principle are out of balance.

Often Donnchadh Bàn addresses the corrie in the second person. The poet has a direct and passionate relationship with nature where each can influence the other. This is the position of man and nature in pagan Celtic mythology where the goddess is both mollified and cajoled into displaying a helpful attitude to man. The Jewish philosopher Martin Buber makes a distinction between the fundamentally different perceptions of the world involved in myth and philosophy. In myth the external world is viewed as Thou, while in philosophy it is viewed as a third person. 'An I–It relationship is detached and intellectual. An I–Thou one is involved and emotional' (Segal 2004, 41).

Crun-lùdh: Romanticism: a Celtic sensibility?

In the above I do not mean to imply that Donnchadh Bàn would have had an active knowledge of the pre-Christian goddess, but that that system formulated attitudes to man's place in nature, of stewardship rather than of dominance. It may be coincidental that these attitudes resonate with certain features of Romanticism that grew up from a quite different basis in reaction to the dominance of nature assumed to be the way to power by early modem philosophy and science.

Some of Donnchadh Bàn's attitudes described above are recognisable as trends in Romanticism: the personification of nature, the attribution of emotions to nature; the poet's passionate involvement with his environment; man's state reflecting that of nature and vice versa; anthropomorphism. I have suggested they are all ultimately connected to the presence of the goddess. Though their origin is independent of Romanticism, the end result can be remarkably similar: an inability to distinguish man from his natural setting, nature 'sending messages', the pathetic fallacy. In Celtic works, the 'pathetic fallacy' results from the goddess's human consort dying; but the end-result looks like its Romantic counterpart with nature reflecting human emotion. It is at least as old as the twelfth century. In Créide's Lament for Cáel, both nature and the girl die with grief for the drowned warrior (in translation):

> The haven roars over the fierce stream of Reenverc: the drowning of the warrior from Loch Dá Chonn is what the wave striking the shore laments.

> A heron calls loudly in the marsh of Druim Dá Thrén: she is unable to protect her live ones − a two-coloured fox is on the track of her birds.

> Sad is the cry the thrush makes in Drumkeen: and no less sad is the note of the blackbird in Leitir Laíg.

> Sad is the sound made by the stag in Drumlesh: dead is the doe of Druim Síleann; a mighty stag roars now that she is gone.
>
> (Murphy 1956, 148 fol)

In the Welsh tradition, Gruffudd Ab Yr Coch laments the death of Llewelyn ap Gruffudd, the last independent Welsh prince, killed by Edward I in 1282 (in translation):

> See you not the way of the wind and the rain?
> See you not the oaktrees buffet together?
> See you not the sea stinging the land?
> See you not truth in travail?
> See you not the sun hurtling through the sky,
> And that the stars are fallen?
>
> (Clancy 1970, 130)

131

A happy productive goddess lies behind Giolla Críost Brúilingeach's description of Moylurg under Tomaltach, who died in 1458, abounding in red wheat, cows in milk, and fruits on every branch:³ likewise Donnchadh Bàn has Coire a' Cheathaich abound in deer, men, hounds, all types of grass, bees, fruits and nuts. What can we say about Suibhne Geilt, cursed by St Ronan for attacking his clerics, left mad, beyond human society, with special powers and insights flying through the trees? He is a perfect romantic type, five hundred years before Romanticism. 'Boile Shuibhne' has the framework of a Christian parable about the power of St Ronan to curse and of St Mo Ling to forgive, but there is more than this in the many twelfth-century poems attributed to him. He is the archetype of the wild man, passionately involved with nature and seeing what those caught up in society cannot see. And what of the druid Amairgin in *Lebar Gabála*? Is his shape-shifting merely a trick to confound and impress his enemies, or does it represent the ultimate interaction with nature, as he diverts his own life-force into other life-forms?

Ruskin associates an interest in landscape with regret and nostalgia. He famously said of the Romantic age, 'No-one ever cared about blue mountains before.'⁴ His contention was that the medieval mind found distant peaks an irrelevance in the daily task of food production, their being neither accessible nor fertile, and that it was not until the advent of Romanticism that they became both symbolic and symptomatic of the dislocation and longing of urban people, safe from starvation but hungry in other ways. Sorley MacLean too felt that the constantly plaintive tone of many nineteenth-century poets surveying deserted glens was something new to Gaelic poetry, resulting from the massive dislocation of the Clearances. 'As compared with 18th century Gaelic poetry, 19th century poetry is flabby and anaemic; it lacks power, gusto, spontaneity, joie de vivre' (MacGill-Eain 1985, 57). Donnchadh Bàn's 'Òran Dùthcha' and 'Cead Deireannach nam Beann' are early examples of this type of clearance verse.

On the surface, the spectacle in the latter poem of Beinn Dòbhrain covered in sheep looks like a proof of Ruskin's link between blue mountains and nostalgia: the change in the mountain that Donnchadh Bàn had imagined immutable represents his shock on finding his homeland cleared of its people:

> Bha mi n-dè san aonach
> 'S bha smaointean mòr air m' aire-sa,
> Nach robh an luchd-gaoil a b' àbhaist
>   bhith siubhal fàsaich mar rium ann;
> 'S a' bheinn as beag a shaoil mi
> Gun dèanadh ise caochladh,
> On tha i nis fo chaoraibh
>   'S ann thug an saoghal car asam.

Yesterday I was on the moor,
and grave reflections haunted me:
that absent were the well-loved friends
who used to roam the waste with me;
since the mountain, which I little thought
would suffer transformation,
has now become a sheep-run,
the world, indeed, has cheated me.

('Cead Deireannach nam Beann', 5576–83)

However, a mythopoeic interpretation is also possible. The final line, 'the world has cheated me', expresses anger rather than longing. The world is constructed wrongly: land and tribe have been separated. The case for this interpretation can be strengthened by noting the right the deer have to the hill in 'Moladh Beinn Dòbhrain':

Tha an eilid anns an fhrìth
mar bu chòir dhi bhith

The hind is in the forest
as she ought to be

('Moladh Beinn Dòbhrain', 2934–5)

And the same word, 'còir' = right, is used by Uilleam Ros at about the same time when another mountain, Blaven, complains about her lack of an earthly lord of Clan MacLeod: 'Ach tha mi gun triath talmhaidh còir.' We have then a convergence in style of two distinct formulations: romantic and mythic.

Songs of nostalgia expressed through a longing for place are well established in the Gaelic tradition long before Romanticism, e.g. the many poems attributed to Colum Cille expressing his regret at leaving Ireland, or to Oisean, outliving the other Fenians, and left to lament their glorious past. In 'Agallam na Senorach' and 'A Bé Find' we have regret expressed for the glories of a pagan past before Christianity had sullied our *joie de vivre* with the notion of sin.

Conclusion

Flona Stafford has given us a rationale for understanding James Macpherson's project of presenting supposed translations of ancient Gaelic poetry to the world (Stafford 1988, Chapter 2). She presents him as a PR man for the culture which he saw disparaged and humiliated in the aftermath of Culloden. Under the tutelage of Blackwell, professor of Greek at Aberdeen University, Macpherson recognised that many of the ingredients required to produce the poetry of Homer had also been present until recently in Highland society. Above all, the heroic ethos of both societies unified action and thought. As in the unsettled times of early Greek society, Macpherson saw that warring Highland society had produced the tumultuous conditions that are productive of great art. It was a common belief of Romanticism that while poetry civilises, civilisation destroys creativity. Art is therefore self-defeating. In reaction to the rationalism of the Enlightenment, Blackwell saw in Homer's heroes, and Macpherson saw in the Highlands, a people uncorrupted by civilisation, educated by nature alone, a people in their natural state – emotional, spiritual, agile, whose ancient language, unlike English, was strong, richly metaphorical, uncorrupted by the artificiality of philosophy. He may genuinely have believed that the Fenian lays of his childhood were the fragments of some great epic that he could reassemble for a public anxious to find a sublime savage near at hand, the last blast of a recently lost Golden Age, of Paradise Lost. His statement that his poems were translations of written texts was perhaps necessary to gain the respect and credulity of a culture that had forgotten the power of oracy. He changed the language to English, the form to prose, and the atmosphere, it is often stated, to the sensibility of the eighteenth century, with its love for refinement, nostalgia and feeling. The Sheridans used Macpherson's work among their acquaintances as a thermometer of fineness of feeling. The same sensibility provided Goethe with a model for *The Sorrows of Werther*, of a young man laid prone by an abundance of feeling.

Various writers, David Hume, Sorley MacLean, Derick Thomson and Malcolm Chapman among them, have dismissed this atmosphere as an invention of James Macpherson's, predicated on the way the 'Celt' was constructed by Romanticism. To add insult to injury, it was then imitated by other Gaels who started to represent themselves as epitomising those very feminine features of non-aggression that sped the emasculation of their culture. In the aftermath of Culloden, the Clearances and emigration, it is easy to see how an aesthetic based on nostalgia for past glories and current passivity was both comforting and a self-fulfilling prophecy. It was against the escapism provided by this sort of poetry that Sorley MacLean railed in articles like 'Realism in Gaelic Poetry' and 'The Poetry of the Clearances'.[5] His own poetry and that of his generation reacted to its soft focus by scrutinising their own times with unveering clarity. They insist that in the native Gaelic aesthetic, nature does not illustrate man's condition, sends no messages, has no soul, nor do the poets draw ethical conclusions from it, nor move from the general to the particular. (Dùghall Bochanan is of course exceptional here as 'Òran dhan Gheamhradh' is primarily a religious poem.) By contrast, they say, Gaelic poetry is concrete, objective, exhaustive, never introspective, and deals in realism.

But is it valid to use the word 'realism'? Is it possible to look at anything neutrally without putting a particular spin on it? Far from being 'neutral', I believe Donnchadh

Bàn's songs came from a particular world view, just as does every human endeavour. We make human constructs to make sense of a possibly senseless world. As Kant says, we cannot see things in themselves, only through our human spectacles, and, may I add, through myriad cultural varifocals.

I hope I have demonstrated in the foregoing that such features as nostalgia, a passionate involvement with nature, nature reflecting the state of man, do have a place in the native Gaelic tradition just as they do in Romantic literature. Their construction in pre-Christian myth and in the thinking of Rousseau, Matthew Arnold and Ernst Renan are of course quite different, but their manifestations in literature are often quite similar. Pre-Christian mythology about man's place in the world chimes with modern man's sense about what is lost when the world is seen as a machine or as a resource for exploitation.

I think we are wrong to dismiss all romantic stances in Gaelic as a projection of Lowland and European Romanticism. Gaelic literature can demonstrate the possession of many such features from the earliest times. Romanticism picked up a lot of momentum from 'uncontaminated' Gaelic thought both in Macpherson's work (dare I say it) and in 'unimproved' Gaelic literature. It might be argued that much of Romanticism in the Lowlands and beyond is a long projection, even a metempsychosis, a shape-shifting, of the goddess.

Notes

Line references and translations are to MacLeod, A., 1952, *Òrain Dhonnchaidh Bhàin/The Songs of Duncan Bàn MacIntyre*, Edinburgh, The Scottish Gaelic Texts Society.

1   This was first proposed to me by Dr John Purser a few years ago.
2   MacLeod 1952, 1480.
3   Watson 1987, 32, vv 9, 10, 11.
4   Ruskin 1856, *Modern Painters*, III.
5   MacGill-Eain 1985.

References

Bate, J., 1991, *Romantic Ecology: Wordsworth and the Environmental Tradition*, London, Routledge.

Chapman, M., 1978, *The Gaelic Vision in Scottish Culture*, London, Croom Helm.

Clancy, J. P., 1970, *The Earliest Welsh Poetry*, London, Macmillan.

Clancy, T. and Márkus, G., 1995, *Iona, The Earliest Poetry of a Celtic Monastery*, Edinburgh, Edinburgh University Press.

Gillies, W., 1977, 'The Poem in Praise of Ben Dobhrain', *Lines Review* 63, Loanhead.

Kennedy, John, 1888, *Celtic Magazine*.

Lorimer, R., 1948, 'Duncan Ban McIntyre, a Modern Interpretation', *An Gaidheal*, Leabhar XCIII, Earrann 8, an Cèitean.

MacGill-Eain, S., 1985, 'Realism in Gaelic Poetry' and 'The Poetry of the Clearances' in *Ris a' Bhruthaich*, Stornoway, Acair Limited.

MacLeod, A., 1952, *Òrain Dhonnchaidh Bhàin/The Songs of Duncan Bàn MacIntyre*, Edinburgh, Scottish Gaelic Texts Society.

Mitchell, I., 1998, *Scotland's Mountains before Mountaineers*, Edinburgh, Luath Press.

Murphy, G., 1956, *Early Irish Lyrics, Eighth to Twelfth Century*, Oxford, Clarendon Press.

Newton, M., 2000, *A Handbook of the Scottish Gaelic World*, Dublin, Four Courts Press.

Ross, A., 1986, *The Pagan Celts*, London, Batsford.

Segal, R., 2004, *Myth: A Very Short Introduction*, Oxford, Oxford University Press.

Sjoestedt, M. L., 1940, *Gods and Heroes of the Celts*, Paris.

Smith, I. C., 1988, *Duncan Bàn MacIntyre's Ben Dorain*, Newcastle upon Tyne, Northern House.

Stafford, F., 1988, *The Sublime Savage: a Study of James Macpherson and the Poems of Ossian*, Edinburgh, Edinburgh University Press.

Thomson, D., 1974, *An Introduction to Gaelic Poetry*, London, Gollancz.

Watson, W. J., 1987, *Scottish Verse from the Book of the Dean of Lismore*, Edinburgh, Scottish Gaelic Texts Society.

MARGERY PALMER MCCULLOCH

The lasses reply to Mr Burns:
women poets and songwriters in the Lowlands

Much progress has been made in recent years in recovering neglected women writers of the past, so that their names are more regularly to be found in scholarly reviews. With earlier periods in particular, however, critical recovery too often stops with the giving of a name and some biographical details or the reprinting of a few poems or quotations from a prose work. There never seems to be enough space to allow a more detailed discussion of what such women contributed to and tell us about their society; or to suggest why, artistically, we should be campaigning for their inclusion in the literary canon of their period. And if one is foolish enough to attempt to make out a case for female poets in the eighteenth century, then, as Roger Lonsdale has commented, the response is likely to be 'the politely sceptical question, "Were there any?"'.[1]

Scotland, generally, has not been in the advance guard in relation to the recognition of women writers and this is especially the case with eighteenth-century women. Of recent historical guides to Scottish literature, only Catherine Kerrigan's *Anthology of Scottish Women Poets* (1991) and *A History of Scottish Women's Writing* edited by Douglas Gifford and Dorothy McMillan in 1997 offer reasonable documentation and discussion of eighteenth-century women poets. However, even in these accounts there are surprising omissions and a lack of discrimination between the various 'traditional' forms, while ballads and songs are discussed primarily as printed word-texts. Song itself has been a poor cousin in the literary tradition. As Tom Crawford comments in the opening chapter of his *Society and the Lyric* of 1979: 'In countries with a strong tradition of puritanism there has always been a tendency to look down on sung lyrics because they do not take up much room on the page and their idea-content is often slight'.[2] He should perhaps have added: 'and because their singers and tradition-bearers are most often women'.

My primary focus here will be on three representative eighteenth-century Lowland women writers in the hope that by examining more specifically a selection of their poems or songs I can begin to suggest why such women should be considered seriously in any account of eighteenth-century Scottish culture. In addition, my three poets and song writers all have some connection with the life and/or work of Robert Burns, the major Lowland Scottish writer of the period. They are: Janet Little, a self-educated poet from a farming family, born in the same year as Burns and, like Burns, a *literary* artist as opposed to a ballad singer or folk poet; Isabel Pagan, a poet in the folk tradition; and Carolina Oliphant, Lady Nairne, one of the most successful writers of *composed* traditional songs in the late eighteenth century, but a writer who went to great lengths to have her compositions printed anonymously – an approach which perhaps tells us something about the oddity of being a published woman writer at that time.

Janet Little was born in 1759, the daughter of George Little, a cottar or hired farm labourer in Ecclefechan, Dumfriesshire. She had only basic schooling, but had the good fortune to go into service first of all with a clergyman in whose home she had access to books and where she began to write poetry. She later entered service with Mrs Frances Dunlop, Burns's patron, first of all at Dunlop House and then at Loudon Castle in Ayrshire, where she supervised the dairy for Mrs Dunlop's daughter Susan, Mrs Henri. Hence the nickname by which she was known, 'The Scotch Milkmaid', just as Burns himself was commonly referred to as the 'Ploughman Poet'.[3]

Mrs Dunlop greatly encouraged her milkmaid *poetess* – and I use this word advisedly, for despite her championship of Janet Little, Mrs Dunlop clearly thought that male and female writers were creatures different in *kind*. She wrote to Burns on 11 December 1789 that 'I have never yet seen what I thought a female poet. I am even writing this in the house with Jenny Little.' And in a letter of 24 December she added: 'glory you are a man'.[4] Despite such gender discrimination, Mrs Dunlop did all she could to encourage Janet Little and to encourage Burns to take an interest in her work. Burns, for his part, kept his distance. Perhaps he had had too many labouring-class poets trying to follow in his footsteps; perhaps he felt that whatever uses women might have, writing poetry was not among them; or perhaps he just did not like Little's poems. Whatever the reason, he was most dilatory and devious in his responses to Mrs Dunlop's solicitations. After she had encouraged Janet to write him an epistle, he replied, not to Janet, but to her patron, saying:

> I had some time ago an epistle, part poetic and part prosaic, from your poetess, Miss J. Little, a very ingenious, but modest, composition. I should have written her as she requested, but for the hurry of this new business. I have heard of her and her compositions in this country; and, I am happy to add, always to the honor of her character. The fact is, I know not well how to write to her: I should sit down to a sheet of paper that I knew not how to stain. I am no dab at fine-drawn letter-writing.[5]

A present-day reader familiar with Burns's collected letters might well consider him a 'dab' at putting on an attitude on this occasion. Clearly, in his view, Janet Little had no qualifications to be a Clarinda to his Sylvander. He did, on the other hand, become one of the subscribers for the collection of her poems.

Janet Little has received almost no attention from recent Scottish scholars. Valentina Bold gives an account of her work in the article 'Janet Little "The Scotch Milkmaid" and "Peasant Poetry"' in the November 1993 issue of *Scottish Literary Journal* and later mentions her briefly in the chapter 'Scottish Women Poets of the Nineteenth Century' in *A History of Scottish Women's Writing*.[6] Her name is absent, however, from other recent historical accounts as well as from poetry anthologies, including Kerrigan's. Hilton Brown's essay in the *Burns Chronicle* of 1950 would appear to have been too readily accepted by later academics as a definitive judgement. In the opening of his 'Burns and the Scottish Milkmaid', Brown comments: 'Perhaps Janet was just good enough to be, not certainly a rival, but a disquieting imitation'. He concludes: 'Not a great deal could have been made of Janet [. . .] There are those whom even Pegasus cannot lift above the ground, and it is a waste of time for Pegasus to try.'[7]

In recent times, on the other hand, Little has been recognised by North American scholars in particular as having a significant place in any study of eighteenth-century women's writing or labouring class writing; and her poetry is included in several major eighteenth-century and (less relevantly) Romantic period anthologies and critical studies edited and published outwith Scotland. This new interest may well have arisen as a result of the growth of feminist, postcolonial and class studies in the later twentieth century. For example, in Donna Landry's *The Muses of Resistance*, the work of Little, 'the Scotch Milkmaid', is considered alongside that of Phillis Wheatley, 'Negro Servant to Mr John Wheatley, of Boston, New England', and in the context of the 'narrative of imperialism'. The 'hybridity' of their respective discourses is discussed in terms of Homi Bhaba's account of 'native mimicry' and its subversive challenge to the imperialist culture. In relation to the bilingualism Little shares with Burns, Landry sees a linguistically hybrid poem such as 'Given to a Lady Who Asked Me To Write A Poem' (which I will return to later) as 'Little's rewriting of literary history to accommodate both herself and Burns as Scottish writers who refuse to be silenced or colonized by Anglographic cultural hegemony'.[8]

Landry's 1990 study was an important landmark in the presentation or *re*-presentation of lower-class eighteenth-century women writers, and in the Scottish context can now be seen as bringing Janet Little's poetry forward for serious analysis for the first time. Her postcolonialist reading was extended into feminist and other theoretical contexts by studies such as Moira Ferguson's 1995 essays in *Romantic Women's Poetry* and *Eighteenth Century Women Poets: Nation, Class and Gender*, and by Leith Davis's 'Gender and the Nation in the work of Robert Burns and Janet Little' published in *Studies in English Literature* in 1998. Davis's account is especially interesting since, in addition to its investigation of issues relating to gender, class and national representation in Little's work, it provides a perceptive reading of the *formal* qualities and achievements of her poetry, pointing in particular to the irony through which she presents many of her themes and scenarios. It was this 'foreign' interest, and in particular Leith Davis's paper at a Strathclyde University Burns Conference in 1996, which first brought Little's name to my attention and led me to explore her 1792 collection for myself.

It has to be acknowledged that Little's collection does not immediately proclaim itself as a subversive Scottish challenge to the various hegemonies discussed by recent cultural critics – and this may be no small contributory factor in her neglect in the Scottish academic scene. The majority of the poems, on a first reading, appear conventionally Augustan in form, with themes relevant to a female writer in a dependent position. Many, such as the dedicatory poem to the young Countess of Loudon, are 'praise' poems for her patrons. Some, like the series of pastoral and dialogue love poems, could be seen as conforming to the fashionable taste of a largely female readership. This is not the place to give a detailed critique of Little's collection as a whole, although it does repay further study. There is a freshness in her handling of Augustan forms and themes while her poems to her patrons never lose a sense of her own selfhood. What is of more relevance to this present essay, however, is a small but significant group of poems in which Little departs more courageously from convention, demonstrating that she is able to combine and negotiate both Scots vernacular and Augustan English forms and idiom and that she has an insider's knowledge of the work of Burns and his predecessors as well as of her Augustan models. In these poems, Little also shows herself deeply conscious of her situation as an aspiring *woman* writer, in addition to being, like Burns, an aspiring *lower-class* writer and a *Scottish* writer. I will therefore focus here on a few examples from this particularly characterful group of Scottish-themed poems.

Although her poems have recently been discussed in the context of both Romantic period and eighteenth-century writing, it seems to me that Janet Little is most firmly rooted in the eighteenth century. Her poetry does not have that 'pre-Romantic' element which makes Burns such an interesting transitional figure. Instead, she employs in her poetry what one might call a formal decorum, choosing verse form and language register to fit her material. For example, 'On Halloween' (167) is written in Scots and in the 'bob and wheel' verse which came into eighteenth-century use through Allan Ramsay's collections of sixteenth- and seventeenth-century poetry. Little's scene is a Scottish rural scene of everyday life where the emphasis is on the friendship and sexual equality between the young people who gather to play out the folk traditions of Hallowe'en. There are no 'cutty sarks' as in Burns's *Tam o' Shanter*. Both sexes, young and old, are equally involved in the fun:

> A candle on a stick was hung,
> An' ti'd up to the kipple:
> Ilk lad an' lass, baith auld an' young,
> Did try to catch the apple;

Which aft, in spite o' a' their care,
Their furious jaws escaped;
They touch'd it ay, but did nae mair,
Though greedily they gaped,
Fu' wide that night.

The poem offers a window into Scottish folk customs and superstitions as well as displaying its confident use of Scots language and poetic form. Its participants depart 'reluctantly [. . .] In hopes [. . .] To hae sic like diversion/Some future night'.

Little's 'An Epistle to Mr Robert Burns' (160), which received no reply from the nation's Bard, is an ambitious poem despite its mock modesty. In the very writing of a poem titled 'An Epistle', one could argue that Little was addressing Burns as an equal in *kind*, as one poet to another; and in her approach to him she uses 'Standart Habbie', now commonly known as the Burns stanza, with accomplishment. There is an interesting and knowledgeable interaction between language registers and references throughout the poem as she brings forward the various qualities of Burns's poetry and the responses it arouses. 'Lov'd Thallia', the muse who 'seem'd long shut up as a recluse [. . .] Till Burns arose' takes her place alongside Burns's Caesar and Luath who 'into human nature keek,/An' knots unravel;/To hear their lectures ance a week./Ten miles I'd travel.' Although the speaker claims at the end of her poem that she herself would never have the skill to praise Burns as he should be praised:

If I should strain my rupy throat,
To raise thy praise wi' swelling note
My rude, unpolish'd strokes wad blot
        Thy brilliant shine,
An' ev'ry passage I would quote
        Seem less sublime.

the reader realises that she has indeed praised him with skill and with an appreciative understanding of the features which make his poetry outstanding as well as the traditions which nurtured him. Her poem deserved a response from the Bard.

On the other hand, 'On a Visit to Mr Burns' (111) demonstrates Little getting something of her own back for Burns's lack of courtesy in refusing to meet her or to correspond with her. Irony is the keynote of this poem and the spurned female poet is the one in control of the discourse. Since the Bard will not come to visit his admirer, she creates in poetry her own visit to him with an outcome very different from what might have been envisaged. The rhetorical questioning, exaggerated imagery and hint of breathlessness in the opening stanzas overtly suggest hero worship on the part of the imaginary speaker, while at the same time ironically subverting this.

One might find a sexual *frisson* in stanza three where the speaker remembers 'excursions made [. . .] at midnight hour' to him in her dreams; but again this is undercut by self-mockery: 'This bliss in dreams was premature,/And with my slumbers fled.' One senses that head and poetic imagination are in control in this poem, rather than the untrustworthy heart. The second half moves openly into the mock heroic when 'a dire alarm' instead of celebratory trumpets announces the arrival of the poet/hero. He, it seems, has fallen from his winged horse Pegasus and broken his arm. It is therefore left to the persona of his female admirer and fellow poet to take control of the situation and offer comfort in the form of a short sermon on human frailty:

> 'No cheering draught, with ills unmix'd,
>   Can mortals taste below;
> All human fate by heav'n is fix'd,
>   Alternate joy and wo.'

Yet in the final stanza we notice how, as so often in her writing about Burns, Little holds the balance between the mock heroic portrait of the national icon and a genuine non-ironic acknowledgement of his achievement:

> With beating breast I view'd the bard;
>   All trembling did him greet:
> With sighs bewail'd his fate so hard,
>   Whose notes were ever sweet.

My final word from Janet Little in this brief account of some of her Scottish poems is 'Given to a Lady who asked me to write a Poem' (113). This poem for her female patron is one which uses its ironic register widely to subvert not only the gender hierarchy of the two previous Burns-related poems, but also to challenge more openly the literary, national and social hierarchies of the time. The quotation marks which enclose the major part of this poem advertise its author's adoption of the persona of the kind of male critic she so dislikes (a dislike documented also in the poem 'To my Aunty'): a North British Augustan critic (perhaps one of the Edinburgh literati who tried to persuade Burns to modify his Scottishness) who dismisses all who do not conform to his views of what literature should be. The milkmaid author mocks such views by her clever playing with language registers and verse rhythms. The sense of the speaking voice is omnipresent: orality and relevant literary reference interact with each other to achieve her desired effects.

Beginning in Augustan register and iambic tetrameter rhyming couplets – 'In royal Anna's golden days,/Hard was the task to gain the bays' – the poem's decorum is quickly undermined by its imagery and by the intrusion of Scots-language elements:

142

Hard was it then the hill to climb;
Some broke a neck, some lost a limb.
The vot'ries for poetic fame
Got aff decrepit, blind an' lame:
Except that little fellow Pope,
Few ever then got near its top:
An' Homer's crutches he may thank,
Or down the brae he'd got a clank.

Stanza two recovers briefly from that demotic 'clank' when the reference to Pope's translation of *The Iliad* is joined by the 'learned age' of 'Swift, Thomson, Addison an' Young [who] made Pindus echo to their tongue'; and by 'Doctor Johnson [who] unto posterity did show/Their blunders great, their beauties few'. The word 'dead' in the phrase 'But now he's dead' then provides a significant transition point. Read with the eyes in an English-language register, but read aloud with Scots pronunciation, 'dead/deid' opens up a move into Scots for the remainder of the critic's discourse, until the milkmaid poet persona takes over in English for the final verse.

This poem makes an assault on all three hierarchies in relation to literary recognition – nation, class and gender. The Augustan 'norm', imitated by ambitious Scots writers as well as by the English, is displaced by the voice of a Scotch critic who, even while he indignantly expresses his puzzlement at Burns's temerity and success, publicises through his complaints the very different qualities offered by Burns's poetry: qualities which endorse Scottish Enlightenment values:

'Yet Burns, I'm tauld, can write wi' ease,
An' a' denominations please;
Can wi' uncommon glee impart
A usefu' lesson to the heart;
Can ilka latent thought expose,
An' Nature trace whare'er she goes [. . .]'

The poem needs to be read as a whole – and preferably read aloud – for its full effect to be appreciated, but it is noticeable even in a few excerpts how Little controls the discourse, allowing a number of viewpoints to interact with each other, while at the same time she directs her reader by means of imagery and ironic register towards what she considers the desired reading. In stanza six, gender is added to the attack as the critic splutters over the impertinence of 'a milkmaid poem-books to print', his scornful incredulity marked by the increased tempo, then by breaks in the rhythmic flow of the lines:

'A milkmaid poem-books to print:
Mair fit she wad her dairy tent;
Or labour at her spinning-wheel,
An' do her wark baith swift an' weel [. . .]
Does she, poor silly thing, pretend
The manners of our age to mend?
Mad as we are, we're wise enough
Still to despise sic paultry stuff.'

When we come to the last stanza, we notice that the inverted commas and the male critic persona have disappeared. Here we have the milkmaid poet speaking for herself. Despite the use of terms such as 'slunk' and 'dread' and 'trembles', this is not an intimidated woman, but one challenging Augustan criticism on its own English-language ground: 'My hand still trembles *when* [not *if*] I write.'

Read with attention to poetic detail, Janet Little's poems have much to tell us about the social mores and literary hierarchies of her time, and about the position of a Scots-language writer and labouring-class writer – as both Burns and she were. They speak especially, even if often implicitly or ironically, about the difficulties of a woman from the wrong class who has literary ambition and the determination to try to fulfil that ambition.

In contrast to Janet Little, Isabel Pagan was a folk poet and singer based in Muirkirk in Ayrshire. She herself could not write and a local tailor, William Gemmell, is credited with being the amanuensis for the collection of poems she published in 1808. An account of her life is given in James Paterson's *Contemporaries of Burns*. Pagan was apparently very well known for her poems and songs which documented the life of her local area. Paterson comments that she was 'famed for her sarcastic wit, as well as for her vocal powers' and that 'her cottage may be truly said to have been the favourite *howff* of all the drunken wags and "drouthy neeebors" in the district'.[9] In her 'Account of the Author's lifetime', she herself writes:

But a' the whole tract of my time,
I found myself inclin'd to rhyme:
When I see merry company,
I sing a song with mirth and glee.[10]

Her verses both celebrate and castigate or mock the characters and activities of Muirkirk, praising benefactors and decrying a growing lack of honesty in present day dealings. There are songs about the shooting parties on whom she depends for patronage, and in some of these she laments the fact that the 'new sportsmen' who now come to the area do not ask after her, thus reducing her income. There is no 'proto-feminist' agenda

144

in Pagan's poems and songs, but we understand from them how difficult it must have been for a woman in her situation to support herself. Several verses advocate adaptability and praise contentment as a virtue or invent scenarios where marrying for wealth is rejected in favour of a love-match, as in 'The Gear and the Blathrie o't' (14–16):

> Some they do marry for riches in store,
> But wisdom and virtue are what I marry more;
> If riches is the motive that makes you tie the knot,
> You will soon curse the gear and the blathrie o't.

Some verses have the name of a popular tune attached, such as 'Campbells is coming' for 'The Duke of Gordon's Fencibles' (16); or 'The Flowers of the Forest' air of Jean Elliot's famous song which is used by Pagan both for 'McLellan's Lament for his Master's Death' (54) and, less suitably (in relation to the matching of words and melody), for a song of happiness at finding true love: 'For he was my choice, and he has been my fortune/And who lives so happy as Johnny and me' (67).

As with Janet Little, Isabel Pagan's name does not appear in most recent guides to Scottish literature, but she does appear as the author of a version of the song 'Ca' the Yowes to the Knowes' (usually ascribed to Burns) in both Kerrigan's *Anthology of Scottish Women Poets* and in Bold's article in *A History of Scottish Women Writers*. It is clear from Paterson's account that her claim to the authorship of the song was a subject of discussion in her own time and throughout the nineteenth century; and this claim would appear to have been furthered in the twentieth century as a result of the growth of feminist studies. Paterson himself seems doubtful about Pagan's authorship, commenting that 'this is a sweet little lyric; and its superiority to the other known effusions of Isobel is well calculated to raise a doubt whether it be really hers or not'.[11] In regard to the claim for Burns's authorship, Burns's letter to George Thomson of September 1794, which accompanied his reworking of the song, makes it clear that he believed it was due to him that 'ever it saw the light':

> About seven years ago, I was well acquainted with a worthy little fellow of a Clergyman, a Mr Clunzie, who sung it charmingly; & at my request, Mr Clarke took it down from his singing. When I gave it to Johnson, I added some Stanzas to the song & mended others, but still it will not do for *you*. In a solitary stroll which I took today, I tried my hand on a few pastoral lines, following up the idea of the chorus, which I would preserve. Here it is, with all its crudities & imperfections on its head.[12]

James Kinsley and Donald Low include both versions of 'Ca' the Yowes' in their respective collections of Burns's poems and songs; Kerrigan's 'Isobel Pagan' version is derived from the 'mended' version Burns sent to Johnson; Paterson begins his article on Pagan with the mended version minus its significant third stanza where the girl questions her suitor's motives ('omitted for its indelicacy'); and Tom Crawford's anthology *Love, Labour and Liberty* adds to the confusion by including a fragmentary version of a song called 'Ca' the Ewes' among its dialogue and work poems.[13] Crawford's fragment strongly suggests that the origins of the song are in the folk tradition:

> Ye's get a maid baith stout and stark
> To milk yere kye and work your wark,
> And I will kiss you i' the dark –
> My bonny dearie.
> *Ca' the ewes etc.*

(Crawford 40)

In his Introduction to *The Songs of Robert Burns*, Donald Low emphasises that 'a Burns song should be thought of in terms of the union of its words and melody. [. . .] When words and melody have been heard together (and not before) we are entitled to ask: do the words suit the tune, and does the tune gain in performance by the words Burns has given it?'[14] This is a useful test to apply to the two contested versions of 'Ca' the Yowes', but it is a test more easily and confidently applied through the act of singing as opposed to discussion on the printed page. Here below is the melody which is given for both versions of the song, together with the shared chorus and a stanza of the Burns/Thomson version.

260   *Ca' the yowes to the knowes*

Tune: *Ca' the yowes*

CHORUS   Ca' the yowes to the knowes, Ca' them whare the hea-ther grows,

Ca' them whare the bur-nie rowes, My bon-ie Dea-rie.

> Ca' the yowes to the knowes,
> Ca' them whare the heather grows,
> Ca them whare the burnie rowes,
> My bonie Dearie.

146

Hark, the mavis' evening sang
 Sounding Clouden's woods amang;
Then a faulding let us gang,
 My bonie Dearie.

(Kinsley 585)

We notice from the above (and from the rest of this well-known version) how appropriately melody and words interact with each other. The tempo is marked 'slow' and the trochaic metre of chorus and stanza, with its emphasis on the first syllable, together with the predominance of long vowels – *au, aa, aw, oo, ee* – in words given Scots-language pronunciation (*whare the heather grows; sounding Clouden's woods*) allows the music to linger and to develop that mood of idealised longing, a mixture of sweetness and potential sadness, which is characteristic of much early Romantic-period *lied* and which occurs in several of the late songs of Burns.

On the other hand, the singer attempting the first version of the song, whether it be by Pagan or Burns, immediately becomes aware of some incongruity in relation to the matching of words and melody. The chorus is the same in both versions (apart from the spelling of 'ewes' in the first), with trochaic metre and long vowels. However, instead of continuing this pattern as in the song sent to Thomson, the stanzas of the earlier version move to a predominantly iambic metre and employ shorter vowel sounds which push the singer towards a more lively, skipping pace as opposed to the 'slow' demanded by the printed tune:

As I gaed down the water-side
There I met my Shepherd-lad,
He row'd me sweetly in his plaid,
 And he ca'd me his Dearie.
 Ca' the etc.

(Kinsley 294)

The sense of this being a different *kind* of song from the Thomson version is strengthened when we add stanza three, generally accepted by Burns scholars as having been one of his additions and the stanza omitted by Paterson because of its 'indelicacy'. In this stanza the girl gives a strong-minded response to her lover's suggestion that they 'gang doon the water-side':

I was bred up at nae sic school,
My Shepherd-lad, to play the fool;
And a' the day to sit in dool,
 And naebody to see me.

(Kinsley 294)

147

And her response seems to achieve the desired effect since the lad promises 'gowns and ribbons meet,/Cauf-leather shoon upon your feet'. What we have here is a folk poem of a love-dialogue kind (although more sophisticated than the labouring version included by Crawford) where a youth and girl argue out their conditions for taking each other as partners. It has a long history in folk culture and a history also of passing into more sophisticated literary culture as, for example, in Christopher Marlowe's late sixteenth-century lyric 'Come live with me and be my love' and Walter Raleigh's response 'If all the world and love were young'.[15] The form frequently appears in Romantic period German *lieder* and its influence can be seen in a Burns song such as 'Last May a braw woo'er' where, although the girl is the only speaker present, her narrative communicates the interactive dialogue with her lover. What this kind of folk dialogue needs, musically, is a lively tempo which allows the argument to be passed backwards and forwards between the characters. And this change of pace and mood is what the *singer* recognises is necessary in order to present the first version of 'Ca' the Ewes' authentically. In contrast, Burns's 'revisioning' of the folk song source in his second version transforms it into a conscious artistic work of the early Romantic period, just as Hugh MacDiarmid in a later time was to transform the folk song 'Jenny Nettles' into the modernist poem 'Empty Vessel'.

From such a comparison of the two versions of the song as well as from a reading of the poems in Isabel Pagan's collection, I myself would conclude that it is most unlikely that she was the *originator* of the first version. It does not appear in her printed collection and there is no poem in the collection that matches it in sophistication. If this song was indeed in her repertoire, then my view would be that she would sing it as a 'tradition-bearer' and that what she sang may have been a version of the song existing before Burns began his mending of it. To say this is not to be reductive either towards Isabel Pagan or folk song. The debate about authorship is interesting, not because of any wish to dethrone Pagan in favour of Burns, but because it shows how source material can be transmitted and transformed in the hands of different kinds of poets. It also demonstrates the negative effect of our neglect of oral tradition and song culture in favour of print-based literature. We no longer know how to judge and present the various forms of our 'traditional' culture.

One of Burns's reasons for rewriting the words of songs in his late great song-collecting period was that he felt that the *tune* – often a traditional fiddle tune – was the locus of national identity. Where he felt that the words which had come with a tune were inferior to the quality of the tune itself, then he rewrote them to make them worthy. One tune which meant much to him was 'Hey tuttie taitie' which he said 'often filled my eye with tears'.[16] Burns associated this melody with Robert the Bruce's March to Bannockburn for which he composed the poem 'Scots Wha Hae', the words of which bring together sentiments of national identity and freedom. In this final part of my discussion of the contribution of women poets and songwriters to eighteenth-century culture, I will compare Burns's 'Scots Wha Hae' with the use of the same 'Hey tuttie taitie' melody by Lady Nairne for her song 'The Land of the Leal', believed to have been written to comfort a friend who had lost her first child.

Lady Nairne is representative of the many upper-class educated women who yet were familiar with Scots language and culture and who, apart from Burns, were the principal *composers* of Scottish traditional song in the eighteeenth century. Her songs were immensely popular and she had clearly learned from the example of Burns. Indeed, as she published anonymously, many of her songs were for many years thought to have been written by Burns himself. In *Lady Nairne and her Songs*, first published in the late nineteenth century, the Rev. George Henderson of Perthshire suggests that she consciously followed Burns in 'the purifying of national song' from 'coarse and worthless words'. He also quotes the view expressed by the notable critic David Masson:

> There is a real moral worth in them all, and all have that genuine characteristic of a song which consists of an inner tune preceding and inspiring the words, and coiling the words, as it were, out of the heart along with it.[17]

The musicologist Francis Collinson described songs such as 'The Auld Hoose' and the Jacobite 'Will ye no come back again' as 'treasures of Scots song for all time'.[18]

'The Land of the Leal' is one of the songs that was for many years attributed to Burns and much confusion and argument grew up around it. Of more relevance to my current exploration of women's writing, however, is Nairne's transformation of the 'Hey tuttie taitie' melody from Burns's martial context to a female-centred song of loss and comfort. Here is Burns's 'Scots Wha Hae' with its martial tempo and dotted rhythms which combine with his words to create a rousing call to *act* for freedom.

Tune: *Hey, tutti taitie*

246   *Scots, Wha Hae wi' Wallace bled*

Scots, wha hae wi' Wal- lace bled, Scots, wham Bruce has af- ten led,

Wel - come to your gor - y bed   Or to vic - tor - ie!

Now's the day, and now's the hour; See the front o' bat- tle lour,

See ap- proach proud Ed - ward's power –   Chains and sla- ver- ie!

149

When we turn to Lady Nairne's song, on the other hand, we might well not recognise that we have the same tune. The tempo of the melody has been slowed, so that the dotted notes are not so 'staccato' in nature, but have been evened out; her choice of words provides long vowels which again extend the musical phrase, allowing it to linger, instead of giving it the marching quality which pushes it onwards in the Burns song.

208 *Land o' the Leal*

The sentiments in the song draw on that eighteenth-century belief in our capacity to empathise with those less fortunate than ourselves. Although Nairne has been criticised in modern times for sentimentality, the feeling expressed in these songs, although full of sentiment and piety, is very different from later Victorian-period sentimentality and piousness. There is a real sense of pain communicated in the *sound* of the second stanza phrase 'And oh we *grudged her sair*/to the Land o' the Leal'.

This is a very beautiful and moving song, which achieves its emotional effect through its long, slow phrases, and the intimate, lingering 'John' breathed out at the end of the phrase. It is a very different treatment of 'Hey tuttie taitie' from what we find in Burns's 'Scots Wha Hae', yet it does have some affinities with songs like Burns's 'John Anderson, my Jo' which also communicates its feeling through a slow tempo and the repetition of the 'my jo, John' phrase. This repeated intimate 'John' in both songs has the effect of being breathed or sighed out in relation to the content of the song, while the *j* consonant moving into the broad *aw* vowel allows the singer quietly to sustain the sound.[19]

Lady Nairne's songs may be more limited in range than those of Burns, more conventional in their aspiring, but like the songs of Burns they have drawn from and have become part of a many-stranded tradition of vocal music in Lowland Scotland. In addition, as with the literary poetry of Janet Little and the folk poetry of Isabel Pagan, Nairne's composed songs make available to us perspectives from the women of the period, so that our understanding is stretched beyond the customary accounts of male-centred philosophy, historical studies and poetry. Women's values should have their place in the documenting of our times.

Notes

1. Roger Lonsdale (Ed.), *Eighteenth Century Women Poets: An Oxford Anthology* (Oxford: Oxford University Press, 1990), p. xxi.
2. Thomas Crawford, *Society and the Lyric: A Study of the Song Culture of Eighteenth Century Scotland* (Edinburgh: Scottish Academic Press, 1979), p. 1.
3. A brief account of Janet Little can be found in James Paterson, *The Contemporaries of Burns and the More Recent Poets of Ayrshire* (Edinburgh: Hugh Paton, Carver & Gilder, 1840), pp. 78–91. She is included in Lonsdale's anthology, pp. 453–5. There is also information about her throughout *Robert Burns and Mrs Dunlop: Correspondence Now Published in Full for the First Time* (London: Hodder and Stoughton, 1898). The phrase 'The Scotch Milkmaid' was used by Little in the title of her collection of poems of 1792, *The Poetical Works of Janet Little the Scotch Milkmaid*, published by subscription and printed by John & Peter Wilson

in Ayr. Quotations from individual poems will be referenced by page number after the title of the poem.

4. *Robert Burns and Mrs Dunlop*, pp. 226, 228.

5. Ibid, p. 204.

6. In addition, my own article 'Women, Poetry and Song in Lowland Scotland', which includes discussion of Janet Little, was published in a Scottish issue of *Women's Writing* 10.3, 2003, pp. 453–68.

7. Hilton Brown, 'Robert Burns and the Scottish Milkmaid', *Burns Chronicle* 2nd series 25 (1950), pp. 15, 20.

8. Donna Landry, *The Muses of Resistance: Laboring-Class Women's Poetry in Britain, 1739–1796* (Cambridge: Cambridge University Press, 1990), pp. 217–37.

9. *Contemporaries of Burns*, pp. 113–23 (p. 116).

10. Isabel Pagan, *A Collection of Poems on Several Occasions by Isabel Pagan* (Glasgow: Niven, Napier & Khull, 1808), pp. 3–4. Paterson spells her Christian name 'Isobel', but it is spelled with an 'a' in the title of her collection. Quotations will be referenced by page number after title of poem.

11. *Contemporaries of Burns*, p. 113.

12. Robert Burns, Letter to George Thomson, *The Letters of Robert Burns* 2nd edn, ed. by G. Ross Roy, vol. 2 1790–1796 (Oxford: Clarendon Press, 1985), pp. 305–6.

13. James Kinsley (ed.), *Burns: Poems and Songs* paperback edn (Oxford: Oxford University Press, 1971), pp. 294, 585; Donald Low (ed.), *The Songs of Robert Burns* (London: Routledge, 1993), pp. 218, 664; *Contemporaries of Robert Burns*, p. 113; Thomas Crawford (ed.), *Love, Labour and Liberty: The Eighteenth-Century Scottish Lyric* (Manchester: Carcanet Press, 1976), p. 40.

14. Low, Introduction, *The Songs of Robert Burns*, p. 2.

15. Kenneth Muir (ed.), *Elizabethan Lyrics: A Critical Anthology* (London: Harrap, 1952), pp. 69–70, 70–1.

16. Letter from Burns to George Thomson [about 30 Aug 1793], *The Letters of Robert Burns*, vol. 2, p. 235.

17. George Henderson, *Lady Nairne and her Songs* third edn (Paisley and London: Alexander Gardner, 1905), p. 51.

18. Francis Collinson, *The Traditional and National Music of Scotland* (London: Routledge, 1970), p. 131.

19. In her contribution to Robert Crawford's *Robert Burns and Cultural Authority* (Edinburgh: Edinburgh University Press, 1997), pp. 46–8, Kirsteen McCue mentions the conviction of Alexander Crichton that 'The Land of the Leal' was Burns's 'deathbed valediction' and that 'John' at the end of the lines should be 'Jean' in reference to Jean Armour. This, however, is another example where proof lies in the *singing*. The substitution of the narrow-vowelled 'Jean' completely destroys the complex of emotional effects achieved by 'John' with its capacity for gentle, sustained sound. Burns would never have made such a mistake. Nor would Lady Nairne.

E. MAIRI MACARTHUR

Fresh fields for inquiry: travellers to the Highlands in the eighteenth century

He desired pastures new, fresh fields for inquiry

This simple sentence, from the biographical sketch of Richard Pococke, Archdeacon of Dublin, neatly encapsulates the spirit of his times: the late eighteenth century, the Age of Enlightenment. Born in Southampton in 1704, Pococke travelled widely in Europe as a young man, this being an accepted part of a gentleman's education. Then, over three visits – the last of which was in 1760 – he rode on horseback all over Scotland and as far north as the Orkney Isles.[1] Through the letters which record this experience we glimpse something of life and landscape in the middle of the century which is the subject of this volume.

Anyone studying the general or local history of the Highlands can spend many absorbing hours poring over the impressions of the men of science, letters and the church who sought to journey, both literally and intellectually, into uncharted territory at this period. The tour undertaken in 1773 by Dr Samuel Johnson, along with his companion James Boswell, was to become perhaps the most famous of such excursions and, as with Pococke, had the lure of novelty at its heart. Johnson had declared himself 'much pleased' with Skyeman Martin Martin's rich account of the Western Isles at the close of the seventeenth century. He had read this at an early age and it had instilled 'a notion that we might there contemplate a system of life almost totally different from what we had been accustomed to see.'[2]

Such outsider observations provide a valuable addition to our understanding of the topography, economy, society and culture of a part of the country where surviving written sources from an inside perspective are meagre. Travellers to the Highlands remain, understandably, a source of fascination and aspects of the topic have been dealt with over the years in a range of articles and anthologies.[3] A major contribution has been made recently with the completion of a PhD thesis by German scholar Martin Rackwitz: 'Travels to terra incognita: the Scottish Highlands and Hebrides in early modern travellers' accounts ca. 1600 to 1800'.[4] This outstanding and comprehensive study not only examines the journeys and accounts from over a hundred visitors, in the context of social and economic changes then underway, but also, crucially, looks back to the Middle Ages and the myth-ridden images of Scotland which help explain its status for so long as 'unknown land'.

A short paper such as this can only summarise what motivated the travellers and highlight a few examples of their written legacy. The pattern through the eighteenth century, however, is by no means even. If a travel documentary team was transported back three hundred years, it would find suitable subjects thin on Scottish ground in the early 1700s. This was partly due to the practical obstacles of rough countryside and poor communications. Real improvement only began with General Wade's road-building programme from 1725, later followed by the pacification, as it was perceived, of the Highlands in the aftermath of the 1745 Jacobite uprising. Edmund Burt, sent north at the start of the Wade road project, as rent collector from the forfeited estates, stressed how inaccessible, in every way, the area appeared:[5]

> The Highlands are but little known even to the inhabitants of the low country of Scotland, for they have ever dreaded the difficulties and dangers of trav-elling among the mountains . . . But to the people of England, excepting some few, and those chiefly the soldiery, the Highlands are hardly known at all: for there has been less, that I know of, written upon the subject, than of either of the Indies.

A glance through the pages of *A Contribution to the Bibliography of Scottish Topography*, begun by Sir Arthur Mitchell and brought into print by C. G. Cash, confirms the patchy picture.[6] A handful of travel accounts were then extant from the first decades of the eighteenth century; only by the last quarter did this trickle swell to a steady stream. Psychological barriers, too, made a venture north a daunting prospect. What, one wonders, was in the letter from 1701 listed by Mitchell and Cash: *Scotland charac-terised . . . to a young gentleman to dissuade him from an intended journey thither*? And what did *The Comical Pilgrim* in 1722 actually contain, subtitled *Travels of a cynick philosopher thro' the most wicked parts of the world, namely England, Wales, Scotland, Ireland and Holland (etc) (mainly abusive)*? Scurrilous and satirical accounts of Scotland did abound in the seventeenth and eighteenth centuries, reinforcing stereotypical views of a barbarous people surviving in an untamed wilderness. These must have acted as a deterrent to many.

In the dedication to his *Tour in Scotland*, undertaken in 1769, zoologist Thomas Pennant admitted to a revelation similar to that of Pococke or Johnson: '. . . struck therefore with the reflection of never having seen Scotland, I instantly ordered my baggage to be got ready and in a reasonable time found myself on the banks of the Tweed.'[7] Though the initial impression here is of transportation by the magic cap or scarf of folk-tale, the traveller still faced an arduous journey, inhospitable terrain and accommodation that offered few home comforts. Professor Thomas Garnett shared his hut on Iona with what he termed 'the light infantry etc in the beds', several chickens, a tame lamb, two or three pigs, a dog and some cats who skulked in and out of the thatch all night; in Fort William he found the service bad and the beds quite simply 'abominable', though in Inverness he was pleased to report that Mrs Ettles kept a very civil and reasonable inn.[8] For his part, John Knox calculated that he had covered some 3,000 miles in the final six months of 1764, calling it 'a hazardous and fatiguing enterprise'.[9]

Why then did they travel north at all? Firstly, many of the visitors from the second half of the century were actively curious. They were imbued with that spirit of inquiry alluded to earlier; they came to observe with their own eyes the natural environment, the economic state, the human condition and the social mores of an area that had, until recently, seemed virtually impenetrable.

Several of the most useful accounts did not result simply from a desire to travel for its own sake, however. The Reverend John Walker, who was also a botanist and geologist, combined in his Hebridean tours of 1764 two reports he had been specially commissioned to write: one on education and religion for the General Assembly of the Church of Scotland; the other a survey of agriculture, fishing and industry for the Commissioners of the Annexed Estates.[10] These resulted in a mass of detail on just about everything, including stock rearing and tools for tillage, types and yields of grain, transport and clothing, population density and rental values, and the vestige of 'whatever is marvellous and supernatural' in the people's religious observance.

That same year, 1764, brought John Knox to the Highlands for the first time 'through motives of curiosity' but the poverty and distress of the people made an impression which, he wrote, 'has ever since engaged my thoughts'. It was this that led eventually to a commission in 1786 to tour the Highlands and Hebrides at the behest of the British Society for Extending the Fisheries. Thomas Garnett was driven by similar intentions. Professor of Natural Philosophy and Chemistry in the Royal Institute of Great Britain, he was conscious of the agricultural and economic changes afoot in the Highlands and had improvement as an avowed aim:

> I expect that what I have said of the wretched situation of the inhabitants
> . . . will give offence to some persons, and particularly to those who have it
> in their power to ameliorate their condition; but I was activated only by a
> desire to increase the comforts and remove the distresses of the natives.

These travellers were aware of each other's trips and accounts. Garnett paid tribute to Thomas Pennant's 'excellent Tour', admired also by Dr Johnson. Knox praised both Pennant and Johnson and the good Doctor's journal became, in time, probably the most quoted book in the annals of travel literature with many following quite literally in his steps. Maximilien Lazowski, who visited the Highlands in 1786 as companion to Alexandre de La Rochefoucauld, had dinner in Edinburgh with Dr John Walker.[11] Draughtsmen often accompanied these gentlemen and, encouraged by the Society of Antiquaries – founded in London in 1707 and then in Scotland in 1780 – a market soon developed for topographical prints. The illustrations in many travellers' accounts are a real bonus, for these captured not only antiquities and scenery but also housing, boats, field patterns, people. Especially memorable, for example, are some of the sketches in Pennant: conical sheilings on Jura; men spearing a shark in Lochranza Bay; women on Skye turning a quernstone and waulking tweed with their feet. The names of Moses Griffiths, John Cleveley and W. H. Watts, for example, deserve as much recognition as those of Pennant, Banks and Garnett with whom, respectively, they journeyed. The authors of a book on Iona through the eyes of artists make a convincing case that the study of that island's history has benefited greatly from the sketches and paintings, at various stages, of the famed ecclesiastical remains.[12] The earliest, and among the most charming, depictions of Iona come from the late eighteenth century.

The notion of the Highlands as hunting and fishing grounds is usually considered a Victorian preoccupation but Dennis Rixson devotes an interesting chapter to the draw of sport over a much longer period. It became a specific attraction once the region began to open up in the late 1700s. He cites Faujas de Saint Fond, the French geologist, who was ascending Ben More on Mull in 1784 with the young Maclean of Torloisk, when the latter offered the visitor use of guns and dogs, 'for he could not imagine that we should wish to climb so rugged a mountain for any other purpose than the pleasures of the chase, which he passionately loved himself.'[13]

This same rugged scenery, once frightful and ominous, came to be a strong pull in itself. As the century wore on, the Highland hills were transformed into a backdrop of sublime splendour, the picturesque setting for a heroic and mythical past, as the Romantics of art and literature moved into full gear and Ossian stepped into the limelight, courtesy of James Macpherson and his purported translations of the ancient bard's verse. The immense enthusiasm, at home and abroad, which greeted Macpherson in the 1760s has been well documented and is addressed elsewhere in this volume. And the impact is reflected in many travellers' accounts. For instance, Garnett regretted that the grandeur of Glencoe, 'this stupendous scene' as drawn for him by Watts, could not be adequately conveyed on paper:

> On the right is Malmor, a mountain celebrated by Ossian; on the left Con Fion, or the hill of Fingal. The valley is closed by some other grotesque mountains, which were almost covered with mist, and which seemed to shut the inhabitants of this romantic glen completely from the world.

Dr Johnson, on the other hand, clashed famously and publicly with Macpherson, challenging the authenticity of his published work.

One travel experience which brings together scientific curiosity and Ossianic fervour is that of Joseph Banks who, in 1772 and en route for Iceland, was delayed off the coast of Morvern. There he heard about the wonders of Staffa and about the greatest of its caves – whose name may first have meant 'the melodious one', Uamh Bhinn, but now became irrevocably linked with Fionn or Fingal, reputedly the father of Macpherson's Ossian. 'Compared to this', wrote Banks of Fingal's Cave, 'what are the cathedrals or the palaces built by man? . . . Where is now the boast of the architect?' Donald B. MacCulloch records that there could be a downside to the glowing and fantastical descriptions of Staffa which swiftly followed Banks's account, published in the *Gentleman's Magazine* and *Scots Magazine* and incorporated into Pennant's *Tour*.[14] One pilgrim asked the boatman at Ulva to sail him in and out of the marble pillars of Staffa, as if through trees in a forest. When told that the island was in fact composed of black rock, massed together, he packed up and left in disgust. Another was so sea-sick that he begged the boatman to turn back and vowed he would leave in his will a forfeiture of every penny of his property if his heirs ever dared to visit Staffa.

Harsh reality had a habit of impinging on a visitor's overly romantic anticipation. Edward Clarke, Professor of Mineralogy in Cambridge University, stepped ashore on Iona in 1797, recalling the words of Dr Johnson as he did so:[15]

> We were now treading that illustrious island, which was once the luminary of the Caledonian regions, whence savage clans and roving barbarians derived the benefits of knowledge and the blessings of religion.

At once, however, he was assailed by a crowd of locals, whom he viewed as:

> . . . a dismaying spectacle . . . a miserable idiot grinned horribly in my face, while on my right hand a raving lunatic, seizing my elbow, uttered in my ears a loud and fearful cry . . . It seemed the hospital of the Hebrides, a general infirmary for the reception of every malady that could afflict human nature . . . A few trifling donations soon dispersed the major part of this melancholy assembly, all but the madman . . .

By this last, relatively benign, term he meant the guide. Clarke's problem was this: 'All the warm feelings excited by the ruins of Iona or the retrospect of its former glory were in one moment obliterated.' He had been prevented from basking in a Dr Johnson moment.

Had Clarke stayed longer, would the experience have been more balanced? Most visitors gained only fleeting impressions, from a few hours ashore somewhere or at most a day and night in one place, although their accumulative experience, plodding across whole areas of the country, often adds up to something substantial. Even if someone came from the outside to dwell for a number of years, as missionary minister

John Lane Buchanan did between 1782 and 1790 in Harris, there could be pitfalls.[16] Buchanan was born and educated in the Lowlands although his surname implies a family link with the Hebrides and he spoke Gaelic. The meticulous information he gathered – on natural history, cultivation, animal husbandry, housing, dress, customs – is of great interest today. Unfortunately, it also includes personal, highly critical attacks on individual tacksmen and clergy, some of them witnesses in the Presbytery prosecution of Buchanan, on grounds of sexual misconduct. For this he was eventually deposed. An extended stay, in this case, clearly led to some serious falling-out and undermines the overall value of his journal.

In conclusion, eighteenth-century visitors to the Highlands and Islands were inspired or instructed to trek north for a variety of reasons. Whatever the motive, however, they were alert to a wide range of topics and concerns and have bequeathed a wealth of fascinating detail on a host of subjects relevant to the life of the people. As with all sources, travel accounts are most usefully considered alongside other material: parish or estate documents, statistical records, oral testimony, archaeological evidence and so on. They can also be a highly enjoyable read. This paper closes with a sample of the vivid 'word pictures' which enliven many of the texts and stay in the reader's mind.

Bishop Pococke, in a poor woman's house on Iona, received a wooden vessel of new milk which was passed around those present in a simple ceremony. By contrast, under the hospitable roof of Maclean of Torloisk on nearby Mull, Faujas de Saint Fond breakfasted on oatcake and barley bread, smoked beef, salt herring and cheese served on mahogany trays, eggs and cream, jams and jelly, tea, coffee and Jamaica rum.

On Skye, a young couple pursued Pennant and the minister, who was going part of the same route, 'in order to have their nuptials celebrated'. So a cottage was commandeered, the minister performed the ceremony there and then, and Pennant observed, with amusement, that 'the bridegroom put all the powers of magic to defiance, for he was married with both shoes tied with their latchet.'[17]

Maximilien Lazowski got nearer than he expected to the Jacobite experience when he asked a boatman hired in Fort William about the young Pretender: '. . . and after that our conversation became really interesting. His first response was to raise the sleeve of his jacket and show me a long scar on his wrist: "My memento of Culloden" he said.'

At Loch Arnisdale John Knox described a charming sight as, within a gunshot of the shore, salmon played in among a shoal of herring: 'It may be supposed that every fish partook of the enjoyment which leaping out of the sea, in a fine sunshine day, afforded.'

The new century was to bring much improvement in stage-coach services, more inns and guidebooks, the graceful passenger steamships and, eventually, the railway. There are hints of Oban's future role as a busy gateway to the Western Highlands even as the eighteenth century closed. George Douglas arrived there in the summer of 1800:[18]

> Every apartment of the small inn is occupied by tourists . . . the Hon. Mr Ward is at present here with a large party and the Hon. Mrs Murray is also exercising her graphic talents in an adjoining lodging . . . we consider ourselves lucky in getting any accommodation whatever. I find my friend Auchterlony with his fellow Pedestrian tourists were here two days ago and seem much delighted with their excursions.

The writings left by the ambulant observers of the age that had just passed, seeking out their own 'fresh fields for inquiry', have informed and delighted very many of us ever since.

Notes

1 *Pococke's Tours in Scotland*, edited by D. W. Kemp (Scottish History Society, Edinburgh, Volume 1, 1887).
2 Samuel Johnson, *A Journey to the Western Islands of Scotland* [1773] (1st edn, London, 1775). Martin Martin, *A Description of the Western Islands of Scotland* (1st edn, London, 1703).
3 For example: T. C. Smout, 'Tours in the Scottish Highlands from the Eighteenth to the Twentieth Centuries' in *Northern Scotland* vol. V (1982), pp. 99–121; E. M. MacArthur, 'Among Sublime Prospects: Travel Writers and the Highlands' in *The Polar Twins*, edited by Edward J. Cowan and Douglas Gifford (John Donald Publishers, 1999), pp 171–186; Elizabeth Bray, *The Discovery of the Hebrides: Voyages to the Western Isles 1745–1883* (Edinburgh, 1996); Derek Cooper, *Road to the Isles: Travellers in the Hebrides 1770–1914* (Routledge & Kegan Paul, 1979; MacMillan, 2002); Denis Rixson, *The Hebridean Traveller* (Birlinn, 2004).
4 Supervised by Professor Dr Thomas Riis, University of Kiel, and by Professor Allan Macinnes, University of Aberdeen, and examined in 2004; available online (e-diss.uni-kiel.de/diss_1362/).
5 Edmund Burt, *Letters from a Gentleman in the North of Scotland to His Friend in London*, 2 volumes (1st edn, London, 1754).
6 A. Mitchell and C.G. Cash, *A Contribution to the Bibliography of Scottish Topography* (1917).

7   Thomas Pennant, *A Tour in Scotland and Voyage to the Hebrides 1772*, 2 volumes (London, 1776).

8   Thomas Garnett, *Observations on a Tour through the Highlands and part of the Western Isles of Scotland*, 2 volumes (London, 1810); the tour was in 1798.

9   John Knox, *A Tour through the Highlands of Scotland and the Hebride Isles in 1786* (London, 1787).

10 John Walker, *Report on the Hebrides of 1764 and 1771*, edited by M. M. Mackay (Edinburgh, 1980).

11 *To the Highlands in 1786: the Inquisitive Journey of a Young French Aristocrat*, edited and translated by Norman Scarfe (Boydell Press, 2001); original by Francis and Alexandre de la Rochefoucauld and Maximilien Lazowski.

12 J. Christian and C. Stiller, *Iona Portrayed. The Island through Artists' Eyes 1760–1960* (New Iona Press, 2000).

13 B. Faujas de St Fond, *Travels in England, Scotland and the Hebrides*, 2 volumes (London, 1799). See Rixson, note 3 above.

14 Donald B. MacCulloch, *The Wondrous Isle of Staffa* (1st edn, Glasgow, 1927).

15 W. Otter, *The Life and Remains of Edward Daniel Clarke* (London, 1825) vol. 1, chapter 4.

16 John Lane Buchanan, *Travels in the Western Hebrides from 1782–1790* (1st edition, 1793); reproduced 1997 by Maclean Press, with introduction by Dr Alasdair Maclean.

17 During the ASLS conference, a selection of travel accounts were on display in the Sabhal Mòr Ostaig library. Entirely by coincidence, Pennant's *Tour* was open at the page explaining this belief, namely that to ensure the success of his wedding night, a groom should leave one shoe-lace untied.

18 George Douglas, 'Tour in Hebrides AD 1800' (National Library of Scotland, MS 213). He mentions the Hon. Mrs Sarah Murray of Kensington whose book *A Companion and Useful Guide to the Beauties in the West Highlands of Scotland and in the Hebrides* appeared in 1803, with much practical advice for the benefit of nineteenth-century travellers.

DOMHNALL UILLEAM STIÙBHART

Highland rogues and the roots of Highland Romanticism

The second most famous anecdote concerning the late-seventeenth-century poet Màiri nighean Alasdair Ruaidh recounts how MacLeod of Dunvegan – possibly Ruairidh son of Iain Breac – forbade her for a second time to make poetry, this time neither within nor without her house. She is supposed to have composed her work standing over the *maide-buinn*, the threshold.[1]

Clearly, this anecdote can be unpacked in a number of ways. It alludes to the well-known Gaelic *adunaton*, usually in the form of a riddle, concerning an item found neither inside nor outside the house. *Glutadh*, peat-dust insulation, is the canonical, if not the most interesting, answer. The tale also suggests how Màiri's songs, and indeed Màiri herself, were regarded not only by posterity, but perhaps also by her contemporaries. Her work was a synthesis: both public, in the sense that it dealt – overtly and covertly – with political themes; and personal, in the sense that its genre, its metre, its starting-point, were specifically female and therefore ostensibly domestic in character. Her compositions are for within the home, and also for without. Màiri herself is neither entirely in the domestic nor in the public sphere.

Returning to the anecdote once more, one can be relatively certain that it also refers to a specific method of *dèanamh na frìthe*, a procedure of divination in which the diviner walks in a circle about the fire reciting a rhyme, goes to the threshold, opens his or her eyes, and then interprets the future according to the first living creatures seen.[2] Màiri nighean Alasdair Ruaidh's position in tradition is thus emphatically liminal, not just between the public and the personal, between male and female, but indeed between this world and what was to come.

The theme of 'crossing the Highland [and for that matter Lowland] Line' allows the writer to stand astride quite a few thresholds, real or imaginary, useful or arbitrary: Gàidhealtachd and Galldachd; Scotland and England; orality and text; turns of the century; poetry and song; perhaps also feminine and masculine.

The fundamental importance of song – and indeed all forms of heightened language – must be emphasised, in a Gaelic world saturated by words in all their forms, from the Ossianic epic to the briefest anecdote, from prayer to charm to curse to work-song. These were sung, chanted, recited and discussed from dawn to dusk and beyond. In the absence of outside institutions, the crucial importance of the spoken or sung word in shaping and controlling social norms cannot be stressed too highly. The position of the poet as arbiter of public reputation was paramount. Thus we find the Rev. Alexander MacDonald of Islandfinnan requesting that a MacMhuirich bard aid him in the social control of his parish, and his son, the great poet Alasdair mac Mhaighstir Alasdair, performing the same role himself as a catechist in Ardnamurchan in the 1730s.[3] But we must be careful: about the same time Allan Ramsay is being asked to compose a poem 'lashing this Goth [who had] blown up with gunpowder the ancient Celtick stones of Abury'.[4] As ever, we are not dealing with absolute differences between the two halves of Scotland, but rather differences in emphases.

Another basic point concerns the sheer difficulty faced by any scholar attempting to wrestle with the protean nature of Gaelic oral tradition, a tradition whose allusiveness is remarkable even by European standards.[5] A number of interpretations were proposed above for one single anecdote, one single piece of 'heightened language'. What then of the vast corpus of Gaelic poetry, or rather, what of Gaelic song? The situation here is even more intractable. In Scottish Gaelic culture there is a notable lack of ballads in which a story is narrated within and through the song itself. Rather, the audience is expected to be acquainted with the narrative already, to recognise the allusions, to be fine-tuned to the performer's message. Political content is often even more allusive, above all in the majority of songs which tend to be sung from an oppositional, usually Jacobite, perspective, dissenting from the authorities of the day whether local or national, created and performed within a culture where the need to secure assent from a diverse audience meant that references were deliberately kept vague and ambiguous.

An additional caveat is one fundamental to the majority of songs composed during the eighteenth century, but one little discussed in other papers in this collection, given that most of the work under consideration was composed, indeed written and even published by a small group of male poets. In discussing Gaelic songs, we work within a highly fluid oral medium wherein stanzas and occasionally entire songs migrate between different oeuvres, wherein different authors, times, places, and circumstances can, both surprisingly and predictably, somehow produce the same song. With some of this material, namely canonical compositions of the best-known poets, the literary scholar is on fairly firm ground. Most ascriptions, however, inevitably entail varying degrees of scepticism.

Over and above the usual prerequisite deep familiarities with linguistic, literary, and historical contexts, the Gaelic scholar is faced with the challenge of grasping that crucial socio-cultural context, the oral tradition in its widest sense, not just its contents – stretching from proverbs to prose narratives, topography and genealogy to popular belief in all its myriad manifestations – but also the transmission of this material through space and time. The embarrassment of misconstruing Gaelic literature is not only the province of that most intractable Scottish tribe, the 'Highland experts' unable to understand a word of the language of the people whose culture and history they have taken upon themselves to expound to the wider world. Indeed, there are moments when all of us go astray. As I have written elsewhere, 'in the badinage of the céilidh house we are but gauche and obtuse intruders'.[6]

In this paper I shall attempt briefly to sketch out a field of study in which Lowland and Gaelic scholars might cooperate and learn from each other, principally by examining how during the late seventeenth and early eighteenth centuries a certain style of fashionable pastoral art-song, as much in vogue in the London metropolis as in the Scottish Lowlands, crossed the Highland/Lowland literary divide and came to be employed in both men and women's poetry. I hope that this might raise some questions concerning multilingual 'literary space' in these islands during the early modern era, the possibility of long-term cultural chronologies, and indeed the fraught mutual relationship between socio-economic change and change in gender identities and representations.

The confused era following the forfeiture and destruction of the Lordship of the Isles known as *Linn nan Creach*, the Age of the Forays, was a series of decades marked by prolonged regional conflict and internecine strife, especially but not only on the western seaboard. In the mid-sixteenth century widespread and vicious feuding broke out between the Campbells of Glenorchy and their erstwhile allies the MacGregors, resulting in the violent dispossession of Clann Ghriogair and, eventually, their proscription by James VI in one of his last acts before departing for England in 1603. Bands of broken MacGregor refugees scattered and settled throughout the Gàidhealtachd, whether reset by those sympathising with their plight, or else imposing themselves upon reluctant host communities. In an effort not just to maintain their own morale, but in order to provoke widespread sympathy for their cause, the magnificent songs lamenting the desperate state of *Clann Ghriogair air fògradh*, the exiled Clan Gregor, played a pivotal function.[7] Such songs represent the roots of a genre of romantic, or proto-romantic, poetry which was to become exceptionally important in, indeed almost representative of, Gaelic literature as a whole. In such songs, the role of women as providers for and protectors of menfolk who found themselves *fo'n choill'*, outlawed, was paramount.

After the crushing of the Ulster rebellion of Cathair Ó Dochartaigh and the kidnapping of most of the island chiefs in 1608, the Edinburgh authorities were able to extend their control over the western Gàidhealtachd. Estates across the region were reorganised along more commercial lines, with rents raised accordingly. Such political and economic developments provoked dissatisfaction at all levels of society, resulting in intensified feuding and, in its wake, many more dispossessed and outlawed 'broken men'. At the same time, the cattle droving trade grew steadily and exponentially, and markets were established and expanded. Fresh opportunities thus arose for the theft and resale of stolen beasts and stolen goods, together with the protectionist rackets and blackmail inherent in such a trade. Bands of armed men, increasingly experienced veterans of Continental wars, began to operate, generally upon the fringes of the Gàidhealtachd. Deprived of the usual clan ties, often at feud, these men had to find shelter and protection. They did so not only by offering their covert armed assistance to local magnates, but also by appealing to a disaffected populace who feared a similar fate of dispossession for themselves. Despite their dependence upon the new commercial world, the caterans posed as representatives of an older, more traditional, heroic order, attractive and charismatic figures acting out traditional roles increasingly forsaken by clan chiefs themselves.[8] It is hardly surprising that they created a romantic – if we might use this term – persona for themselves, the more so given the often brutal reality of their trade. Their appeal to women was part and parcel of their allure, and it may be no coincidence that almost the only 'photofit' description we have of any criminal in official seventeenth-century records is black propaganda by the Privy Council, wherein Seumas an Tuim, James Grant, outlawed uncle of the murdered Iain Ruadh Charrainn, John Grant of Carron in Glen Moriston, is described as 'a man of little stature, bald headed, braid faced, fair culloured, broun bairded, weake eyed, bow hoghed, fatt bellied and about fiftie yeeres of age'.[9]

Neverthless, women gave Seumas an Tuim and others like him food and shelter, and in contemporary records they appear to a disproportionate extent among the resetters of these characters.[10] They would remain so as long as outlaws operated in the Gàidhealtachd. A song attributed to the later seventeenth-century cateran Domhnall Donn mac Fir Bhoth-Fhionntainn, Donald MacDonald of Bohuntine, supposedly composed upon his capture by his arch-enemy the Laird of Grant, ends with the verses:

Nam biodh fios mi bhith 'n-sàs
Gun dùil ri fuasgladh gu bràth,
'S lìonmhor ghabhadh mo phàirt 's an uair seo.

'S iomadh maighdeann glan ùr,
Chluinnteadh faram a gùin,
A chuireadh na crùin gu m' fhuasgladh.

Gu bheil té dhiubh 'n Srath Spé
'S nam biodh fios aice fhéin,
Nàile, chuireadh i ceud gu luath ann.[11]

If they would know I was captive, with no expectation of release, many would take my part at this time. Many a bright young maiden whose gown would be heard to rustle would give crowns to release me. There is one of them in Strathspey, and if she would know, by Saint Nàile, she would quickly give a hundred.

In order to fashion their romantic personae, the outlaws and cattle thieves drew upon traditional courtly motifs, possibly to an unusual extent compared with previous songs and poems composed by men in the Scottish Gàidhealtachd. In this respect, it should be stressed that such motifs are remarkably scarce in extant vernacular and classical verse dating from the late medieval period and from *Linn nan Creach*.[12] This fact is somewhat obscured in that, despite the paucity of surviving classical courtly verse from Scotland, two of the most celebrated examples of the genre in the entire Gaelic world were in fact composed by members of the foremost bardic family in Scotland, the MacMhuirichs. One of these, *Námha dhomh an dán*, is the work of Eòin MacMhuirich, in the words of literary historian Mícheál Mac Craith 'an chéad fhile gairmiúil a chum dán grá a bhfuil eolas cinnte againn ina thaobh' ['the first professional poet of whom we have certain knowledge who composed a love poem'].[13] The other, *Soraidh slán don oidhche a-réir*, a poem ascribed to Niall Mór MacMhuirich in the Red Book of Clan Ranald, and in which the use of the *alba* motif in the fifth stanza certainly suggests a measure of English influence, is described by the same author as '*an ceann is gleoite ar fad, b' fhéidir*' ('perhaps the most accomplished of them all').[14] Only two Gaelic poems in the admittedly somewhat skewed poetry collection assembled in the *Book of the Dean of Lismore* are entirely courtly in character, although the anthology embraces anti-courtly and non-courtly verse aplenty.[15] The first half of the seventeenth century was a time when the courtly genre was in full bloom in Irish. In Scotland, however – although the great classical poet Cathal MacMhuirich was certainly able to compose a courtly stanza[16] – there are no extant entirely courtly works to be found in the admittedly slender surviving classical corpus. The same also holds true for those vernacular texts which have come down to us. Indeed, in Derick Thomson's survey of 'The earliest Scottish Gaelic non-classical verse texts' we only find various versions of the celebrated song *Cailín o Chois Siùire mé*.[17] Nevertheless, a handful of other songs, or at any rate stanzas within them, may suggest faint echoes of *amor hereos* in the earlier Scottish Gaelic tradition which have been rather stifled by the inclinations of later generations and later compilers.[18]

What we do have from the early seventeenth century onwards are songs composed by outlawed 'masterless men' assiduously cultivating their romantic appeal to women. These outlaws and caterans represent something of a new type in the Scottish Gaelic world. Previously, characters who lived in the wilderness on the margins of society, far from being romantic figures, were rather more akin to fearsome semi-savages occupying a liminal, somewhat ambiguous position.[19] One of the earliest fugitive poets outwith Clann Ghriogair is Fearchar mac Iain Òig, Farquhar MacRae from Kintail in the Seaforth estate, whose wife incited him to the impulsive murder of the factor who had just confiscated his prized copper kettle in lieu of a newly raised rent with grassum. During the next seven years MacRae's wife provided for him while he was *fo'n choill'*, mainly in Coire Gorm a' Bhealaich in Gleann Lic. In his song *Cha b'e dìreadh a' bhruthaich* MacRae ironises the courtly motif of 'troma-cheist', the heavy question or anxiety his wife has placed him under: the consequence of love, certainly; but it was she who had brought about his flight in the first place. His exile may allow him to participate in the aristocratic pastime of the hunt, but it is as much from necessity as from pleasure:

> 'S i do nighean-sa Dhonnchaidh chuir an troma-cheist seo orm:
> Té do'n d' fhàs an cùl dualach 's e m'a guaillean mar òr,
> 'S e sìos mu dà shlinnein anns an ionad bu chòir.
> 'S nuair a thigeadh a' foghar b'e mo roghainn bhith falbh
> Leis a' ghunna nach diùltadh 's leis an fhùdar dhubh-ghorm,
> 'S bheirinn fiadh ás a fhireach 's breac a linne 'n t-Sruith Mhóir.
> O na saoilinn thu m' fhreagairt dhèanainn fead cheann a' mheòir.[20]

> *It is your daughter, Duncan, who put me under this great anxiety: a girl whose curly hair grew over her shoulders like gold, down about her two shoulderblades as was fitting. And when the autumn would come I'd choose to go with the gun which does not misfire and the black-blue powder, and I'd bring a deer from the high ground and a trout from the pool of the Sruth Mór. O, if I thought you'd answer me I'd whistle with my fingertips.*

The most notorious Gaelic outlaws of the early seventeenth century, however, were considerably more formidable characters operating on the other side of the country, on the Gàidhealtachd frontier in Strathspey. Having won a fearsome reputation, Seumas an Tuim, James Grant, was eventually arrested by the authorities in 1630 and incarcerated in Edinburgh Castle. His daring escape, after his wife had smuggled him a rope hidden in a cog of butter, represented a humiliating blow to the Privy Council, which thereupon put a price on Grant's head. Pàdraig Geàrr, Patrick MacGregor, brother of the chief of the clan, turned bounty hunter, in part to obtain government support for his kindred; but the aggressive behaviour of himself and his men alienated the people of Strathspey and he was killed while leading an attack upon Seumas an Tuim. This was by no means the end of the affair. Bloodfeud had now been kindled between James Grant and his supporters on the one hand, and, on the other, the kinsfolk of Pàdraig Geàrr MacGregor under the leadership of his father, Iain Dubh Geàrr, and his uncle, Pàdraig Ruadh, better known as An Gille Ruadh, *anglice* Gilderoy. Thus two outlaw bands at loggerheads were now disrupting the eastern border of the Gàidhealtachd, while the Edinburgh authorities were trying to destroy them both. In the case of the MacGregors at least, this attempt was eventually successful.[21]

Although tradition about Seumas an Tuim was somewhat scant by the time of the first wave of major folklore collectors in the second half of the nineteenth century, a couple of sources record the following stanza:

> Tha mo ghràdh thar gach duine
> Air Seumas an Tuim;
> Ruitheadh tu, leumadh tu 's dhannsadh tu cruinn
> Chuireadh tu treun-fhir a bhàrr am buinn
> Cha do dh' fhàilnich riamh do mhisneachd do
> Thapadh 'nad lùim.[22]

My love over every man is for Seumas an Tuim; you would run, you would leap, and you would dance neatly. You would knock the strong man from the soles of his feet. When leaping, your courage and strength never failed you.

There is the same stress on dancing and agility in the song, or rather port-a-beul, *Ruidhle Thulaichean* or the Reel of Tulloch, supposedly composed by Iain Dubh Geàrr. As we have it today, the song relates how he escaped an ambush in Killin, and then how 'Iseabail Dubh Thulaich' helped him to kill his enemies – her own brother among them – when they launched an ill-advised attack on the outlaw in Strathspey:

> The forsaid song was made by Iain Duth who was Courting a young Lady and an other man was Courting her at the same time and sent for John to meet him in an ale house and had 18 men with him but Black John defeated them all & afterwards run to Strathspey and the pursuit followed him and he tells in the song how the Las[s] behaved in Loading and him shooting.[23]

The romance of such songs, and the numerous local aiders and abettors of the outlaws, should not distract us from the often brutal conduct of the caterans themselves, especially the MacGregors. In the words of the Privy Council:

> thay have broken louse and associat unto thamselffes a lawlesse byke of infamous and theevish lymmars with whome thay go ravagin athort the countrie, and on all places where thy may be maister they sorne upon his Majesteis good subjects, taking from thame all and everie thing that comes narrest to thair hands, and whare they find anie opposition or resistance they threaten his Majesteis subjects with all kynde of extremitie and sometimes with death . . .[24]

John Spalding describes the same band as follows:

Thir lawless McGrigour, wnder cullour of seiking James Grant, opprest the countrie wp and doun, sorning and taking thair meit, defloiring virgynes and menis wyves, and begetting of barnes in hourdome, without pvnitioun quhaireuer thay went.[25]

The Record of the Privy Council describes how Iain Dubh Geàrr viciously turned the tables on John Stewart of Drumquhen by ambushing his intended assailant on Christmas Day 1636:

[he] lurked in the said hous [in Tulloch] whill the said umquhill Johne came there and how soone they gott sight of him they sett upon him with shotts of hacquebutts and musketts, shott him through the thighes, brak his thigh bones, cutted aff his fingers, cutted aff his head and danced and made merrie about him a long time . . .[26]

Motifs, songs and anecdotes concerning cattle thieves are found in profusion and confusion across the region, from female as well as male performers. Confident attribution of these productions is generally unattainable, the more so given that entrepreneurial caterans would adopt the names of their illustrious forerunners. Thus we have an Iain Dubh Geàrr Òg appearing in the sources from 1640 onwards;[27] another Pàdraig Ruadh MacGregor making a name for himself as a cateran in Strathspey in 1670;[28] while the son of the renowned cateran Donald MacDonald – 'Donald mc Ranald vc Allester termed the gawin kennin or quhyt faced stirk' (or the 'Halket Stirk') – adopted his father's title after his death.[29] As with names, so also with poetry: a number of songs ascribed to Domhnall Donn contain facts clearly at odds with the little we know of their supposed creator.[30]

The popularity of songs supposedly composed by the caterans, and anecdotes concerning them, reflect the concomitant growth of popular printed literature about 'rogues' in English. The *beau idéal* of such characters is of course Robin Hood, a figure just as prominent in Scottish Lowland culture as in his own native land. In this regard, a letter written by Robert Campbell of Glenfalloch on 16 November 1638 to his brother, Sir Colin Campbell of Glenorchy, concerning Iain Dubh Geàrr MacGregor, is noteworthy:

thair is na nowells in this c[on]trie bot Jhone Gar and his me[n] is playand Robin Hud and Littill Johnis passagis thay spylled sum est lowlaen me[n] at ye burne of Camis cuming to this merkat . . .[31]

The celebrity accorded their later seventeenth-century successors is clearly analogous to that of contemporary highwaymen in England. An anecdote dating to 1646 concerning

Alexander Fraser, the young Master of Lovat, serves as an example of the notoriety enjoyed by Highland reivers. Feeling snubbed by his guardian John, first earl of Wemyss, the youth threatened peevishly:

> if I be thus used any longer, and that you provoke me to return north again, I will purchase for my selfe, and turn John Dow Gare among yow at last. My Lord Weemes could not understand what he meant by John Dow Gare, and asked Mr William Fraser [of Phopachy] who this was? He told his Lordship that this John was a notorious leading robber and outlaw that troubled all the North with excursions, and never traveled without 20 stout fellowes attending him well armed, put a tax uppon townes and villages as he went through, and made all compon with him, bribing him with loane and soumes of money; and, my Lord, yow will do well to mollify his temper and prevent his youthly forward and froward designs, for if he once take it in his head being my Lord Lovats sone, he will get many to follow him, and if he join with the rebels, he may creat trouble enough and anger yow all.[32]

Whether bluffing or not, Fraser was made a captain in Leslie's regiment.

Despite the ignorance of the earl of Wemyss, the renown of Highland caterans was evidently not confined to the Gàidhealtachd alone, as can be seen from the threats of two brothers in Monkland near Glasgow, James and George Cleland, made against Mr Walter Whiteford, 'sub-dean of Glasgow, one of his Majesty's chaplains', 'assumeing to thameselves the name of James Grant, and threatning to committ mare insolenceis than fell out be him'.[33] The most interesting and unexpected translation, however, is that undergone by Pàdraig Ruadh MacGregor, an Gille Ruadh, whose name, if nothing else, achieved posthumous celebrity in the eponymous English-language ballad *Gilderoy*. The first extant version of the ballad in print is in the collection *Westminster-Drollery* of 1671, while a mention of its hero in John Lacy's play *Sauny the Scot* of 1675 suggests that the text was already well-known to the metropolitan audience.[34] The earliest recorded mention of the 'excellent Scotish tune, call'd Gilderoy' dates from a broadside of 1664, while the introduction to the text in admittedly later eighteenth-century editions might allow us to trace its origin back to the Commonwealth era: 'it is somewhere said of him' that he 'pick'd Cardinal Richlieu's Pocket in the King's Presence, return'd to England, robb'd Oliver Cromwell, hang'd a Judge, and was at length taken and executed in Scotland, a little before the Restoration.'[35] We might tentatively suggest that the earlier version of the ballad – or at least the melody accompanied by a rudimentary narrative – was brought back to London by veterans who had served in Scotland with General Monck; this is certainly the case with some Gaelic airs which enjoyed a contemporary vogue.[36]

Whatever its origins, this first text of *Gilderoy* was superseded in later collections

by a 'version which, with corruptions and expurgations calling themselves "improve-
ments", has come down in unceasing popularity through all the Scottish Song-books
to the present day.'[37] From a literary perspective, the more elaborate later text is somewhat surprising in that, drawing upon imagery in the earlier *Gilderoy* – 'his silken
Garters on his legs,/And the Roses on his shoone'[38] – it explicitly plays down the
Highland connections of its hero:

> *Gilderoy* was a bonny Boy,
>   had roses tull his shun,
> His Stockings made of the finest silk,
>   his Garters hanging down:
> It was a comely sight to see,
>   he was so trim a Boy;
> He was my Joy and Heart's Delight,
>   *my handsom* Gilderoy.
>
> Oh, sike a charming Eyen he had,
>   a breath as sweet as Rose;
> He never wore a Highland plad,
>   but costly silken Cloaths . . .[39]

To label Gilderoy as 'the idealisation of the Highland freebooter'[40] thus appears somewhat wide of the mark – although of course the lines quoted above may very well
have been composed as a reaction against such a phenomenon. The creation, or re-
creation, of the romantic, or proto-romantic, Highland cateran is a phenomenon which
might be dated to some years later, towards the end of the seventeenth century; rather
than being the work of London ballad singers, it appears to have arisen in the Scottish Lowlands.

> LADY SQUEAMISH: Mr Truman, Mr Goodvile, and Ladies, I beseech you
> do me the favour to hear Mr Malagene sing a Scotch Song: I'le swear I am
> a strange Admirer of Scotch Songs, they are the pretti'st soft melting gentle
> harmless things –
> SAUNTER: By Dad, and so they are. – In January last – (*Sings*)
> VALENTINE: Deliver us! A Scotch Song! I hate it worse then a Scotch
> Bagpipe, which even the Bears are grown weary of, and have better Musick.
> I wish I could see her Ladiship dance a Scotch Jigg to one of 'em.
> MALAGINE: I must needs beg your Ladiships pardon, I have forgotten the
> last new Scotch Song: But if you please, I'le entertain you with one of another
> nature, which I am apt to believe will be as pleasant.[41]

During the last quarter of the seventeenth century 'Scotch songs' or 'Scotch snatches' began to win some – although clearly not universal – popularity in the metropolis at all levels of society.[42] Indeed, the enforced sojourn of James, Duke of York, in Edinburgh as a result of the Exclusion Crisis of 1679 – a few years not just of respite but indeed of favour being shown to the clans – might well have led to another wave of interest in Highland culture in the metropolis.[43] From street ballads, the genre was introduced to the stage, taken up by that quintessential early modern cultural entrepreneur Thomas D'Urfey, followed soon afterwards by John Lacy and Aphra Behn. 'Scotch songs' were performed as entr'actes by characters with no connection with Scotland, and indeed as stand-alone pieces too; many of the genre were eventually incorporated into D'Urfey's multivolume song anthologies.[44] With their rural setting, artificial, often insipid and urbane sentiment, abstraction, and clichés, the genre was an offshoot of existing English pastoral song, outfitted with 'Scots' characters with names such as 'Jocky', 'Sawney', 'Jenny' or 'Moggie', and a greater or lesser smattering of Lowland Scots words adding extra vigour. It would appear, however, that at least some of the male parts were sung by characters dressed in tartan trews. In Behn's *Widow Ranter* the heroine is attended by a 'Bag-Piper, Playing before a great Boule of Punch, carryed between two Negro's, a Highlander Dancing after it'. Behn's dancing 'high Land-Vallet' is clearly meant to be clad in a plaid.[45] Generally, however, it is unlikely that late-seventeenth-century London metropolitan audiences made too much distinction between Highlander and Lowlander any more than they do nowadays, the more so given that drovers of the Highland middling sort – and indeed the Highland 'Scotch pedlars' of rather lower social status – swaggering around the streets of London dressed in plaid would of course speak Lowland Scots.[46] In the various versions of Michael Wright's triple portrait of John Lacy, one of the characters he plays is a Scotsman dressed in a plaid, whether Wareston in John Tatham's *The Rump* of 1660, or the playwright's own Sauney the Scot.[47]

The rise of the 'Anglo-Scots art song' during the late seventeenth century is clearly a British phenomenon, 'a part of a general, all-British lyric culture'.[48] It is not sufficient, however, to identify and delineate a particular *éspace litteraire*; one also needs to chart centres of production and patterns of diffusion and dissemination. In this respect, these popular or tea-table songs were created as much on the stage and indeed in the streets of London as they were in Scotland itself. In a protean culture functioning according to market demand, recognising little distinction between 'artificial' and 'popular' genres or for that matter between 'oral' and 'written', wherein tunes, motifs, settings, and manner of delivery were in constant flux, we have 'Scots' songs created by English entertainers, while Scots – and probably English too – adapted existing English songs into Scots versions.[49]

The most influential sub-genre to derive from the phenomenon was that based upon the motif of the 'Bonnie Highland Laddie', celebrating 'the love of a Highland man and a Lowland woman.'[50] The earliest versions of the type suggest that it developed as an offshoot to popular songs from the south in which the patriotic English soldier was exalted by his sweetheart to the detriment of his foreign counterparts.[51] Although the 'Highland Laddie' theme – subsuming the popular *Lizzie Balie* songs among others – clearly draws upon one of the most common, and doubtless one of the oldest, motifs in international love poetry wherein 'an upper-class woman or just an ordinary farmer's daughter goes off with a poor man or an outcast, whether beggar, serving-man, gipsy or highland marauder'[52] into a vogueish pastoral setting, growing interest at the time in the figure of the Noble Savage, a character in which hard and soft masculinities are combined, should also be borne in mind.[53] The rise of the genre in Scotland has been traced in important but still rather neglected studies by Thomas Crawford, William Donaldson, and Murray Pittock.[54] Although these critics have suggested that it was the adaptability of the Highland Laddie songs for political ends which sealed their popularity, one rather suspects that 'the wish-fulfilment role of the Highlander' in contemporary popular culture was not entirely due to Jacobite sympathies alone; witness Edmund Burt's remarks:

> But to return to the Marriages of the Highlanders,– Perhaps, after what has been said of the Country, it may be asked, what Lowland Woman would care to lead a Life attended with so many Inconveniences? Doubtless there are those who would be as fond of sharing the clanish State and Power with a Husband, as some others are of a Name, when they sell themselves for a Title; for each of these Kinds of Vanity is very flattering: besides, there are many of the Lowland Women who seem to have a great liking to the Highlandmen, which they cannot forbear to insinuate in their ordinary Conversation.[55]

Whether the songs were primarily political or not, what is interesting for our present purpose is that it was clearly not long – perhaps only a few years – before the motif of the Highland Laddie began to be employed by Gaelic caterans, men who had learnt such songs either from Lowland soldiers or merchants in the Gàidhealtachd, or else, having crossed the Lowland line, as drovers or soldiers themselves. Thus we have canonical verses of the type such as:

> O'er benty Hill with him I'll run
> And leave my Lawland Kin and Dady
> Frae Winter's Cauld and Summer's Sun
> He'll screen me with his Highland Plaidy.

or:

Thoul't row me in thy tartan plaidy.

being remodelled in Gaelic. For instance, in a song ascribed to Domhnall Donn, *Thogainn fonn gun bhith trom*:

Lùib mi i 'nam bhreacan fhéin,
Liom a b'éibhinn mar thachair.

Biodh sneachd ann 's gaoth-a-tuath,
Phaisginn suas i 'nam achlais.[16]

I folded her in my own tartan plaid, for me it was joyful what happened. Let there be snow and a north wind, I would fold her up under my arm.

In such late-seventeenth- and early- eighteenth-century popular song is to be found the genesis of the creation of the romantic Highlander and the romantic Highlands. Motifs were rapidly adopted and refashioned by Gaelic poets for their own ends, in hybrid compositions which, ironically, have been described as the essence of pure, authentic Gaelic song. In fact, these texts represent the mingling, to a greater or lesser extent, of Gaelic tradition with a new infusion of pastoral and popular song – together with their tunes – from outwith the Gàidhealtachd, from printed English broadsheet sources. It is not only beasts which were being traded or lifted over the line, but motifs, themes, symbols, metres and airs as well.[17]

As the earlier example of *Gilderoy* suggested, it was not until this period that tartan plaid began to be an essential emblem of Gaelic masculine virility. Two conjectures might be advanced as to why this was the case. Firstly, by the late seventeenth century the plaid was increasingly becoming a male garment in the Gàidhealtachd, as women abandoned the traditional female plaid or *earasaid* in favour of contemporary Lowland fashions. In addition, the tartan, that clothing of brawn, vigour, and spectacular display *par excellence*, was more and more being compared to and distinguished from garments of 'renunciation' worn in the south, namely the black hat and cloak worn by Presbyterian ministers, and, on a wider British stage, the rise of that most emblematic whig garment, the sober three-piece suit.[18]

It is hardly surprising, then, that we have women's songs in Gaelic also praising the 'Highland plaidy' and its related accoutrements. The song ascribed to Domhnall Donn's lover the Laird of Grant's daughter has the stanza:

'S math thig féile dhut 's an fhasan,
Boineid ghorm is còta breacain,
Osan geàrr is trì chuir ghartan,
'S glas lann air do chruachan.

The kilt in fashion well becomes you, a blue bonnet and a tartan coat, short hose and thrice-tied garters, and a grey blade on your hip.

A crucial point not to be overlooked, of course, is the reference to fashion: '*'s an fhasan*'. Despite the fact that they did not yet travel across the Lowland frontier as frequently as their male counterparts, female poets were nevertheless well aware of the symbolism of tartan, of its effect upon outsiders. As a praise song to Allan Maclean, tutor of Bròlas, by the Mull woman Mairearad ni'n Lachlainn demonstrates, they could employ the allusive power of tartan as a motif in order to urge the adoption of Jacobite policies. The poet stresses how Maclean's father had been received by the Duke of York's court, in effect a Stuart court in exile, in Edinburgh:

'Nuair a chunnacas na h-àrmainn,
Na fior Ghàidheil gun fhòtas,
Is nach d'iarr iad de dheise orra
Ach breacan is còta,
Is sgiath bhreac nam ball iomad
Air an slinnein gu còmhrag
'S ann a thuirt gach duine,
Siud a' chuladh tha bòidheach!

When the nobles saw the true Gaels without blemish, didn't they want any garment upon them but a tartan plaid and a coat, and a speckled many-bossed shield on their shoulder for fighting. Every man exlaimed, 'What a beautiful garment!'

The veiled erotic imagery of the tartan is dealt with in a rather more straightforward fashion in the following early-eighteenth-century waulking song recorded from a Mrs Mary Morrison by John Lorne Campbell in Barra:

'S truagh, a Rìgh, nach mi 'm breacan
Thug thu dhachaigh o'n fhéill.

'S 'nuair a thilleadh o'n fhrasrach
Bhithinn paisgte fo d' sgéith.

'S 'nuair a rachadh i fhàsgadh
Bhithinn sgaoilte ri gréin.[59]

A pity, Lord, that I am not the tartan you took home from the fair. When you'd return from the shower, I'd be folded under your arm. When it had been wrung out, I'd be spread out in the sun.

The use of 'courtly' motifs in Scottish Gaelic texts of the period by and about caterans is perhaps the most conspicuous example of their wider vogue with contemporary male poets. Among texts in which a synthesis of classical Gaelic influence with that of English and Lowland song might be discerned is *Gura muladach tha mi*, a poem dating from the third quarter of the seventeenth century by Gilleasbaig na Ceapaich, chief of the Catholic MacDonells of Keppoch. The author adopts the romantic persona of one suffering grievously for a lost love, praising not only her beauty, but also her feminine virtues, before turning the song into an aristocratic *jeu d'esprit* with a final exaggerated stanza undermining the melancholic picture of the previous verses.[60]

> Cha ghearaininn bàs dhoibh,
> Nan cuirteadh fo'n fhàd mi, roimh'n àm:
> Ach sùgradh mo leannain
> Bhith aig ùmadaigh balaich, gun taing.

I wouldn't wish death for them, if I were put untimely under the turf, but my darling uselessly courting a clownish dolt.

Although Gilleasbaig na Ceapaich was acquainted with the representative of the MacMhuirich classical bardic family of his time, Niall Mór, and could apparently employ classical *corr-litir* script, he was educated – like many Highland heirs – in Forres, and was evidently proud of the travels he had undertaken throughout Scotland.[61] It is therefore likely that *Gura muladach tha mi* is indebted to Lowland chapbooks as well as to classical *dánta grá*. It is fascinating to see Gilleasbaig apparently using song to bolster the rather uneasy position of his family after the celebrated Keppoch Murder, for instance in the song *'S mór a' bhleid is an stràic* composed against his enemies Domhnall Donn and the piper Donald Campbell.[62]

The love poem *Thugas ceist do mhnaoi ghasda* by Gilleasbaig's son Aonghas Odhar employs the same persona of the suffering lover, albeit speaking rather more earnestly and certainly more directly to the object of his affections.[63] Again, it is likely that the work is indebted to contemporary Lowland songs as well as to the classical Gaelic tradition: lines such as '*Cha robh Diana ri faicinn/Ann an coltas ri d' phearsa mar thrian*' – 'Diana was not to be seen but as a third of your likeness' – probably owe rather more to contemporary parlour songs than to the Mediterranean classical tradition. The resistance of the poet to the persona convention demands be adopted might be suggested by the couplet:

> Dhomhs' cha bheag e mar pheacadh
> Ma nitear mo chasgairt le mnaoi.

For me it is not a small sin if I'm to be slain by a woman.

175

A somewhat more light-hearted example is offered by Anndra mac an Easbaig, Andrew Maclean. His *Thugas gaol nach fàillinneach* plays with courtly conventions and is apparently set to the tune of the great panegyric *Gun tug mi ionnsaidh bhearraideach*.[64] Although ostensibly a love poem, the date given for its composition in Ronald MacDonald's *Eigg Collection* indicates that the song was addressed to a child – Barbara, daughter of Bishop John Fullerton – by a man old enough to be her grandfather.[65] Maclean was to some extent at least versed in the classical Gaelic tradition, as evinced by two somewhat inelegant verses composed in *séadna* metre to Edward Lhuyd for his *Archæologica Britannica* of 1707.[66] It is worth noting that the poet's mother was brought up in Eaglesham, albeit of Gaelic, and indeed ecclesiastical, stock: she was herself the child of a bishop, the Bishop of Argyll. It is virtually certain that Maclean was brought up in two cultures.

Another contemporary 'love song' suffered a rather interesting fate. *Slàn iumradh do'n ùr-mhnaoi* was composed by Mr John Beaton, minister of Bracadale in Skye from 1667 to 1708 and one of the famous Beaton medical family.[67] Although the author employs courtly motifs aplenty, with much praise of the new wife's beauty, his song is emphatically not a love poem composed in the persona of a suffering paramour. Rather, it works as an epithalamium praising her good bearing, civility, learning, and piety:

> Glac gheal a nì 'n sgrìobhadh,
> Gu fìnealt' 'nuair b' àill,
> 'Ga tharraing gu lìonmhor,
> Le ìnnleachd do làmh;
> Leis an leabhar am Bìobla
> Gu cinnteach gach tràth;
> Glac creideas is fìrinn
> 'S lean a-chaoidh ris mar ghnàths.

A white hand which writes beautifully when you wish, the skill of it drawing [the pen] copiously; with the Bible assuredly every time seize belief and truth, and follow them always as your habit.

Beaton's song represents a reworking by a member of the clergy for moral ends of the love poetry so fashionable at the time; it is comparable to the marriage poem *Tha tamall o sguir mi de'n dàn* by Beaton's contemporary the Rev. John Maclean.[68] Indeed, the fact that a number of verses from *Slàn iumradh* also appear in texts of the well-known love song *A' Bhean-Chomainn* might indicate that it was composed to the same tune.[69] A later version of Beaton's song in the MacDiarmid Collection suggests, however, that it was a victim of its own success. Pursuing a rather unusual trajectory for works of this type, *Slàn iumradh* was absorbed into the tradition where, ironically, it was refashioned into a straightforward romantic work – albeit with remnants of its original moral message – sung in the character of a rejected lover. Beaton's first lines '*Slàn iomradh do'n ùr-mhnaoi,/Dh' fhàg mi'n Ugairidh thall*' ('farewell to the new bride I left over in Ugairidh') are converted into '*Tha mo chion air an ùr-ghibht a dh' fhàg mi'n Ugairidh thall*' ('My love on the "new gift" I left over in Ugairidh').[70]

The songs briefly listed above represent a fusion of classical Gaelic with contemporary English and Lowland vernacular verse. They are composed in a high register of vernacular Gaelic with classical inflections, and employ stressed rather than syllabic metre. Courtly, 'romantic' motifs also appear in more popular contemporary Gaelic song by men. Among their number is the love song *Mo Màili Bheag Òg*, clearly something of a hit of its day judging from the fact that Sìleas na Ceapaich recycled both tune and chorus as Jacobite propaganda.[71] It is likely, following the earliest sources, that this obsessively romantic song, and the pathetic murder story behind it, originated in Ulster, a region whose own Gaelic literature was considerably more affected by English than was the case in Scotland: a notable example of how the literary market for songs in the Atlantic Archipelago was rather more complex than we might imagine.[72] The 'Irish youth' having won the heart of 'a nobleman's daughter in the Highlands':

> Having received the lady's consent, he eloped with her. Her two brothers pursued them on horseback, and found them on a Sunday morning in a glen, where they had passed the night; – the struggle commenced between the young gentlemen and the unfortunate lover, who had the inexpressible anguish of killing his sweetheart in the contest, with his own sword. He was then taken prisoner, and carried to jail, where he composed this heart-melting song a few days before his execution.[73]

> 'S truagh a rinn do chàirdean,
> Mo Mhàili bheag òg,
> 'Nuair thoirmisg iad mo ghràdh dhomh,
> Mo chuid de'n t-saoghal thu,
> Nan tugadh iad do làmh dhomh,
> Cha bhithinn anns an àm seo
> Fo bhinne airson gràidh dhut,
> Mo Mhàili bheag òg.

> *Your relations did wrong, my little young Màili, when they forbade my love for you, my portion of the world. If they had given your hand to me, I wouldn't be now under sentence for love of you, my little young Màili.*

In *Mo Màili Bheag Òg*, the usual love motifs are made all too real, intensified through the singer's plight, a martyr for love, and indeed through the compulsively repetitive structure of the text. At one level, *Mo Màili Bheag Òg* can be read as a yardstick of the increasing fashionability of passionate, wholehearted, direct, somewhat unsophisticated, indeed even obsessive love songs. Later traditions ascribe it to a soldier, 'a young Highland officer, who had served under King William on the continent soon after the Revolution'.[74]

At least one other romantic song can certainly be traced to the Flanders campaigns, one which may have enjoyed some popularity at the time. In it we find the stanza:

> 'Nuair bha mis' ann am Flànnras,
> Bha mi thall ann am shaighdear,
> Gur h-ioma bean àillidh
> Le fàineachan daoimean
> Thigeadh gu m' sheòmar
> 'S dh'fhuraineadh pòg orm;
> 'S gum b'annsa Nighean Domhnaill
> Ged nach beò i [*sc.* mi] ach oidhche.[75]

When I was in Flanders, I was there as a soldier, and many a beautiful woman with diamond rings would come to my chamber to ask me for a kiss; but I would prefer Donald's daughter though she [recte I] would only live one night.

The mention of Flanders reminds us that the experience of the Scottish Gael during the late seventeenth century, especially of those involved in soldiering, was rather more widespread than the United Kingdom alone. Indeed, the paradoxical role of the early modern soldier as unlikely proselytiser of new standards of European culture and civility is still badly under-researched.[76] Documentary sources suggest that a surge in the number of Highland cattle-raiders at the end of the seventeenth century was due to the return of veterans, skilled in the arts of foraging as well as fighting, after having been disbanded in 1698 following the Peace of Rijswick. Probably contemporary with *Mo Mhàili Bheag Òg* is *A Mhairghread Òg*, 'Òran an Amadain Bhòidhich' ('The Song of the Beautiful Fool'), another song of somewhat exaggerated emotion, again concerning a forbidden affair in which the beloved – apparently another cateran, indeed a figure often confused with Domhnall Donn himself – is killed by accident. One finds the same stress on pastoral background and agility as in the Highland Laddie type. Hence:

> Shiubhlainn leat an saoghal,
> Mo Mhàili bheag òg,
> Cho fad' ri cùl na greine,
> A gheug as àillidh gnùis,

178

Ruithinn agus leumainn,
Mar fhiadh air bhàrr nan sléibhtean,
Air ghaol 's gum bithinn réidh 's tu,
Mo Mhàili bheag òg.

I would travel the world with you, my little young Màili, as far as the back of the sun, o branch of the loveliest face; I would run and jump like a deer on the mountain slopes, if we could live together, my little young Màili.

The motif is even stronger in *Òran an Amadain Bhòidhich*, with one version as follows:

Ochòn, a Rìgh, mo nighean donn,
Nach robh mi thall am Muile leat.

Ochòn, a Rìgh, etc.
Gum marbhainn iasg is sitheann fhiadh,
'S cha bhiodh, a chiall, oirnn uireasbhuidh.

Gum marbhainn, etc.
'S gum marbhainn coileach dubh air geug,
Mu'm biodh 'na éi[s]teadh iomadh fear.

'S gum marbhainn, etc.
'S an earbag bheag á bun a' phris,
Ged 's clis a chì 's a chluinneas i . . .[77]

Woe, Lord, my brown-haired girl, if only I was over in Mull with you. I'd kill fish and venison, and, my darling, we'd want for nothing. I'd kill the blackcock on the branch, before many men could get into its earshot, and the little roe from beneath the bush, no matter how sharp its sight and hearing.

Just as with the contemporary highwaymen in England and rapparees in Ireland, caterans played a rather uneasy role as folk heroes, denied legal powers, constantly living under the threat of capture by the authories, including their own chiefs. As we have seen with their forebears in the earlier part of the century, the importance of oral culture in enhancing their image was paramount.[78]

Gilleasbaig na Ceapaich, chief of the MacDonells of Keppoch, appears to have used songs in order to bolster his authority; so also with Domhnall Donn, who created a romantic persona for himself not just with text, but also by employing his musical gifts (tradition tells that he could play the clàrsach).[79] Domhnall Donn's songs are somewhat simple and vernacular in character, closer in character to songs made by women than to the classically inflected poetry still being composed by his own social class. At the heart of this self-image is romantic love. One instance of this is a song in praise of his close friend Donald Campbell, the piper of Gilleasbaig na Ceapaich, in which Campbell is eulogised for obtaining his desire among women:

> Thugadh bean leat bho'n Bhreugaich
> 'S an cluinnt' beucadaich mheang.
>
> 'S ro mhath b' aithne dhomh 'n nighean
> A bha 'cridh' ort an geall;
>
> Anns a' ghleannan bheag laghach,
> 'S am biodh tu tadhal os n-àird.[80]

You took a wife for yourself from Breugach, where the bleating of kids was to be heard. I knew very well the girl whose heart was set on you, in the pretty little glen which you would visit openly.

In the songs of Domhnall Donn can be discerned a new concept of Gaelic heroism, in which the poet portrays himself as much courtier as cateran. An example of this is his song *Nach b' fheàrr leat mi agad.*[81] Some versions of this song have stanzas by Fearchar mac Iain Òig interwoven, suggesting that the tune of the two pieces was the same:

> Nach b' fhèarr leat mi agad
> Na mac breabadair beò?
>
> Gar an [*sc.* nach] dèanainn dhuit fighe
> Bhiodh sitheann mu d' bhòrd.
>
> Gum biodh fuil an daimh chabraich
> Ruith ri altan do mheòir.
>
> Is i do nighean-sa 'Dhonnchaidh
> Chuir an truime-cheist mhór orm.

Wouldn't you rather have me than any son of a weaver living? Although I [wouldn't] sew for you, there would be venison on your table. The blood of the antlered stag would run to the joints of your fingers. It is your daughter, Duncan, who put me under this great anxiety.

In metre and vocabulary alike, such stanzas are especially close to women's popular song of the period – indeed, the implication is that Domhnall Donn's work may have been aimed at a female audience in the first place.

The martyr's death suffered by Domhnall Donn sealed his fame as a romantic hero. The songs he composed in his final months, supposedly incarcerated in the Laird of Grant's prison, clearly romanticise his capture in the hope of winning from their audience pity, sympathy, and maybe the money to pay for his release. His posthumous fame meant that Domhnall Donn became the cateran *par excellence*; as has been seen, songs such as *Òran an Amadain Bhòidhich*, items with apparently no connection whatsoever to Domhnall Donn, were nevertheless ascribed to him in tradition.[82] What hearsay we do have concerning Domhnall Donn rather indicates that grubby reality did not live up to his romantic image, let alone his posturing as a 'social bandit'. He abducted 'an nighean donn a bha'n Cataibh'; he killed the son of the bard Iain Lom at Highbridge; he was captured after a drunken spree in a stable.[83] Having suffered smallpox like so many of his contemporaries, he may not even have been particularly handsome; indeed, lines such as *'Ged is crom leibh mo cheann/ 'S ged is cam leibh mo chasan'* ('Although in your eyes my head is bent, and although in your eyes my legs are crooked') might suggest quite the opposite. It is worth noting that the rather curious absence of contemporary documentary evidence regarding the demise of such a notorious cateran might be accounted for if we were to identify Domhnall Donn with the 'Donald Broun' apparently hanged along with a certain Peter Broun at Gallow Hill in Banff in June 1701. This execution took place despite an attempt by the Laird of Grant to have them both forcibly abducted and tried under his own heritable jurisdiction. The two Brouns were captured along with the notorious freebooter 'Macpherson' who is supposed to have composed the famous 'Macpherson's Rant' before his own execution.[84] As with the seventeenth-century MacGregors, we have here a good example of caterans operating on the Highland/Lowland Line who inspired contemporary song in both Gaelic and Scots, manifested and transmitted variously in oral, written, and printed forms.

We have seen how much the rise in the popularity of love songs inspired a slew of sub-genres, whether humorous pastiches or recensions for moral purposes. They also, of course, inspired various anti-courtly songs. A remarkable example demonstrating how the courtly stream might incite its exact opposite can be found in the flyting ascribed in tradition to Domhnall Gruamach – the brother, it will be noted, of Domhnall Donn himself – and the martial poet Iain Lom:

Domhnall Gruamach:
A bhean nam pòg meala,
'S nan gorm-shùile' meallach,
'S ann a tha mo chion falaich
Fo m' bhannaibh do m' ghràdh.

Chan eil mi 'gad léirsinn
Ach mar gum biodh reul ann,
An taic ris a' ghréin so
Tha 'g éiridh gach là.

Iain Lom:
Ar leatsa gur reul i
'S gur coslach ri gréin i,
'S ann a dh' fhàs i ro éitigh
Fo h-éididh a bhàn.

Boladh ùilleadh an sgadain
De dh' ùrla na h-apa;
'S i as cùbaiche faicinn
Tha 'n taice ri tràigh.[85]

Domhnall Gruamach: *Woman of the honeyed kisses, and the deceiving blue eyes, my secret love is bound to my darling. I can only see you as a star, like this sun which rises every day.*

Iain Lom: *You think she is a star, that she's like the sun, but really she's grown loathsome, down under her clothing. Oily smell of the herring, with an ape's face; the furthest bent of those beside the beach [i.e. looking for shellfish].*

The vogue for Gaelic love poetry in the late seventeenth century may well have given renewed impetus to the obscene and anti-female strain in poetry too, that sharp, sardonic voice lampooning romantic rhetoric. We might look at *Marbhphaisg air na mnathan feadhair*, 'Trod nam Ban Eigeach', by Iain Dubh mac Iain mhic Ailein,[86] where the satire against female loquacity gains its very strength and vigour from a description of that loquacity.

Marbhphaisg air na mnathan feadhair
Nach gleadhadh an antlachd!
Tha mo chluasan air fàs bodhar
Le gleodhar an càinte;
Nis bho chaidh iad bho riaghailt
Leigeam srian le'n aimhleas,
'S tàirneamaid gu àite dìomhair
Bho mhìothlachd an càinnte.[87]

A curse on the women of the fair who won't keep their discontent [quiet]. My ears have grown deaf with the babble of their scolding. Now since they've gone out of control, let me take the bridle from their mischief. Let's go to a secret place away from their offensive speech.

This strain is not, of course, aimed at women alone, but revels in matters related to sex and obscenity in general.[88] In *Féill nan Crann* by the Clàrsair Dall,[89] however, and in *An Obair Nodha* by Fear Ghrinneirt,[90] it is female lusts on which the poet dwells. The latter poem is as it were an answer to the religion spread by the Presbyterian Church at the time, as can be seen from the related reference to the '*teagaisg nodha-s*' in a stanza from *Crosanachd de ghné choluadar eadar a' cholainn 's an t-anam* by Donnchadh nam Pìos:

> Thubhairt guth is e 'freagar:
> *An t-anam*: "'S mise t' anam uasal;
> Na gabh fiamh no eagal
> Roimh mo theagasg nuadh-sa.'[91]

A voice spoke in answer: [the soul] 'I am the noble soul; Do not be afraid of my new teaching.'

Again, we cannot understand the full humour of Morison's poem unless we are aware of the context of the growth of small fairs and markets throughout the Gàidhealtachd at the time.[92] The same goes for Sìleas na Ceapaich's answer to Fear Ghrinneirt's poem, 'An aghaidh na h-Obair Nodha', where the market is the place where young men and women meet and court each other, away from their parents' eyes:

> 'Nuair théid sibh thun na féille
> Na géillibh do luchd nan gibhtean;
> Innsidh mi dhuibh reusan
> As feudail nach coisinn mios iad:
> Ged a gheibh sibh làimhnean,
> Fàinne no deise ribean,
> Is daor a nì sibh phàigheadh
> 'Nuair dh' àrdaicheas air a' chriosan.[93]

When you go to the fair, don't yield to folk with gifts; I'll tell you a reason why they're a treasure that won't earn you respect. Although you get gloves, a ring, or a bunch of ribbons, you'll pay for it dearly, when your girdle begins to rise.

I hope that this paper has outlined a field of study which might encourage closer cooperation between literary scholars working with Scottish Gaelic, Scots, and English, inviting wider reflections concerning mutual contact and influence between and among the various literatures of the multicultural early modern Atlantic Archipelago. Such research requires a sensitivity to historical context, processes, and cyclical shifts, an awareness of rapidly changing socio-economic circumstances and of associated transformations in culture and gender relations, of new horizons and opportunities, indeed an increasingly fluid range of feminine and masculine identities. Although, with some notable exceptions, scholars have been content to situate the foundations of Highland romanticism in the later eighteenth century, in the wake of the Jacobite risings and Macpherson's *Ossian*, this is clearly not the case. The construction in the late seventeenth century of the figure of the Highland Laddie, that potent amalgam of heroism, proto-Romanticism, and hard and soft primitivism melded together, was a fundamental step towards the construction of a gendered image for the Scottish Gael/Highlander which would prove highly resilient until the present day. For contemporaries, however, this literary figure represented a reworking of older heroic values, in an increasingly post-heroic age.[94]

Notes

[1] Stith Thompson motif-index H1052; Jan de Vries, *Die Märchen von klugen Rätsellösern* (Helsinki, Folklore Fellows Communications 73, 1928), 198–9; for comparable 'paradoxical tasks', see motif-index F555.3.1; H862; H1051, 1053–77, H1378. Kate MacDonald, 'Hilliù-an, hilleò-an', *Tocher* 27 (1977), 150–1; James Carmichael Watson (ed.), *The Gaelic songs of Mary MacLeod* (1934: Edinburgh, Scottish Gaelic Texts Society, 1965), xi–xvii; Rev. William Matheson, 'Notes on Mary MacLeod', *Transactions of the Gaelic Society of Inverness* xli (1951–2), 15–16; John MacInnes, 'Notes on Mary MacLeod', *Scottish Gaelic Studies* xi (1966), 9–10; idem (ed. Michael Newton), *Dùthchas nan Gàidheal: Selected Essays* (Edinburgh, 2006), 245, 261; Colm Ó Baoill, '"Neither out nor in": Scottish Gaelic women poets 1650–1750', in Sarah M. Dunnigan, C. Maire Harker and Evelyn S. Newlyn (eds), *Woman and the Feminine in Medieval and Early Modern Scottish Writing* (Basingstoke, 2004), 136, 140–1, 150; also Máirín Nic Eoin, *B'ait leo bean: gnéithe den idé-eolaíocht inscne i dtradisiún liteartha na Gaeilge* (Dublin, 1998), 243–55, 283–8.

2 Alexander Carmichael, *Carmina Gadelica* (6 vols, Edinburgh, 1900–71), ii, 158–9; v, 286–97; Rev. John Gregorson Campbell (ed. Ronald Black), *The Gaelic Otherworld* (Edinburgh, 2005), 142–3, 395, n.470.

3 Ronald Black, *Mac Mhaighstir Alasdair: the Ardnamurchan Years* (Inverness, 1986), 21–3; idem (ed.), *An Lasair: Anthology of 18ᵗʰ-century Gaelic Verse* (Edinburgh, 2001), 190–2, 459–60.

4 National Archives of Scotland [NAS] GD18/5023/3.

5 On this point, see especially Thomas A. DuBois, 'Native hermeneutics: traditional means of interpreting lyric songs in northern Europe', *Journal of American Folklore* 109 (1996), 235–66.

6 Domhnall Uilleam Stiùbhart, 'The uses of historical traditions in Scottish Gaelic' in John Beech, Owen Hand, Mark Mulhern and Jeremy Weston (eds), *Scottish Life and Society: Oral Literature and Performance Culture* (Edinburgh, Compendium of Scottish Ethnology 10, 2007).

7 Martin MacGregor, 'A political history of the Clan Gregor until 1571' (University of Edinburgh, unpublished PhD thesis, 1989); idem, '"Surely one of the greatest poems ever made in Britain": the lament for Griogair Ruadh MacGregor of Glen Strae and its historical background' in Edward J. Cowan and Douglas Gifford, *The Polar Twins* (Edinburgh, 1999), 114–53; see Colm Ó Baoill and Donald MacAulay (eds), *Scottish Gaelic Vernacular Verse: A Checklist* (Aberdeen, revised edition 2001) [henceforth *ÓBMA*], [no.] 10: *Moch madainn air latha Lùnasd* (*Griogal cridhe*); *ÓBMA* 408: *'S mi am shuidhe an seo am ònar/Air còmhnard an rathaid*; *ÓBMA* 422: *Tha mulad, tha mulad, tha mulad 'gam lìonadh* (*MacGriogair á Ruadh-shruth*); *ÓBMA* 427: *A mhic an fhir ruaidh* (*Saighdean Ghlinn Lìobhann*). For the choral context of *ÓBMA* 398 and *ÓBMA* 402, see John MacInnes, 'Gaelic poetry' (University of Edinburgh, unpublished PhD thesis, 1976), 337–9. For the possible function of such songs in maintaining MacGregor morale, see ibid., 223–4.

8 Allan I. Macinnes, *Clanship, Commerce and the House of Stuart, 1603–1788* (East Linton, 1996), 32–7; Domhnall Uilleam Stiùbhart, 'An Gàidheal, a' Ghàidhlig agus a' Ghàidhealtachd anns an t-seachdamh linn deug' (University of Edinburgh, unpublished PhD thesis, 1997), 355–78; for comparable developments in Ulster, see Raymond Gillespie, 'The transformation of the borderlands, 1600-1700' in Raymond Gillespie and Harold O'Sullivan (eds), *The Borderlands: Essays on the History of the Ulster–Leinster Border* (Belfast, 1989), 84–7; also Eric Hobsbawm, *Bandits* (Harmondsworth, 1985), especially 18–19, 22, 24, 83–7.

9 *Records of the Privy Council of Scotland* [RPC], 2nd series, IV (1630–2), 544.

10 See *RPC*, 2nd series, VI (1635–7), 215–18, 231–4; VII (1638–43), 487–94.

11 *ÓBMA* 57.

[12] Despite its ostensible classical origins, reinforced in Derick Thomson's editions of the text in 'Bho Làmh-Sgrìobhainnean MhicLathagain (xi)', *Gairm* 144 (Autumn, 1988), 351–2; *The MacDiarmid MS Anthology* (Edinburgh, 1992), 120–5; and also *An Introduction to Gaelic Poetry* (Edinburgh, 1989), 61–2, the poem *'S luaineach mo chadal a-nochd* (*ÓBMA* 219) should be dated to the late seventeenth century at the earliest: Helen Jane Theresa O'Sullivan, 'Developments in love poetry in Irish, Welsh and Scottish Gaelic, before 1650' (Glasgow University, unpublished MLitt dissertation, 1976), 95–9. Its appearance in the Royal Irish Academy MS 24 C 55, 287 suggests that the work possibly originated in Ireland, rather than being the work of the early- sixteenth-century chief Eachann Mór MacLean of Duart as has been suggested. O'Sullivan also casts doubts on the classical origin of the collection of stanzas concerning women known as *Tha bean an crìch Albainn fhuar* (*ÓBMA* 341): 'Developments in love poetry', 99–101.

[13] Mícheál Mac Craith, *Lorg na hiasachta ar na dánta grá* (Dublin, 1989), 61.

[14] Ibid., 225, n.51.

[15] These are *Thugas ró-ghrádh do mhnaoi fir* and *Fada atú i n-easbhaidh aoibhnis*: William Gillies, 'Courtly and satiric poems in the Book of the Dean of Lismore', *Scottish Studies* 21 (1977), 35–6; also Martin MacGregor, 'The view from Fortingall: the worlds of the *Book of the Dean of Lismore*', *Scottish Gaelic Studies* xxii (2006), 71–3; ibid., 'Creation and compilation: *The Book of the Dean of Lismore* and literary culture in late medieval Gaelic Scotland' in Ian Brown, Thomas Owen Clancy, Susan Manning and Murray Pittock (eds), *The Edinburgh History of Scottish Literature* (3 vols, Edinburgh, 2007), i, 215–17; William Gillies, 'Gaelic literature in the later Middle Ages: *The Book of the Dean of Lismore* and beyond', in ibid., 224.

[16] Ronald Black, 'The genius of Cathal MacMhuirich', *Transactions of the Gaelic Society of Inverness* 1 (1976–8), 355.

[17] Derick S. Thomson, 'The earliest Scottish Gaelic non-classical verse texts' in Dietrich Strauss and Horst W. Drecher (eds), *Scottish Language and Literature, Medieval and Renaissance: Fourth International Conference 1984, Proceedings* (Frankfurt am Main, 1986), 533–46; *ÓBMA* 511.

[18] For example, *Tha an oidhche nochd fuar*: John Lorne Campbell and Frances Collinson (eds), *Hebridean Folksongs* (3 vols, Oxford, 1969–81), ii, 207–20; *Trom òr o chalanas*: ibid. iii, 261–5. For a satire on the courtly genre, see *Mòr inghean Ghiobarlain* (*ÓBMA* 450), a song ascribed (probably because of the 'gaberlunzie' allusion) to James V.

[19] A list of such characters would include Dubh-Shìth, Iain Beag nan Saighead, Iain Beag mac Anndra, and Gille Pàdara Dubh.

[20] *ÓBMA* 328; see also the verse preserved in William Mackenzie, 'Leaves from my Celtic portfolio III', *TGSI* viii (1878–9), 28: *'Dheòin Dia cha bhi gillean/Riut a' mire 's mi beò.'*

('With the grace of God boys will not be sporting with you while I am alive.') The song may tentatively be related to the revision of the Seaforth estate rental made by Ruairidh na Còigich, Ruairidh MacKenzie, Tutor of Kintail, after the death of his brother Coinneach, Lord MacKenzie, in 1611.

[21] The career of Seumas an Tuim can be pieced together from *RPC*, 2nd series, IV (1630–2), xlviii–l, 99–100, 164, 204, 544–6, 550–1, 553, 561–2, 576–8; V (1633–5), 500–1, 503, 506–7, 529; VI (1635–7), 17–18, 21–2, 45, 46, 111, 138, 170–1, 176–7, 230, 236, 258, 272, 304, 379–80; William Fraser (ed.), *The Chiefs of Grant* (3 vols, Edinburgh, 1883) I, 226–37; II, 14–15, 58, 59–60, 61–3, 69–70; III, 228, 229, 231, 341, 441–2, 443–4, 448–51; John Spalding, *Memorialls of the Trubles in Scotland and in England. A.D.1624–A.D.1645* (Aberdeen, Spalding Club, 1850), I, 11n., 20, 21–3, 29–30, 43–4, 52–5, 61, 63, 67, 69, 70, 126, 141, 169, 205, 208, 210, 244; II, 338, 341; also I, 390–2, 394, 395, 396, 398, 399, 400, 401, 402, 404; Robert Gordon, *A Genealogical History of the Earldom of Sutherland* (Edinburgh, 1813), 414–16, 420–1, 459–60, 481; James Gordon, *History of Scots Affairs, from MDCXXVII to MDXLI* (Aberdeen, Spalding Club, 1841), III, 71–2; George Bain (ed.), *The Lordship of Petty* (Nairn, 1925), 62–71; National Library of Scotland [NLS] Acc. MS 7708/22. For Pàdraig Geàrr, see Spalding, *Memorialls* I, 44, 46, 52, 61, 69, 126. Iain Dubh Geàrr first appears in 1635 as one of those attempting to capture Seumas an Tuim: *RPC* 2nd series, VI, 529. The career of himself and his brother Pàdraig, an Gille Ruadh, can then be traced in ibid., xxxviii–xl, 128, 207–10, 215–18, 218–20, 231–4, 236, 252, 256, 257, 274, 301 (An Gille Ruadh executed in Edinburgh in July 1636), 304, 308–9, 321–2, 327–8, 363–4, 366–7, 376–7; VII (1638–43), xlviii–l, 21–2, 56–8; Fraser (ed.), *Chiefs of Grant* I, 236, 254; II, 60, 62–3; III, 231, 451–3; Spalding, *Memorialls* I, 94–5, 126, 129, 205, 229, 236 (Iain Dubh Geàrr killed by a bullet on the bank of the Spey in November 1639); Robert Gordon, *Earldom of Sutherland*, 460, 481–2, 496; James Gordon *History of Scots Affairs* II, 267–8; III, 71–2; NAS GD 112/39/62/2, /4, /67/18, /74/8/1, /2.

[22] 'Glenmore' [Donald Shaw], *Highland Legends and Fugitive Pieces of Original Poetry* (Edinburgh, 1859), 89–90; also NLS Acc. MS 7708/22 fo.7. For 'lùim', see *Dwelly's Illustrated Gaelic to English Dictionary* s.v. luim.

[23] EUL Mackinnon MS 10C [by Benjamin Urquhart, 1823], fo.400. *ÓBMA* 163: *O thulaichean gu bealaichean.* There are two Isobels appearing in the Privy Council records in connection with the caterans. Firstly, in the list of those assisting the MacGregors in *RPC*, 2nd series, VI, 215–18, there is a mention of 'William Fettes and [ ] Fettes, Gilleroyes whoore in Cabrach'; later there is a reference to 'Issobell Sandesone, Gilleroyes whoore'. Secondly and rather more likely is the reference of 1637 in ibid., VII, 376–7, to a family in Tulloch who assisted Iain Dubh Geàrr: 'John Grant, alias McJokkie, . . . Grant, his

wife, Issobel Grant, his daughter.' A reference in a 1639 letter by an Archibald Campbell to Sir Colin Campbell of Glenorchy should also be noted: 'if they should prove
that Johne Dow Gaire his wyff and complices haiue bein publictlie resaitt in the Marques
of Huntlie his boundes: That then the Marques does present Johne Dow Gaire and
his complices and to be lyebill for all the wronges that they haue done.'

²⁴ *RPC*, 2nd series, VI, 128.

²⁵ Spalding, *Memorialls* I, 61.

²⁶ *RPC*, 2nd series, VI, 366–7.

²⁷ *RPC*, 2nd series, VII, 487, 488, 490, 492; Spalding *Memorialls* I, 298–9; II, 5, 176,
237–8.

²⁸ Rev. James Fraser (ed. William Mackay), *Chronicles of the Frasers: The Wardlaw MS*
(Edinburgh, Scottish History Society 1st series, 47, 1905) 486–9; also 'Glenmore', *Highland
Legends*, 140–7; Macinnes, *Clanship, Commerce and the House of Stuart*, 32, 126.

²⁹ NAS GD 112/39/106/7, Sir John Campbell of Glenorchy to Lord Glencairn, 12 Sep
1660; for the Halket Stirk, see Fraser (ed.), *Chiefs of Grant* I, 280–2; Paul Hopkins, *Glencoe
and the End of the Highland War* (Edinburgh, 1998), 29, 37, n.49, 393, n.210; also 31–2,
60, 320, 379. For the increase in cattle thieving after the Restoration, see ibid., 28–9;
David Stevenson, *Alasdair MacColla and the Highland Problem in the Seventeenth Century*
(Edinburgh, 1980), 281–3. For further historical context, see Hopkins, *Glencoe and the
End of the Highland War*, 10–82; Macinnes, *Clanship, Commerce and the House of Stuart*,
123–58; Stiùbhart, 'An Gàidheal, a' Ghàidhlig agus a' Ghàidhealtachd', 231–354.

³⁰ See especially *ÓBMA* 52: *A Mhairghread òg, 's tu rinn mo leòn* ('Òran an Amadain Bhòid-
hich') and *ÓBMA* 60: *Thogainn fonn gun bhith trom* ('An nighean donn a bha'n Cataibh').
A similar process has apparently occurred with a number of songs later attributed to
Domhnall Donn's sworn enemy Iain Lom.

³¹ NAS GD 112/39/67/1816. For the popularity of Robin Hood in the Lowlands at the
time, see Stephen Knight, *Robin Hood: a Complete Study of the English Outlaw* (Oxford,
1994), 27–8, 31, 32–9, 108–9, 111.

³² Fraser (ed. Mackay), *Wardlaw MS*, 324.

³³ *RPC*, 2nd series, V, 506–7.

³⁴ Anon., *Westminster-Drollery, or, A Choice Collection of the newest songs & poems both at court
and theaters by a person of quality; with additions* (London, 1671), 112–14; James Maidment
and W.H. Logan (eds), *The dramatic works of John Lacy, comedian, with prefatory memoir and
notes* (Edinburgh, 1875), 362.

³⁵ M.P., *Two Strings to a Bow; or, The Cunning Archer* (London, 1664); the earliest printed
account of Gilderoy's life appears to be in Capt. Alexander Smith, *A Compleat History
of the Lives and Robberies of the Most Notorious Highwaymen, Footpads &c.* (2 vols, London,

1719) ii, 297–304, drawn upon in [Ambrose Philips], *A Collection of Old Ballads, Corrected from the Best and Most Ancient Copies Extant* (London, 1723), 306. For the origins of the phrase 'higher than Gilderoy's kite', see Smith, ii, 303–4.

36 See Hyder E. Rollins (ed.), *Cavalier and Puritan: Ballads and Broadsides Illustrating the Period of the Great Rebellion 1640–1660* (New York, 1923), 70, 315; also Samuel Pepys (ed. Robert Latham and William Matthews), *The Diary of Samuel Pepys* (11 vols, London, 1970–83) vii, 224–5; ix, 130–1.

37 Joseph Woodfall Ebsworth (ed.), *The Bagford Ballads, illustrating the last years of the Stuarts* (2 vols, Hertford, 1878–80), i, 102.

38 Ibid., i, 101.

39 Ibid., i, 105.

40 Thomas Crawford, *Society and the Lyric* (Edinburgh, 1979), 148.

41 Thomas Otway, *Friendship in Fashion* (London, 1678), 30.

42 See, for example, Hyder E. Rollins, *An Analytical Index to the Ballad-entries (1557–1709) in the Registers of the Company of Stationers* (Hatboro, PA, 1967), nos. 222, 2666 and 2757.

43 Macinnes, *Clanship, Commerce and the House of Stuart*, 191.

44 For examples of the genre in the works of Thomas D'Urfey, see his plays *A Fond Husband, or, The Plotting Sisters* (London, 1677), 10; *Trick for Trick, or, The Debauch'd Hypocrite* (London, 1678), 17–18; *The Virtuous Wife, or, Good Luck at Last* (London, 1680), 30–1; *The Royalist* (London, 1682), 32; *A Fool's Preferment, or, The Dukes of Dunstable* (London, 1688), 13–14; *The Marriage-hater Match'd* (London, 1692), 56; *The Campaigners, or, The Pleasant Adventures at Brussels* (London, 1698), 26. Also Aphra Behn's plays *The City-heiress, or, Sir Timothy Treat-all* (London, 1682), 29, 32; *The Widow Ranter* (London, 1690), 19; and her *Poems upon Several Occasions with a Voyage to the Island of Love* (London, 1684), 93–8, 123–5; and Peter Motteux's *Love's a Jest* (London, 1696), 18; William Mount-fort's *Greenwich Park* (London, 1691), 46; Henry Neville Payne, *The Morning Ramble* (London, 1673), 45. See also Thomas D'Urfey, *A New Collection of Songs and Poems* (London, 1683), 14–15, 16–17, 39–40, 48, 74–8; ibid., *Choice New Songs* (London, 1684), 3–6, 14–16; ibid., *Several New Songs* (London, 1684), 1–2; ibid., *A Third Collection of New Songs* (London, 1685), 10–11; ibid., *New Poems, Consisting of Satyrs, Elegies, and Odes* (London, 1690), 132–5, 139–41, 143–4, 183–5; ibid., *A Choice Collection of New Songs and Ballads* (London, 1699), 10; and ibid. *Songs Compleat, Pleasant and Divertive; Set to Musick* (London, 1719), I, 36–7 (The NORTHERN Resenter – *made to a Scotch Tune call'd Robin the High-lander*), 42–4, 53, 121, 148–9, 169, 254–5, 294–5, 304–5, 306–7, 326–7, 330–1; II, 30–1, 83–5, 150–1, 159 (based on 'a bonny young Highland laddy'), 169–70, 200–1, 202–3, 228–9, 265, 268–9 (*The Honest HIGHLANDER's new Health to the QUEEN*), 302–3, 348 (*A PROLOGUE Spoken like a SCOTCH HIGHLANDER with a Sword and Target* – at Preston in

1715); III, 88–9, 225–6, 228–9, 230–1, 231–2, 233–4, 257–8, 259, 262–3, 279–80, 297–8, 307; IV, 65, 90–1, 204–5, 211–12, 230–1, 271, 347–8; VI (from *Pills to Purge Melancholy*), 25, 164–6, 274–6, 350–2, 359–60; also Hyder E. Rollins, *Pepys Ballads* III, 111–13; VI, 282–6; Henry Playford, *A Collection of Original Scotch-tunes, (full of the Highland humours) for the violin* (London, 1700); Wing J758–9A; S950All. See also Martin Martin, *A Description of the Western Islands of Scotland* (London, 1703), 200, concerning the people of Skye: 'There are several of 'em, who Invent Tunes very taking in the *South* of *Scotland*, and elsewhere; some Musicians have endeavoured to pass for first inventers of them by changing their Name, but this has been Impracticable, for whatever Language gives the Modern Name, the Tune still continues to speak its true Original; and of this I have been shew'd several Instances.' For the popularity of the 'Anglo-Scots art song' genre in Scotland, see Patricia H. Wise, 'The alternative tradition in Scottish poetry, 1560–1720' (Australian National University, unpublished PhD thesis, 1982), 280–1.

[45] Aphra Behn, *The Widdow Ranter* (London, 1690), 18, 19; also James Orr Bartley, *Teague, Shenkin and Sawney: being an historical study of the earliest Irish, Welsh and Scottish characters in English plays* (Cork, 1954), 149–51.

[46] Edward Burt, *Letters from a Gentleman in the North of Scotland to his Friend in London* (1754: Edinburgh, 1876), i, 186: 'this you have seen in London, and it is chiefly their Mode of dressing when they are in the Lowlands, or when they make a neighbouring Visit, or go anywhere on Horseback; but when those among them who travel on Foot, and have not attendants to carry them over the Waters, they vary it [the plaid] into the *Quelt* . . .'

[47] The Hampton Court version appears in Ernest Law, *Masterpieces of the Royal Gallery of Hampton Court* (London, 1904), as well as picture 20 in Bartley, *Teague, Shenkin and Sawney*. John Evelyn describes the painting in a diary entry (retrospectively written) on 3 Oct 1662: 'his [Michael Wright] best in my opinion is Lacy the famous *Roscius* or Comedian, whom he has painted in three dresses, a Gallant, a Presbyterian minister, and a *Scots* highlander in his plaid.' [E.S. de Beer (ed.), *The Diary of John Evelyn* III (1650–1672), 338–9]. The portrait and the characters portrayed therein are dicussed in Charles W. Cooper, 'The triple-portrait of John Lacy: a Restoration theatrical portrait: history and dispute', *Proceedings of the Modern Language Association* 47 (1932), 759–65.

[48] Crawford, *Society and the Lyric*, ix.

[49] Crawford, *Society and the Lyric*, 6, 31, 113.

[50] William Donaldson, *The Jacobite Song: Political Myth and National Identity* (Edinburgh, 1988), 57; James Hogg (ed. Murray Pittock), *The Jacobite Relics of Scotland* (Edinburgh, 2003), 115–17, 335, 509–12.

[51] Ibid., 55–7; also John Holloway (ed.), *The Ewing Collection of English Broadside Ballads in the Library of the University of Glasgow* (Glasgow, 1971), 62: *The Coy Cook-Maid*.

52 Crawford, *Society and the Lyric*, 106.

53 The *locus classicus* is Hoxie Neale Fairchild, *The Noble Savage: a Study in Romantic Naturalism* (New York, 1928), 1–49.

54 Crawford, *Society and the Lyric*; Donaldson, *Jacobite Song*, 49–66; Murray Pittock, *Poetry and Jacobite Politics in Eighteenth-century Britain and Ireland* (Cambridge, 1994), 57–8, 141–2.

55 Burt, *Letters* ii, 216–17.

56 *ÓBMA* 60.

57 The migration of song tunes between the Gaelic- and English-speaking regions of these islands remains to be researched. For melodies originating in the latter area, one method might be to investigate Gaelic songs composed in an iambic rhythm apparently more suited to English than to Gaelic scansion. See (although it should be noted that she herself discounts the influence of English) Allison Ann Whyte, 'Scottish Gaelic Folksong 1500–1800' (Glasgow University, unpublished BLitt dissertation, 1971), 36–7, 41, 74, 136. For an early example, see *ÓBMA* 98 (*Mi gabhail Srath Dhruim Uachdair* by Iain Lom); also *ÓBMA* 3 (*Tha iongnadh air an Dreòlainn*); 18 (*Tha thu 'd mhac do Fhear Bhoth Fhionntainn*); 84 (*An deicheamh latha de thùs a' Mhàirt*); 197 (*Tha mulad mór, tha mìghean orm*); 377, 460 (*Tha mulad, tha sgìos orm,/Tha mìghean, tha gruaim*); also 483 (*Tùrsa mo mheanmainn, tùrsa is ainm dhom*), 'Irished to the toon qn the king coms home in peace again'. Note also the problems encountered by members of the Synod of Argyll in translating the Psalms from English into Gaelic, but preserving the metre: *An ceud chaogad do Shalmaibh Dhaibhidh, ar a dtarraing as an Eabhra, a meadar dhana Gaoidhilg, le Seanadh Earraghaoidheal* (Glasgow, 1659), 2–3.

58 See David Kuchta, *The Three-piece Suit and Modern Masculinity: England, 1550–1850* (Berkeley, CA, 2002).

59 Black (ed.), *An lasair*, 12–13.

60 *ÓBMA* 69.

61 See *ÓBMA* 67 (*Chuireas làmh do sgrìobhaireachd*); 68 (*Chunna mi eaglais Ghlaschù*); 72 (*'S mairg a dhiomol ceòl is caismeachd*); Somerled MacMillan, *Bygone Lochaber: Historical and Traditional* (Glasgow, 1971), 149; NLS MSS 1334 fo.79; 3784 fos.56ᵛ–57.

62 *ÓBMA* 73.

63 *ÓBMA* 48. For Aonghas Odhar's wild character, which may have led to him effectively being outlawed, see Hopkins, *Glencoe and the End of the Highland War*, 461, 463, 464; NLS MSS 1305 fo.63; 1307 fos.171, 175, 177; Charles Fraser-Mackintosh (ed.), *Letters of Two Centuries, Chiefly Connected with Inverness and the Highlands, from 1616 to 1815* (Inverness, 1890), 146–7. Aonghas Odhar married in 1703 or 1704 the widow of John Fraser of Cnoc Choilleim: Ó Baoill (ed.), *Bàrdachd Shìlis*, xxxviii–xxxix. In the opinion of his brother, Colla nam Bò, Coll MacDonell of Keppoch: 'my Broyr is like to be ruined by

this unhappie marriage qch he did rashlie wtout my Consent or knowledge': NLS MS 1305 fo.71 (Coll MacDonell to John MacKenzie of Delvine, 17 May 1704).

[64] *ÓBMA* 204. See Colm Ó Baoill (ed.), *Bàrdachd Chloinn Ghill-Eathain: Eachann Bacach and Other Maclean Poets* (Edinburgh, Scottish Gaelic Texts Society, 1979), 78–80, 247–52, 293–6; also Thomson (ed.), *MacDiarmid MS*, 83–98. The same satiric aims are to be found in the poetic debate *Thoir soraidh gu Iain Manntach uam*, between Briain, am Bàrd Asainteach, and Iain Lom: *ÓBMA* 99.

[65] Raonuill MacDomhnuill (ed.), *Comh-chruinneachidh Orannaigh Gaidhealach* (Edinburgh, 1776), 300; see Ó Baoill (ed.), *Bàrdachd Chloinn Ghill-Eathain*, 248.

[66] Ibid., 76, 244–7, 293.

[67] *ÓBMA* 2; John Bannerman, *The Beatons: a Medical Kindred in the Classical Gaelic Tradition* (Edinburgh, 1986), 64–70.

[68] *ÓBMA* 255; also Ó Baoill (ed.), *Bàrdachd Chloinn Ghill-Eathain*, 104–10.

[69] *ÓBMA* 518 (*Is ann feasgar Di-haoine*).

[70] Thomson (ed.), *MacDiarmid MS Anthology*, 57–63.

[71] *ÓBMA* 486; Ó Baoill (ed.), *Bàrdachd Shìlis*, 16–18, 127–9, 226–9.

[72] For the song's origins, see NLS MS 14949b fo.16 ['The Original supposed Irish']; and compare John Mackenzie (ed.), *Sàr-obair nam bàrd Gaelach: or, The Beauties of Gaelic Poetry* (Edinburgh, 1877), 368, with his earlier account in the (anonymously compiled, but clearly by Mackenzie) *Co'chruinneachadh de dh' oranan taoghta* (Glasgow, 1836), 16; also Ó Baoill (ed.), *Bàrdachd Shìlis*, 229. Note also the tradition ascribing the song to an Irishman 'Lachlann Ògaidh' recorded in Carmichael, *Carmina Gadelica* ii, 340–1; but see [Mackenzie (ed.)], *Co'chruinneachadh*, 28–9. See Énrí Ó Muirgheasa (ed.), *Céad de cheoltaibh Uladh* (Dublin, 1915), 78–9, 243–5; also 88; idem (ed.), *Dhá chéad de cheoltaibh Uladh* (1934: Dublin, 1969), 383–4.

[73] [Mackenzie (ed.)], *Co'chruinneachadh*, 16.

[74] Mackenzie (ed.), *Sàr-obair*, 368.

[75] Edinburgh University Library MS MN C fo.21; also Thomson (ed.), *MacDiarmid MS*, 132.

[76] Domhnall Uilleam Stiùbhart, 'Highlanders in the Low Countries', *Dutch Crossing* 29 (2005), 107–24.

[77] Gilleasbuig Mac-na-Ceàrdadh (ed.), *An t-Òranaiche* (Glasgow, 1879), 523. The fashion for impassioned love song reaches its height during the 1720s with the feverish, tragic compositions of Mac Fir Dhail an Easa (*ÓBMA* 131–3), whose songs, and persona, greatly influenced Uilleam Ros later in the century.

[78] See Somhairle MacGill-Eain, *Ris a' Bhruthaich: Criticism and Prose Writings* (Stornoway, 1985), 211–34.

79 Rev. Alexander Maclean Sinclair (ed.), *The Gaelic Bards from 1411 to 1715* (Charlottetown, 1890), 171.

80 *ÓBMA* 59 (*Slàn iomradh do m' ghoistidh*).

81 *ÓBMA* 58.

82 See MacGill-eain, *Ris a' Bhruthaich*, 231–3.

83 For traditional accounts of Domhnall Donn, see William Mackenzie, 'Leaves from my Celtic portfolio, first series', *Transactions of the Gaelic Society of Inverness* vii (1877–8), 56–7; William Mackay, *Urquhart and Glenmoriston* (Inverness, 1893), 187–90, 487–9; Alexander MacDonald ('Gleannach'), *Song and Story from Loch Ness-side* (1914: new ed. Inverness, 1982), 79–91.

84 Crawford, *Society and the Lyric*, 148–53; also Fraser (ed.), *The Chiefs of Grant*, i, 325–6; James Grant (ed.), *Records of the County of Banff 1660–1760* (Aberdeen, New Spalding Club, 1922), 104–5; John Stuart (ed.), *The Miscellany of the Spalding Club* iii (Aberdeen, Spalding Club, 1846), 175–91; Somhairle MacGill-Eain, 'Domhnall Donn of Bohuntin', *Transactions of the Gaelic Society of Inverness* xlii (1953–9), 91–110; and Hopkins, *Glencoe and the End of the Highland War*, 29, 361, 442, 477, n.36–7.

85 *ÓBMA* 100. The influence of such poetic debates on Alasdair mac Mhaighstir Alasdair's *Moladh* and *Diomoladh Mòraig* will be immediately apparent. See also *ÓBMA* 368 (*Chualas naidheachd o t'armailt*) by Donnchadh Dubhshùileach Stiùbhart, Colla na Ceapaich's standard-bearer, satirising Kenneth MacKenzie of Suddie who was killed at the Battle of Mulroy in 1688.

86 *ÓBMA* 79; Colm Ó Baoill (ed.), *Iain Dubh: òrain a rinn Iain Dubh mac Iain mhic Ailein* (*c.1665–c.1725*) (Aberdeen, 1994), 21–2, 48–50; also 83–4.

87 Ibid., 21; see also Nic Eoin, *B'ait leo bean*, 176–82.

88 See, for example, Derick S. Thomson, 'Niall Mór MacMhuirich', *Transactions of the Gaelic Society of Inverness* xlix (1974–6), 22; and stanzas ascribed to the Clàrsair Dall and Iain Lom in NLS MS 14876 fos.43ᵛ–44ʳ: '2 Verses of a Satyr made on John Maundaghe by Rory Morison' and 'John Maundaghe retorts on him'.

89 *ÓBMA* 355.

90 *ÓMBA* 178 (*Gun do labhair Màiri*).

91 *ÓBMA* 315 (*Chualas guth air mhadainn*). For another use of the contemporary meaning of *nodha*, see *ÓBMA* 239 (*'N àm dol sìos* by Iain mac Ailein).

92 Ronald Black, 'Scottish fairs and fair-names', *Scottish Studies* 33 (1999), 1–75.

93 *ÓBMA* 152. See also *ÓBMA* 149 (*'S mór mo mhulad 's mi 'm ònar. 'Laoidh air Bàs a Fir agus a h-Ighne*).

94 See MacInnes, *Dùthchas nan Gàidheal*, 265–319; Stiùbhart, 'An Gàidheal, a' Ghàidhlig agus a' Ghàidhealtachd', 311–54.

WILLIAM GILLIES

The poetry of William Ross

The credentials of William Ross for inclusion in the present conference are cast-iron.[1] He is one of the 'big names' of Gaelic poetry in the eighteenth century, having been dubbed 'the Gaelic Burns', 'the Gaelic Keats' and so on. Not only has he been seen as the counterpart of these Lowland and English poetic luminaries, but his work has been seen by his main twentieth-century editor, Rev. Dr George Calder, as actually indebted to that of Burns, which makes him a prime candidate for scrutiny under the heading of our conference theme of 'Cross-currents'. To this I would add that his all too brief *floruit* in the 1780s and early 1790s coincided with a key period in Highland history and in the history of Gaelic culture. At this time, we may recall, we see the beginnings of the culturally conscious work of Gaelic societies such as the Highland Society of London and the Highland Society of Scotland, the repeal of the Disclothing Acts, the creation of Highland regiments, and a growth in Gaelic publication, including the beginning of the long haul to bring the Bible into contemporary Scottish Gaelic. As a third reason for pressing the claims of William Ross to consideration by the present gathering, if further justification is needed, I would merely add that the Skye connection is self-sufficient and obvious.

In a forthcoming study of the textual foundation and literary characteristics of William Ross's poetry I conclude by emphasising the following qualities.[2] He is a poet with a well-developed, self-conscious sense of a Gaelic literary tradition and of his place within it. He displays an equally self-conscious sense of the linguistic differentiation in the different genres of Gaelic poetry, and a readiness to experiment eclectically. It is possible to diagnose Lowland–Highland crossovers in his life and work. Amongst these crossovers, I argue, one can detect attempts to come to terms with the overshadowing presence of Macpherson's *Ossian*. A crucial element in the theory of literature implicit in his poetry is a conviction, bearing comparison with similar ideas lying behind the work of Robert Burns, that the bardic 'franchise' includes the invitation, or perhaps the mandate, to collect and recycle, even to appropriate traditional and other pre-existing songs and poetry. And I conclude there (not altogether unexpectedly or originally, but I hope with better grounds than previous critics have had) that Ross's undoubted distinctiveness derives from a brew containing some highly traditional poetic qualities, some that pertain to his age, and some that are more idiosyncratically his own. My aim in what follows here is to develop some of these points further and to add in some complementary considerations that show what makes him tick as a poet. In keeping with the specific theme of the conference I shall be especially concerned to flag up bicultural issues and aspects of his work.

Ross was born near An Sìthean, about a mile south of Broadford on the Torrin road in Strath Suardal, here in Skye, in 1762.³ He was the son of John Ross, whose family seem to have been settled in Skye for a number of generations, and Margaret, daughter of John Mackay, the piper and poet known as Am Pìobaire Dall, who was piper to Sir Hector Mackenzie of Gairloch. Tradition says that he was sickly as a child, but at the same time showed signs of superior intelligence. His biography relates that his parents removed to the mainland so that he could go to school in Forres. The details of his short adult life are not clear, but it would appear that when his parents moved back west they settled in Badachro in Gairloch rather than returning to Skye; that his father became a packman and that William accompanied him on some of his travels; that William spent his last years (from c.1786?) as a schoolmaster in Gairloch until his death (probably from consumption) at a young age in 1791; and that he also spent some time in Edinburgh, whether working or studying or seeking medical help. As is well known, he met his *femme fatale* and major poetic inspiration, Mòr Ros, in Stornoway, but she married another. This unfortunate love-suit, plus his poetical outpourings on the subject, gave rise to further traditions about William Ross, in which he figures as the poet who died for love, and Mòr as the *belle dame sans merci* who eventually reaped the reward for her cruelty. Although we have very little in the way of factual record about his life, it happens that we do have some record evidence concerning Mòr Ros of Stornoway and her marriage to Captain Samuel Clough of Liverpool. This is a useful control over the burgeoning traditional accounts of how she was visited by him in Liverpool at the moment of his death. Suffice it to say for now that these historical glimpses are consistent with certain references contained in Ross's surviving poems, which is reassuring in regard to the authenticity of at least the core of the traditional biography.

Fifteen of William Ross's poems (a little under half the known corpus of his work) appeared for the first time in 1804 in Alexander and Donald Stewart's collection of Gaelic songs.⁴ His collected works were first published independently by John Mackenzie (Inverewe) in a volume dated '1830'. Mackenzie brought out a revised and expanded edition in 1834 which was subsequently reissued on several occasions in the later nineteenth century. Mackenzie also included a substantial selection of Ross's poems in his influential anthology *Sàr Obair nam Bard Gaelach* ('The beauties of Gaelic poetry'), first published in 1841.⁵ Finally, Ross received his first scholarly treatment with the publication of Rev. Dr George Calder's 1937 edition.

Ross himself was traditionally supposed to have burned his poems before death; and John Mackenzie was reputed to have taken them down orally from the recitation of an aged Gairloch informant, Alasdair Buidhe mac Iamhair (Campbell), who had been poet to Sir Alexander Mackenzie of Gairloch in Ross's heyday, and also a personal friend of Ross himself. But there are several reasons for doubting this account, including the demonstrably close relationship between Mackenzie's versions and those printed by the Stewart brothers two years before Mackenzie's birth. I suggest elsewhere that both the Stewarts and John Mackenzie may have had access to a written copy or copies of the majority of Ross's poems, most likely kept by someone from the Gaelic-friendly circle of the house of Mackenzie of Gairloch.[6]

Although we thus have several printings of his poems, Ross is not particularly well served. John Mackenzie was well known for interfering with his texts in both predictable and erratic ways, and examples of his editorial interference can be seen in his successive treatments of Ross's poems. As for Calder's edition, his editorial basis (Mackenzie's 1834 edition) is suspect, not least in that he gives no consideration to the versions of the songs contained in the Stewarts' collection. Moreover, he follows Mackenzie's example of tampering with the text by omitting poems and verses which do not accord with his preformed vision of the poet's temperament and genius. I also regard his handling of the oral tradition (including the question of oral and orally based versions of William Ross songs from sources other than Mackenzie) as shaky. And although he has solved many of the linguistic problems in Ross's poems, he has unfortunately cloaked his conclusions in a translation that, to the modern ear, ranges from inept to appalling. There is clearly more work to be done on the texts of Ross's poems before we can say that justice has been done to them. Perhaps further research will reveal further contextual information, e.g. in regard to his schooling in Forres, his travels to Edinburgh or Stornoway, or his life as a schoolmaster in Gairloch. Perhaps some currently unquestioned information will need to be taken away, e.g. if it is discovered to be based on the editor's deductions from the poetry, and to have no independent basis. William Ross really needs a proper new edition, and thoroughly deserves one.[7]

In what follows I propose to look briefly at three of Ross's poems which give valuable insights into his attitudes and methods: Calder's No. 28, *Òran cumhaidh* ('Song of lament'), composed on hearing of Mòr Ros's departure to England with her man; Calder's No. 1, *Còmhradh eadar am Bàrd agus Blàbheinn* ('Conversation between the Bard and Blaven'), the poem which heads both Mackenzie's and Calder's editions; and Calder's No. 5: *Òran air Gaol na h-Òighe do Chailean* ('Song about the Maiden's love for Colin'), a Highland pastoral idyll. I have, in other words, eschewed the famous songs like *Òran an t-Samhraidh* and *Feasgar Luain* and *Òran eile air an adhbhar cheudna*, which are the ones that have been decently translated or discussed by such scholars as Sorley MacLean, Derick Thomson, Iain Crichton Smith and Ronald Black. I believe these three slightly less well-known works are worth a wider exposure, and will discuss them in turn, viewing them firstly as specimens of Gaelic poetry functioning within the Gaelic tradition, and secondly in relation to the wider influences to which they appear to be indebted in different ways. In this way, I hope, the relevance of these productions to the theme of Highland-Lowland 'cross-currents' will become apparent.

Òran cumhaidh

This is the òran to which the celebrated Òran eile air an adhbhar cheudna ('Another song on the same theme') is eile, the theme being the hopelessness of the poet's love for Mòr Ros. The title means 'A song of lament', and uses a term which is most usually associated with the finality of the grave. The short superscription continues as follows: A rinn am Bard 'nuair a chualadh e gun do phos a Leannan ('Which the Bard made when he heard that his Beloved had married').[8]

The opening (v. 1) makes use of a common opening formula in Gaelic verse: 'Although I have long been drowsing it is time for me to arouse myself – (to declare) why I, who used to be so blithe, have now lost my sparkle.' Here the powerful traditional idea is that the bard is stung into poetic action, moved to bestir himself by a 'wrong' that needs to be drawn to the communal attention. 'Why should I be miserable about the maiden,' he continues, 'when she has no feeling for me?' –

> ged ghlac i an lùib a gràidh mi
> le àmhailtean Chupid

> *although she ensnared me in love for her*
> *by the ambuscades of Cupid.*

In v. 2 he goes on: 'Let people speculate as to how I was wounded [i.e. pierced, as by a dart] by her love . . . I am reluctant to admit it, or to grant her a release.' How should he proceed in the circumstances? His answer is:

> Thig m' uirsgeul o Apollo,
> mar sheòlas an Naoinear

> *My exemplum comes from Apollo,*
> *as the Nine (Muses) direct.*

Here an alternative source of poetic prompting is invoked. In effect, the classical framework lets the poet retreat from the sense of public responsibility claimed by the Gaelic bard, since he is in the hands of the God of vaticination and it is the Muses who inspire his words. His use of the term *uirsgeul* is noteworthy. This word, which usually means 'fable, fiction, legend',[9] was also used by the classical bards in a technical sense to denote the 'apologue' or *exemplum* which very frequently occupied the central section of a classical Gaelic eulogy.[10] I believe this meaning may well have been in the mind of the poet at this point. At all events, he proceeds to cite a literary precedent bearing on his own case, just as a classical *filidh* would have done, before adducing the *applicatio*, i.e. the 'application' of the precedent to the present circumstances.

Ross's precedent is a harper called Cormac, who played music to extinguish the memory of his unattainable love. It is explained in a footnote accompanying the poem that Cormac was an Irish harper attached to the household of MacLeod of Lewis. He had fallen in love with MacLeod's daughter but presumably had no prospect of persuading her father to agree to a match. In desperation, he played magical sleep-music, put MacLeod and his household to sleep, and then drew his knife to slay MacLeod, so that he could elope to Ireland with the daughter. At that moment MacLeod's son came in from the hunt, and told Cormac to desist: 'You had better not, as you will get your choice of a thousand virgins in Scotland, by far fairer than my sister, without committing so cruel a deed.' This mixture of common sense and brotherly candour did the trick, for Cormac replied, 'You speak truly, my young man; hand me my lyre, that I may banish the virgin's love with the sound of my harp.' The actual poem does not tell the story in as connected a fashion as that, but verses 3–6 are consistent with the account I have just summarised.

Now there are some problems as to the status of this story. Professor Colm Ó Baoill, in his 'Some Irish harpers in Scotland', was inclined to look for a historical identification for Cormac – conceivably the Diarmaid Ó Cairbre who murdered Angus, son of John of the Isles in 1490.[11] I am not so sure. Earlier Gaelic literature is well supplied with references to different sorts of magical music, including sleep-music designed to enable a pair of lovers to thwart the girl's family.[12] Moreover, the second musical reference, i.e. to harp music drowning out the (siren?) sound of the girl, reminds one of the musicians in *Oidheadh Con Culainn* playing as loud as they could to drown out the sound of the *Badhbh* who was trying to lure Cú Chulainn to battle and death.[13] On that basis I am tempted to claim this reference for literature rather than history, i.e. as an allusion to a literary romance or a *sgeulachd* about the love of a noble girl and a harper.[14] But whatever the source of the *uirsgeul*, the point I wish to make is that we are dealing here with the native Gaelic tradition. Although he has invoked Apollo and the Muses, Ross is not looking to the slopes of Mount Parnassus or Mount Helicon to find his precedent.

However, the parallel turns out not to be an exact one. For the 'punch-line', or original twist that concludes this part of the poem (v. 6) is that the precedent does not work for Ross:

> . . . cha d'fhuair mise sgeul
> ann am Beurla no Gàidhlig
> a dh'innseadh dhomh mar dh'fhaodainn
> an gaol ud a smàladh.

> *I have not found a tale*
> *in English or in Gaelic*
> *to tell me how I might manage*
> *to smoor that love (of mine).*

His unquenchable love can find no parallel in either native or exotic literature. The second half of the poem contains an extended declaration of the poet's suffering. Critics have sometimes associated this with a confessional, personal side of William Ross's poetry, but we have to be careful here. The *maladie d'amour* was part of the stock-in-trade of poets all over Europe from the twelfth century at latest, in the courtly love tradition. Its references to love as an 'illness', a 'prison', 'madness' or 'life-in-death' are highly conventional. They had intermingled with native attitudes and conventions long before Ross's day to produce distinctive Gaelic patterns and tropes.[15] The same is true of comparisons and descriptions of the beloved: there is a strong international reservoir of commonplaces drawn on by poets in Gaelic as in other European linguistic traditions, with a complex background of borrowing, imitation and re-creation between the 'native' and 'exotic' versions. So when William Ross says his Marion is *binne na an smeòrach no cuach sa' mhadainn Mhàighe* ('more melodious than the song-thrush or a cuckoo in a May morning') it is no criticism of his sincerity or his poetic competence to say that he is using well-worn images. And when he goes on to ask, *Carson nach d'rugadh dall mi / gun chainnt is gun léirsinn?* ('Why was I not born blind / without speech and vision?'), he is quoting – and not for the only time – not just a sentiment but also a phrasing that was well established in Gaelic song before his time.[16]

It is true that, in the verses following v. 12, Ross seems to become more 'personal': perhaps one could think of his greater reliance on the traditional epithets and motifs in the earlier verses as a build-up, a sort of launching pad from which the individual poet can spread his wings.

> Ach fàgaidh mi mo dhùthaich,
> gun diùchnaich mi pàirt dheth,
> ro-mheud 's a thug mi 'rùn
> dha do chùl buidhe fàinneach.

> *But I'll leave my native land*
> *till I forget part of it,*
> *how great an excess of love I gave*
> *to your yellow ringleted head.*

The reason becomes clear in v. 13: she has departed with another man (a Captain Samuel Clough from Liverpool, as we know from the documentary evidence).

Interestingly, Ross adds a reason: the other man is more *stòrasach* ('wealthy') than the poet. This was doubtless true, but the opposition between true love that knows no social or financial gradations and the pragmatic reality of arranged marriages was also a prime convention of Gaelic and European popular and courtly love lyrics. The intense pain of admitting that his love has gone off with another perhaps compelled Ross to retreat to the shelter of the convention.

Even more interestingly, he now seems to find some degree of resolution or closure, for a moment at least (v. 14). If she has to go, then she should go with his blessing:

> Biodh soireann air na speuraibh,
> gun éirigh air mór-thonn,
> a dh'aisigeas le réidh-ghaoith
> gun bheud thu go seòlaid.

> *Let there be a (favourable) breeze in the skies,*
> *with no great swell arising,*
> *to ferry you with a steady wind*
> *safely to harbour.*

Despite the hurt she has caused him, he cannot bring himself to wish anything but good for her. But he is not finished yet; for in a haunting and (to me at least) ambivalent conclusion (v. 15), Ross returns to the comparison with Cormac:

> Mar sud bha uirsgeul Chormaic
> cho dearbhta 's a sheinn e:
> e fèin 's a chomunn òg
> 's iad glè bhrònach m'a thimcheall;
> e 'gabhail cead le pòig dhi
> gun chòmhradh, gun impidh,
> 's e 'dìoladh guth an còmhdhail
> na h-òighe gu 'm pill e.

> *That's how the story of Cormac was*
> *as efficacious as he played –*
> *himself and his young associates,*
> *and they so sad about him;*
> *him saying farewell to her with a kiss*
> *without converse, without entreaty,*
> *and he pledging (?) that he will return*
> *to meet up with the maiden.*[17]

I take the 'young associates' to be Young MacLeod and his sister; but I confess I'm not quite sure how this is all meant to be applied to Ross himself.

In this poem the 'cross-currents' are mostly native ones. A classical ripple may disturb the surface, in the references to Cupid, Apollo and the Muses. But they are no more than superficial. And there may be a sensation of *amour courtois*. But if there is, it had reached William Ross in a form that was already well assimilated, at both learned and vernacular levels, in Gaelic poetry. In other respects, including both the form and the substance of the apologue, this is a thoroughly 'Gaelic' song containing, as it does, many backward glances to older Gaelic literature.

Còmhradh eadar am Bàrd agus Blàbheinn

The explanatory legend to this poem may be translated as follows: 'Composed by the bard as he looked from a hilltop in Gairloch in the direction of Strath in Skye – the hereditary homeland of his forefathers. He entreats the Ben to tell the history of "the Age that has gone". The Ben, as it were, answers him, declaring that various troubles have afflicted it since the poet's forefathers ceased to frequent it.'[18]

After the briefest of *entrées*, simply locating the poet on a *tulach* ('knoll') and in pensive mood, Ross launches into a eulogistic address to the Ben, praising it as an unmistakable sight, and as the place where the poet's ancestors used to hunt, though it is now distant and untrodden by the poet. This moves him to beg the Ben to respond,

'S labhair an t-uirsgeul o shean
le bhith toirt fainear gach àm
o na làithean a chuaidh
dh'ionnsaigh an tràth thruaigh so th'ann.

And enunciate the legend from long ago,
paying heed to every era
from the days that have departed
to this wretched present age.

The Ben obliges: *B'eòl dhomh t'aitim 's b'ait am beus* ('I knew your race and enjoyed their style'). But they have been missed for some time now:

Chaill na h-ionadan am blàth
is thriall gach àrmunn àigh g'a uaigh.

The (special) places have lost their bloom
and every triumphant warrior has gone to his grave.

The sound of the harps has been silenced, and Echo (*Mac Talla*) has become dumb. The Ben is all that remains:

> Tha mise mar bha mi riamh
> o na shoillsich grian an là,
> o na dhealraich gealach oidhche
> chuireadh mo ghaibhlean-sa an sàs.

> *I am as I always was,*
> *since the sun (first) illumined the day;*
> *since the moon lit up the night*
> *my forks have been firmly planted.*

The Ben has been rooted since antediluvian times, and will be unshakeable for ever. But a terse conclusion reveals that Blaven is not a happy Ben:

> Tha mi gun triath talmhaidh còir:
> mo choire air Sìol Leòid, lèoir an cron;
> ach nam faodainn-sa dhol thairis
> dhìoladh Dùn Can' air a shon.

> *I am without a proper earthly prince:*
> *I blame the MacLeods, their fault is abundant;*
> *but if I could go over*
> *Dùn Cana would pay for it.*

This is an interesting little poem for several reasons. Its unevennesses of language and irregularly accented rhythm, aping the syllabic *rannaigheacht* metre, are reminiscent of some versions of the heroic *laoidhean*, and give it a distanced, formal, antique flavour. The sententious second couplet in v. 1 (which he uses here not for the only time)[19] adds to this effect:

> Cluain an domhain, truagh an dàil
> gur cobhartach don bhàs gach feòil.

> *The deceitfulness of the world – sad the circumstance*
> *that all flesh is prey to death.*

In Gaelic song-poetry the poets very often take their tune from well-known earlier compositions, whose associations establish the mood and reinforce the message of the new work. In this case it must be significant that the tune given is entitled *Tuireadh na[m] Fiann* ('The lament for the Fenian Heroes').[20]

Again, there is an echo of the famous *Òran na Comhachaig* ('The Song of the Owl') in v. 2: Ross's *Os ionmhain leam na chì mi thall* echoes the earlier poem's panorama of beloved bens in the Loch Tréig area, each introduced by *chì mi*. The *Comhachag* was already 'old' in the literary sense by the late eighteenth century, so the effect is similar to the points already cited. In fact it seems to me that the poet's overall purpose is in keeping with these indications. He seeks the *uirsgeul* ('legend')[21] of an age that contrasts with *an tràth truagh seo*, i.e. 'this degenerate age', which suggests the recurrent idea of *Linn an Àigh* ('The Age of Prosperity'), the nearest Gaelic expression to 'the Golden Age'. In short, he seeks stabilising, reassuring, comforting wisdom from the Ben.

Now dialogues are well established in Gaelic poetry, from Ross's day right back to the Middle Ages. The repertoire of stock confrontations includes the notion of a 'dialogue with the ancients', as in the late Middle Irish poem of Fintan and the Hawk of Achill.[22] It is fundamental to the sixteenth-century *Òran na Comhachaig* which we have just mentioned. Closer to home, Roderick Morrison, An Clàrsair Dall ('The Blind Harper'), has it in his famous *An Talla am bu ghnàth le MacLeòid* (i.e. 'The Hall in which Macleod was wont'), which likewise contains a dialogue with Echo, and contains the same message of degenerate times – in this case the contrast between his glorious days at Dunvegan and his subsequent exile to Glenelg.

Indeed, closer still to home, William Ross's maternal grandfather, John Mackay, Am Pìobaire Dall ('The Blind Piper'), has another such dialogue in his *Cumha Choire an Easa(in)*. This poem contains an elegy for a benevolent patron whose death has prompted the poet to visit the Corrie where the *àrmuinn* ('warriors') used to hunt. Lacking his patron, the poet is moved to compose an *ealaidh gun duais* ('a song without a fee') to the Corrie; and the Corrie answers him.

So far, so good; and so traditional too: everything seems firmly set within the 'Gaelic continuum'. However, we should also note a striking element within the vocabulary of this poem. At the outset of the poem the poet is sitting on a *tulach* ('knoll') that is *faoin*, which usually means 'soft, faint, feeble'. It is not *gorm* 'green', nor *lom* 'bare', nor is he *'na aonar* 'alone', or any of the usual things one expects to find when a Gaelic poet sits on a Highland knoll.[23] Again, the poet asks the Ben (l. 11) to answer him *le comas diamhair*, i.e. by a 'secret' or 'mysterious' ability. Especially, at l. 22 the poet listens and hears a sound from the Ben: 'a distant whisper *(fathann)* . . . in a feeble voice *(guth fann)*'. These words, taken together, suggest to me the pull of Ossianism, in which words like 'faint', 'feeble' and 'weak' are omnipresent.[24] Given the metrical and linguistic tendencies already mentioned, they reinforce one's impression that Ross was being self-consciously experimental in this poem, and further suggest that the mood or atmosphere he was trying to conjure up had brought him within the gravitational pull of Macpherson.

The point of the poem seems to be the contrast between the immutable, unshakable Ben and the disappearance of the people who used to frequent it. As we have seen, the mountain's foundation posts were driven in a long time ago (l. 40), and no amount of strength can ever shift them (ll. 42–4). Yet just as Ben Doran, Duncan Bàn Macintyre's eternal Mountain, deceived him at the end by exchanging deer for sheep, so Blaven has a surprise for William Ross. Duncan Bàn, in his *Cead deireannach nam Beann* ('Last farewell to the Bens') says:[25]

> 'S a' Bheinn as beag a shaoil mi
> gun dèanadh ise caochladh,
> on tha i nis fo chaoraibh,
> 's ann thug an saoghal car asam

> *Since the Mountain, which I little thought*
> *would suffer transformation,*
> *has now become a sheep-run,*
> *the world, indeed, has cheated me.*

It had been unthinkable, up till that point, that the symbol of permanence could alter. In the same way, Blaven's closing words (ll. 47–8) are arresting:

> Ach nam faodainn-sa dhol thairis
> dhìoladh Dùn Can' air a shon.

> *But if I could go over*
> *Dùn Cana would pay for it.*

For the personification involved in the idea of Blaven going over to Raasay to 'punish' Dùn Cana is grotesque in Gaelic. One of the *impossibilia* in the song *Mac Òg an Iarla Ruaidh*, where the girl says she will never marry the 'Young son of the Red Earl' until certain outlandish things happen, is the thought that 'the Ben down yonder' should change places with 'the Ben up yonder'.[26] The whole conceit is a bit awkward, and it is at least suggestive that the only mediating conceptual link that comes readily to mind is the link between the Fenian heroes and the landscape, whereby natural features can be associated with, or even represent Fionn or another of the Fiann.

It is possible to guess at the circumstances which caused the poet to evoke this mood of cosmic disorder. In 1789 Charles Mackinnon, chief of the Clan Mackinnon, sold off the Strathaird estate, the last remaining part of the Mackinnon patrimony, to Alexander Macalister. As Rev. Alexander Maclean Sinclair put it, 'The Mackinnons were now a landless clan.'[27] The sale had provoked strong feelings locally, and there was an attempt at an eighteenth-century equivalent of a 'buy-out' with the aim of preserving a Mackinnon landlord, if not a Mackinnon chief:[28]

> At the time of the sale the tenantry of Strathaird offered to place the means of purchasing the estate at the disposal of Mackinnon of Corry, but their chief opposed this, saying he was resolved if the estate went out of his own family, none other of the same name should possess it.

Now the chief's mother was Janet MacLeod, daughter of MacLeod of Raasay. When her husband, Iain Dubh Mackinnon, died in 1755, Janet's brother, John MacLeod, was appointed tutor to young Charles and his brother. MacLeod at once initiated proceedings to recover the Mackinnon estates from Mackinnon of Mishnish who had been their 'caretaker' during the period when the old chief, Iain Dubh, had been incapable of holding them.[29] A bitterly contested lawsuit ended with what was left of the Mackinnon estates, i.e. Mishnish and Strathaird, being secured for the young chief by MacLeod's efforts. Whatever local feeling may have been at the conclusion of the lawsuit, it looks as though people were deeply unhappy when Charles, once he had come of age, sold first Mishnish and then Strathaird. It is not hard to imagine that MacLeod may have been seen as the bogeyman, either for ejecting the 'caretaker' Mackinnon of Mishnish or for leaving the estates with such financial burdens that the young chief was forced to sell them. All this would have had a major impact on the family of William Ross, who lived very close to Corry during the time of these perturbations. I strongly suspect that all this came flooding back to Ross when the last estate was sold in 1789 and that the present poem was composed at about that time and conveys Ross's feelings about the sale.

If that is a correct inference, it is no wonder that the wisdom of the Ben was not comforting: the warriors who have departed, the *clàrsach* that is no longer played, and the missing *triath talmhaidh còir* ('proper earthly ruler'), will all relate to the disappearance of the ancient patrimony of the Mackinnon chiefs. We can draw a parallel with the alarm sounded by Duncan Bàn Macintyre in his *Cumha Choire a' Cheathaich* ('Lament for Misty Corrie'), where the absence of a 'proper ruler' is likewise the explanation for current malaise.[30] In Ross's case the 'message' is about 'ancient heroes and modern pygmies', whereas Macintyre uses the image of the 'changeling' (*tàcharan*). Ross's message is correlated more explicitly with the idea of 'Golden Age versus Degenerate Age', but the concept would not have been alien to Macintyre. The fact that Blaven can articulate the *impossibile* of uprooting and going to attack Dùn Cana is an expression of the *Clockwork Orange*-like dysfunctionality of the times.

In terms of our present focus, the theme of the symbiosis between ruler and land which is implicit in the reference to the *triath talmhaidh* ('earthly prince') is just about as traditional as one could get in Gaelic verse. But in attempting to go one better than his grandfather's *Cumha Choire an Easa(in)*, William Ross seems to have found it expedient to invoke the shade of Ossian; and this results in an instructive crossover: a neat example of how the Ossianic tone could repopulate the territory that originally spawned it.[31]

Òran air Gaol na h-òighe do Chailean

The lengthy preamble to 'A song on the Maiden's love for Colin' (no. 5 in Calder) lets us know what we are to expect: a pastoral idyll. The superscription is worth quoting in full.[32]

Air do'n Bhard a bhi siubhal air feadh Gàidhealdachd Siorramachd Pheirt, thàrladh dha tuiteam air achadh fàsaich far an robh nighean tuathanaich eireachdail maille ri seirbheisich, air àireachas le spréidh a h-athar. Dh'fhiadhaich i'm Bàrd le caoibhneas gu *fantuinn leo rè beagan laithean, a sgìos a chur seachad, agus iadsan aonaranach, 's déidheil air cuideachd:* ghabh e 'n tairgse gu toileach agus dh'fhan e leo. Air dha féin agus do'n chailin èolas math a chur air a chéile, dh'innis i dha gu'n robh – '*A h-aigne òg go trom fo leòn,*' le i-féin agus òganach àraidh *da'm b'ainm Cailean a bhi'n déidh air a chéile, agus nach fuiligeadh a càirdean di a phòsadh, do bhrìgh nach robh e cho saibheir no cho mòr-inbheach rithe-se.* Geàrr mar a bha 'n ùin a chaith am Bàrd 'na fochair, chunnaic e gu tric an ribhinn àigh agus Cailean a' còmhlachadh a chéile, ann an glacagan uaigneach an fhàsaich ri conadal diamhair, far an do shònraich iad latha pòsaidh, an ni fa dheòidh a thachair mu'n d'fhàg e-féin an t-achadh. Chum iad e ri chuid de'n chuirm phòsaidh, a's sheinn e 'n t-òran a leanas do na chàraid shona, agus thriall e air a thuras, a' guidhe – 'Sòlas gun chrìch do'n chomunn chiùin.'[33]

It is worth remarking that the Gaelic does not say that the girl *lived* in the 'pastureland', merely that she was herding there; and the poet left the pasture (*achadh*), not 'the farm'. There is therefore no hint or innuendo that the girl's parents had become reconciled to the match, or were present, or aware of the goings-on; the writer of this paragraph envisioned 'the Highlands of Perthshire' as a cross between a sin-free Celtic Otherworld and Arcadia.

As the poem opens we are transported to a May morning, with Phoebus's rays lighting a rosy sky. A beautiful girl is singing a song. In fact, it is just like the well-known English folk-song that begins, 'Early one morning just as the sun was rising / I heard a maiden singing in the valley below.' Her beauty is almost indescribable (ll. 29ff.):

Slios geala-mhìn mar eala
no mar canach nan gleann,
's a h-anail chùbhraidh mar chaineal
o beul meachair gun mheang

(Her) side smooth-white like a swan,
or like the cotton-grass of the glens,
and her breath fragrant like cinnamon
from her tender, flawless mouth.

As for her hair (bearing in mind that the Gaelic poets were always very concerned about hair), it was (ll. 33ff.):

. . . cama-lùbach bòidheach
bachlach òrbhuidh', 'na dhuail,
cas-bhuidh' snìomhanach fàinneach
an neo-chàramh mun cuairt

. . . curvaceously wavy, lovely,
tight-curled, golden, in a plait,
tumbling-yellow, spiralling, ringleted
in disorder all around.

Here the last line contains a big 'giveaway'. For this is a pose: the hair 'in disorder' is clearly a calque. The girl has a carefully disordered 'rural look' to balance the Mrs Siddons-type ringlets and curls. Calder hit the right note when he translated this as 'in a dishabille whirl', for it is 'designer' dishevelment. No wonder the poet's 'head swam' (*shnàmh mo smuaintean*, l. 17) as he 'fell into confusion' (*thuit mi'n caochladh romhór*, l. 18), and 'stood, carved like a statue' (*sheas mi snasaichte mar ìomhaigh*, l. 19). The presence of a foreign diction, perhaps an actual model, is palpable.

The maiden heads for the shade of the wood, and starts to sing. The poet wonders if he should listen: modesty forbids, but compulsion drives him forward, and he follows the voice into the wood. She is singing a love-song (ll. 59–60) to

òg-laoch nan ciabh òr-bhuidh'
an Leitir Laomainn nan cuach

the young hero with the golden locks,
in Lomond-side of the cuckoos.[34]

The birds gather round to provide a backing choir, as she sings to her Colin, 'Why won't you come?' Her song then contains an autobiographical flashback, for the poet's benefit, and ours: 'Colin and I were young together, gathering flowers, resting together on the bank, accompanied by the bird-choir' (ll. 79–80),

> . . . 's bhiodh na cruitearan sgiathach
> cur ar cianalais uainn
>
> . . . *and the winged harpers*
> *would banish our pining.*

In case we (her audience) should have been tempted to think otherwise, she states unequivocally that 'our dalliance was innocent (*neo-chiontach*), with no thought of "cheating" (*foill*), even though Cupid was drawing us, children as we were, to love' (ll. 82–84). Now, she goes on, she often leaves the cattle and comes to the glade (ll. 94–95)

> gu bhith taomadh mo dhosgainn
> ann am fochair nan geug
>
> *to pour out my injury*
> *in the vicinity of the branches.*

She suffers from a common problem: 'my relations are angry with me' (*tha mo chàirdean fo ghruaim rium*) since Colin is poor. But why, she asks, should that stand in the way of love?

Thus the gentle maiden sang 'the sincere origins of her love' (*tòsan tairis a gaoil*, l. 106, translated by Calder as 'her faithful love lay'), and pledged her undying love to her Colin. Then she turns and addresses a wider audience (ll. 109ff.):

> Gach òigh eile da cluinn so,
> gun robh a h-inntinn gu bàs
> gu bhith leantainn an t-samhl' ud,
> gun a h-anntoil thoirt dha
>
> *Every other maiden who hears this,*
> *may her intention till death*
> *be to follow that example,*
> *and not give it her displeasure.*[35]

At this point, who should appear but the Hero (ll. 117ff.):

chunn'cas òganach gasda
teachd o leacainn a' chrò
's e le uile shàr imeachd –
's b'ann gu innis nam bó

I saw a handsome young man
coming from the slope of the cattle-fold,
making his very best speed –
and heading for the pasture of the cattle.

He receives a verse of praise for his beauty (just one verse in his case) as the poet dwells on the welcome sight. Then he espies the girl and his heart lights up and they embrace warmly (ll. 140ff.):

is o'n bha ['m] furan cho tairis
's nach b'fhuras aithris cho fial,
ghuidh mi sonas gun dìth dhoibh
gu là na crich' is mi triall.

and since their welcome was so sincere
that one could not easily describe its generosity,
I prayed for happiness without want for them
until the final day, as I departed.

In other words, the poet realised it was time for him to make a sharp exit, and the poem ends quite abruptly.

This poem obviously bears comparison – even without the hints of linguistic borrowing or thematic debt – with the ballads and pastorals and folk-songs of the Scots- and English-speaking world, to go no further afield. It equally obviously contrasts with what Sorley MacLean called the Old Songs (*seann òrain*), whose tone is more red-blooded, whose diction is more direct, and which lack the coyness we sense here. A contrast exists at the presentational level too: in the present poem, the frame and flashback and asides to the audience set it apart from the 'old songs'. It is not that the latter lack dramatic complexity; but they do not customarily have stage directions or commentary on the action embedded in the body of the text.

There is thus something novel afoot, from the Gaelic point of view, in poems like 'The Maiden's love for Colin'. This is perhaps easiest demonstrated in the case of the linguistic innovations (i.e. from lines like *sheas mi snasaichte mar ìomhaigh*, quite literally 'I stood carved like a statue'), but once one is on the lookout for it, it becomes obvious also in other ways related to language. For Ross's Gaelic in this poem is best described as eclectic. The innovations coexist with 'unmarked' contemporary Gaelic poetic language (e.g. in the description of the girl's hair); and Ross also introduces (or reintroduces) archaic or archaistic forms like *chunnacas* 'I saw' and *dhiuchd* 'came'. In Anglophone terms, the effect is not unlike what we meet with in ballads and folk-songs. For here too one comes across idiomatic vernacular usages cheek by jowl with stilted, 'old-fashioned' diction, as in 'I did salute my love most courageously', or 'But aye she loot the tears doon fa' (for Jock o' Hazeldean)', and so on.

Of course, some elements of this 'international' love poetry were already embedded in Scottish Gaelic, if not quite as spectacularly as in Irish Gaelic, as Seán Ó Tuama's *An Grá in Amhráin na nDaoine* showed. The famous song *Cuachag nan Craobh* ('The Cuckoo (?) of the branches') which popular pressure forced John Mackenzie to include in the second edition of William Ross's works, though it (or something closely similar to it) clearly pre-dates him (or at least his love-life), has all the trappings: the woods, the dew, the birdsong, the flowers. But in *Gaol na h-Òighe do Chailean* we find a new sensibility, answering to a new world of *soirées* and dance-halls and other metropolitan influences to which William Ross was clearly beholden, whether in the big town of Stornoway or in the big city of Edinburgh. In this poem, then, the attempt to do something new for Gaelic is manifest, just as clearly as in the recreations of Isaac Watts's hymns which Professor Meek has delineated for us in the *laoidhean spioradail* of Dugald Buchanan.

This does not exhaust discussion of the poem, of course. For one thing, we ought to consider it, in more explicitly critical terms, along with other poems in which Ross seeks ways to project, sublimate or externalise his personal feelings in his compositions. There is also room for refinement of our sense of both Highland and Lowland analogues and influences, e.g. the 'voyeuristic' note of reportage that surfaces towards the end of the poem, which begs comparison with texts of the highly ambivalent, semi-Ossianic *Miann a' Bhaird Aosda* ('The Aged Bard's desire'). Again, one needs to take into account the metre and tune which Ross has used here – and elsewhere – when assessing the poem in a rounded way. Nevertheless, the pastoral framework which we have emphasised in this brief treatment was clearly a central concern of the poet's, and one that singles it out for mention in the context of Highland–Lowland 'cross-currents'.

There are also other poems which it would have been apposite to introduce here. These would include, for sure, *Cuachag nan Craobh*; but similar questions of ascription and authorship are also raised by *Bruthaichean Ghlinn Bhraoin* ('The Braes of Glen Broom'), within the wider perspective of late eighteenth-century attitudes towards collecting and adapting or improving older songs. Again, the 'merry' and satirical songs omitted or truncated by Calder are ripe for exploration, having 'native' analogues in (e.g.) Rob Donn's *Briogais Mhic Ruairidh* ('MacRury's Breeks') and *Banais Mhic Asgaill* ('MacAskill's Wedding'), attributed to John MacCodrum, but also palpable points of comparison with Burns and others in the Lowland tradition. Here social and psycho-logical analysis would form the general backdrop.

While it has not been possible to touch on these and similar points, I hope I have given some useful instances of William Ross's poetic interests, methods and style, and also something of the flavour of working in this phase of eighteenth-century Gaelic literature. In general it seems to me that Ross's relationship to the wider world of Scottish literature bears comparison with that of Lowland Scottish poets to the wider world of English literature; it will be worth exploring this perception further and asking whether it can be utilised to illuminate the work of other Gaelic literary figures. The more specific points I make tie in pretty well with the estimations of Ross that have emerged from the critical works of Sorley MacLean, Derick Thomson and Ronald Black, as a poet who could be vulnerable, sensitive and self-absorbed, but simultan-eously faithful to the more public, community responsibilities that came the way of a Gael who had a way with words and tunes.[36] I hope to have added some flesh to the bones, and supplied some additional colouring to the portrait of William Ross.[37]

Notes

1   I wish to thank Ronald Black, David Hewitt, John MacInnes and the editors of this volume for helpful suggestions at the conference or subsequently.

2   '"Merely a bard?" William Ross and Gaelic poetry', forthcoming in *Aiste*, 1 (2007).

3   Most of the known or assumed facts about Ross's life are contained in the biograph-ical sketch prefaced to John Mackenzie's editions of his poetry, beginning with *Orain Ghaelach le Uilleam Ros* (Inverness, 1830), restated with some additions in G. Calder, *Gaelic Songs by William Ross* (Edinburgh, 1937). Oral traditions which in some respects supplement the 'canonical' printed accounts are found in J. H. Dixon, *Gairloch* (Edin-burgh, 1886); E. MacCoinnich, 'Dà bhard à Gearrloch', *Transactions of the Gaelic Society of Inverness* [hereafter *TGSI*] 44 (1964–66), 297–309; and in the Sound Archive of the School of Scottish Studies.

4   A. agus D. Stiùbhart, *Co-chruinneacha Taoghta de Shaothair nam Bard Gaeleach* (Edinburgh 1804).

5   For details of Mackenzie's editions of Ross, including the doubt about the date of the first edition, see D. Maclean, *Typographia Scoto-Gadelica* (Edinburgh, 1915), pp. 334–5,

and, for *Sàr Obair*, id., pp. 247–9. In addition to the poems contained in these printed editions, a handful of other songs have been persistently associated with Ross in popular tradition.

[6] See "'Merely a bard?'" (note 2).

[7] The truth of all these assertions is demonstrated in "'Merely a bard?'", where I also express the intention to tackle the editorial challenge in due course.

[8] Cited from the '1830' edition, p. 103. Note that in fact Mòr married before leaving Stornoway: see W. Matheson, 'Mór Ros', *Gairm* 12 (Summer 1955), 339–42; D. S. Thomson, 'William Ross', *An Gàidheal*, 1959, 26–8.

[9] In Calder No. 1, v. 3, the poet addresses Blaven as follows: *[L]abhair an t-uirsgeul o shean / le bhith toirt fa-near gach àm* ('Enunciate the legend from long ago, paying heed to every era'). The more usual meaning occurs in the last verse of the present song, where *uirsgeul Chormaic* means 'the story of (= about) Cormac'.

[10] See L. P. Ó Caithnia, *Apalóga na bhFilí* (Dublin, 1984).

[11] See *TGSI*, 47 (1971–2), 143–71 (143–4); cf. W. Matheson, *The Blind Harper* (Edinburgh, 1970), p. lvi.

[12] See, e.g. M. Dillon, *The Cycles of the Kings* (Oxford, 1946), pp. 4–7 (*Orcuin Denna Ríg*); cf. K. Ralls-MacLeod, *Music and the Celtic Otherworld* (Edinburgh, 2000), p. 84.

[13] Transl. K. H. Jackson, *A Celtic Miscellany* (2nd edn, London, 1971), pp. 42–8. A more tenuous connection might be made to the episode in *Fingal Rónáin* where the king's son comes into his father's hall after a day spent hunting on the hill; see M. Dillon (ed.), *Irish Sagas* (Dublin, 1968), p. 165.

[14] Compare the story of the Irish poet Cearbhall Ó Dálaigh and the daughter of the King of Scotland in J. Doan, *The Romance of Cearbhall and Fearbhlaidhe* (Dublin, 1984), which contains a pastiche of motifs from Early Irish literature along the lines which I wish to identify here.

[15] For the European dimension see P. Dronke, *Medieval Latin and the Rise of the European Love Lyric* (2nd edn, Oxford, 1968). For the Gaelic reflexes see S. Ó Tuama, *An Grá in Amhráin na nDaoine* (Dublin, 1960); M. Mac Craith, *Lorg na hIasachta ar na dánta grá*, (Dublin, 1989); W. Gillies, 'Courtly and satiric poems in the Book of the Dean of Lismore', *Scottish Studies*, 21 (1977), 35–53.

[16] See "'Merely a bard?'" for this jackdaw-like quality in Ross, which has been taken in different ways by critics.

[17] I have altered the punctuation in the first and last couplet in an attempt to make better sense of this verse.

[18] This is taken from the 1834 edition. The first edition has only an asterisk against 'Blaven' in the text and the explanatory gloss 'A mountain in the Isle of Skye'.

[19] He uses it again in 'An Suaithneas Bàn', except that there it comes out as *gur cobhartach gach feòil don bhàs* for metrical reasons.

[20] This identification first appears in the 1834 edition. *Tuiridh nam Fiann* is the title given to one version of a heroic ballad also known as *Caoidh Oisein*, which appears in the Book of the Dean of Lismore with the first line *An so chonnaic mé an Fhéinn* (see N. Ross, *Heroic Verse from the Book of the Dean of Lismore* (Edinburgh, 1939), no. XVII). It lists in successive verses the departed Fenian heroes whom Oisean, the speaker, has known. Its metre, in the versions printed by J. F. Campbell, *Leabhar na Féinne* (London, 1872), pp. 47–9, is a crude form of *rannaigheacht mhór*.

[21] I.e. in the sense of 'literary or fictive tale', as we recall. Calder translates this as 'romantic tale', which is not quite the same.

[22] See J. F. Nagy, *Conversing with Angels and Ancients* (Ithaca, 1997), for the roots and development of this powerful *leitmotiv*.

[23] Calder translates this 'lonely', which stretches the Gaelic somewhat. His Explanatory Note A (p. 180) is completely obscure to me, but at least suggests that he too was puzzled by this verse.

[24] References to departed warriors (l. 30), silent harps (ll. 31–2) and stilled Echo (l. 33) reinforce the note of melancholy and nostalgia.

[25] Angus MacLeod, *The Songs of Duncan Bàn Macintyre* (Edinburgh, 1952), pp. 390–1 (ll. 5580–3).

[26] See, e.g. L. Mackinnon, *Cascheum nam Bard, Earrann I* (Inverness, 1939), p. 15: *Gus an cuir a' bheinn ud shìos / cùlaibh ris a' bheinn ud shuas.*

[27] 'The Clan Fingon', *Celtic Review*, 4 (1907–8), 31–41 (39).

[28] Quoted from 'A Genealogical Account of the Family of Mackinnon' by A. Cameron, *The History and Traditions of the Isle of Skye* (Inverness, 1871), p. 132.

[29] He had been attaindered as a result of participating in the 1715 Rising, and had had to live away from home. He had eventually returned to Skye and married Janet MacLeod in 1743 (his son and heir by an earlier marriage having died young), but then participated in the 1745 Rising and spent a further period in compulsory exile.

[30] See MacLeod, *Duncan Bàn*, pp. 174–83 (especially ll. 2550–665) and cf. Meg Bateman's contribution to this volume.

[31] One remaining puzzle may be mentioned. When the Ben says to the poet 'your people used to frequent me' (and the poet himself says the same at the outset, so it is no slip) this could only be addressed to a Mackinnon. Does this tell us something about William Ross's Skye forebears, or does it suggest that the poem was composed as though spoken by a member of the Mackinnon family?

[32] It appears first in the 1834 edition of Ross's songs. The italics are the editor's, not mine.

[33] Calder's translation reads: 'When the Bard was travelling through the Highlands of the County of Perth, he chanced to light on a pasture-land where a tacksman's handsome daughter lived with her servants, taking charge of her father's cattle. She kindly invited him to stay with them for a few days to recover from his fatigue, they being also lonely and fond of company: he willingly accepted the offer and stayed with them. When he and the maid had established a good acquaintance with one another, she told him that "her young heart was heavy with grief" owing to herself and a certain young man named Colin being fond of one another, and her relations would not allow her to marry him, because he was not so wealthy or of so high a position as herself. Short though the time was that the Bard spent in her company, he often saw the adorable nymph and Colin meeting together in lonely dells of the pasture-land in secret conversation where they fixed a day for marriage, an event that finally took place before he himself left the farm. They included him with those of the marriage party, and he sang the following song to the happy pair, and proceeded on his journey with the prayer: "Unending joy to the quiet company".'

[34] 'Lomond-side' is intriguing, since the best-known Lomonds are in the Lennox and Fife, whereas 'the Highlands of Perthshire' in the superscription may suggest Rannoch as the Arcadian location (cf. the well-known song *Bothan àirigh am Bràigh Raineach*, 'A shieling hut in the Braes of Rannoch', for this association). Did the poet locate his Arcadia in the Trossachs, and was the superscription composed by someone other than the poet who did not notice the difference, or did not judge it important? Or are we to assume that Colin was a far-roving boy, as well as being landless?

[35] The verse containing these lines is not in the first edition. I tentatively regard it as an omission there.

[36] For MacLean see *Ris a' Bhruthaich* (Stornoway, 1985), e.g. pp. 38–9; for Thomson see especially his *Gaelic Poetry in the Eighteenth Century* (Aberdeen, 1993), pp. 145–67; for Black see *An Lasair* (Edinburgh, 2001), pp. 304–9. Further references to critical writing on William Ross will be found in the notes to '"Merely a bard?"'.

[37] In addition to the last cited work see '"No bonnier life than the sailor's": A Gaelic poet comments on the fishing industry in Wester Ross', forthcoming in *Studies in Scottish Literature*, 35 (2007).